The ISO 9001:2015 HANDBOOK

A Practical Guide to Implementation

The ISO 9001:2015 HANDBOOK

A Practical Guide to Implementation

LORRI HUNT
JOSE DOMINGUEZ
CRAIG WILLIAMS

Chico, California

Most Paton Professional books are available at quantity discounts when purchased in bulk. For more information, contact:

Paton Professional
PO Box 44
Chico, CA 95927-0044
Telephone: (530) 342-5480
e-mail: books@patonprofessional.com
Web: www.patonprofessional.com

© 2016 by Lorri Hunt, José Domínguez, and Craig Williams. All rights reserved. Printed in the United States of America

20 19 18 17 16   10 9 8 7 6 5 4 3 2 1

ISBN: 978-1-932828-15-3

Notice of Rights
No part of this work covered by the copyright herein may be reproduced or used in any form or by any means—graphic, electronic, or mechanical, including photocopying, recording, taping, or information storage and retrieval systems—without permission in writing from Paton Professional.

Notice of Liability
The information in this book is distributed on an "as is" basis, without warranty. Although every precaution has been taken in the preparation of the book, neither the authors nor Paton Professional shall have any liability to any person or entity with respect to any loss or damage caused or alleged to be caused directly or indirectly by the information contained in this book.

Staff
Publisher: Scott M. Paton
Editors: Laura Smith and Daniel Taylor
Book design: Anita Jovanovic
Cover design: Miguel Kilantang

Dedications

In memory of our dear friend and colleague Peter Papakostantinu, who left this world at almost the exact minute the first working draft of ISO 9001:2015 was completed. We miss you every day.

Lorri Hunt

To my niece Madison, who always makes time for me around my difficult travel and work schedule. You are simply the best!

José Domínguez

To Paola—the love of my life—and to my parents, brothers, and sisters. Their love and support have helped me to be the man that I am.

Craig Williams

To Caroline, Alex, and Matthew for living with the pace, travel, and overall craziness that is our lives and still loving and supporting me to make it all worthwhile!

Acknowledgment

We would like to acknowledge our colleagues in ISO TC/176 Subcommittee 2, Working Group 24 and Subcommittee 1, Working Groups 1, 2, and 3 for their contributions to ISO 9001:2015 and ISO 9000:2015. This group of technical experts are not only our colleagues, they are also our friends.

Contents

SECTION I
Introduction and Overview of ISO 9001:2015 1

CHAPTER 1
Introduction 3

CHAPTER 2
ISO 9001:2015 Overview.................................. 5

CHAPTER 3
ISO 9000:2015 Overview................................. 13

CHAPTER 4
ISO Standards Development Process...................... 25

CHAPTER 5
Introduction and Annexes 31

CHAPTER 6
Process Approach and Risk-Based Thinking 33

SECTION II
Clause-by-Clause Analysis 39

CHAPTER 7
Clause 4—Context of the Organization 41

CHAPTER 8
Clause 5—Leadership 53

CHAPTER 9
Clause 6—Planning 65

CHAPTER 10
Clause 7—Support 73

CHAPTER 11
Clause 8—Operation 99

CHAPTER 12
Clause 9—Performance Evalutaion 141

Chapter 13
Clause 10—Improvement 159

Section III
Implementation and Integration 167

Chapter 14
Engaging Leadership 169

Chapter 15
Certification vs. Declaration of Conformity................ 173

Chapter 16
Implementation 181

Chapter 17
Procedure Writing 205

Chapter 18
Internal Audit Process................................. 219

Chapter 19
Adding Value to the Quality Management System 231

Section IV
Transition.. 243

Chapter 20
ISO 9001:2008 to ISO 9001:2015 Transition................ 245

Chapter 21
ISO 9001:2008 to ISO 9001:2015 Correlation 249

Section V
Appendices 255

Appendix A
Integrated Management System Standards................. 257

Appendix B
The Relationship Between ISO 9001 and ISO 14001......... 261

Appendix C
Compliance Standards vs. Excellence Models 267

Appendix D
ISO 9000 Family of Standards........................... 273

Appendix E
Quality Management System Checklist.................... 275

Index.. 277

Section I

Introduction and Overview of ISO 9001:2015

This section will provide a broad overview of ISO 9001:2015, a brief review of the standards-development process, a summary of ISO 9000:2015 and its use as a normative reference, and other background information related to understanding ISO 9001:2015.

Chapter 1

Introduction

The decision to implement an international standard such as ISO 9001 can be based on many factors. You may have customers or other interested parties that are requesting it, your parent company may be mandating it for the entire corporation, management may be seeking to differentiate the organization from its competition, or you may need a methodology to provide controls.

Regardless of the reason, most organizations that implement an ISO 9001-based quality management system (QMS) face challenges in understanding its requirements and implementing them without disrupting business operations or the bottom line.

To determine what level of implementation will be necessary, you need to truly understand ISO 9001's requirements, related supporting materials, and the processes to implement them. Without this fundamental understanding, your organization may flounder when determining the actions needed to close gaps or make changes to existing processes to meet requirements.

The most successful ISO 9001 implementation efforts are those that have a robust implementation plan and a clear understanding of it. Implementation plans will differ for different organizations and their varying needs. These differences may be based on what the organization must do to complete its implementation, the resources available to assist with the implementation, or the current state of its QMS.

The release of ISO 9001:2015 has provided additional challenges to organizations—both those with an existing ISO 9001-based QMS and those that wish to implement one. ISO 9001:2015 is the first significant revision of the standard since 2000. It contains new requirements, new concepts, a new structure, and a different way of looking at the role of the QMS in an organization. ISO 9001:2015 also removed some requirements, leaving many organizations wondering what to do now. We'll take a deep dive into the new standard, beginning in chapter 2.

This handbook is divided into five sections:

I. *Overview of ISO 9001:2015.* This section will provide a broad overview of ISO 9001:2015, a brief review of the standards-development process, a summary of ISO 9000:2015 and its use as a normative reference, and other background information related to understanding ISO 9001:2015.

II. *Clause-by-clause analysis.* As the title suggests, this section provides a clause-by-clause analysis of ISO 9001:2015's requirements, keys to understanding those requirements, and guidance on transitioning to the new requirements.

III. *Implementation and integration.* This section provides practical guidance on how an organization implementing ISO 9001 for the first time or integrating multiple management systems should conduct the implementation and integration activities.

IV. *Transition.* This section gives readers an understanding of what is needed to move from an ISO 9001:2008 QMS to meet the requirements of ISO 9001:2015.

V. *Appendices.* This section provides additional information that's helpful to understanding ISO 9001:2015 and its relationship to other standards and other excellence models, as well as more information on the entire ISO 9000 family of standards. We've also included a sample QMS checklist.

The concepts in this handbook are based on a practical approach to implementing ISO 9001:2015 taken from lessons learned from real-life experiences of the authors. It will provide information around the 2015 revision and associated materials, and afford the reader an understanding of the considerations prior to implementation and integration. Finally, it will provide practical guidance to an organization in developing an implementation plan based on the individual needs of the organization.

The key to a successful transition to or implementation of ISO 9001:2015 is to take ownership of the QMS. This handbook is meant to be used to help readers achieve that goal. It can be read cover-to-cover or used to review the application of a specific requirement. However you use this handbook, the goal is simple: to be a practical guide to your ISO 9001:2015 implementation journey.

Chapter 2

ISO 9001:2015 Overview

ISO 9001:2015 is the first major revision to the standard since the 2000 version. The intent of the 2015 revision was simple: Consider the technological changes in business during the last 15 years, develop requirements that could be dynamic enough to adjust when additional changes occur in industry, and include requirements that could be audited for conformance.

Any changes in requirements should enhance a customer's confidence in the organization's quality management system (QMS) and help the organization achieve intended results. A common criticism of past versions of ISO 9001 was that organizations could meet the standard's requirements but deliver products that didn't meet customer requirements. ISO 9001:2015 includes requirements that focus on achieving intended results. This new approach focuses on the performance and effectiveness of the QMS.

By making the standard less prescriptive and more reliant on risk-based thinking to determine the level of complexity needed for an organization's QMS, ISO 9001:2015 accomplishes what many users have requested. However, this introduces new challenges.

For this reason, ISO 9001:2015 includes an annex that provides the rationale for some of the changes.

It's important to know how to read ISO 9001:2015. Many readers tend to skip the introduction and head straight to the requirements section in clause 4. This may be because when we began reading as young children, we would skip the introduction pages of books and go straight to the first chapter. Most of us also learned never to jump to the end of the book lest we ruin the ending

In this case, however, it's best to start with the introduction section of the standard, skip all of the clauses, and read annex A at the end. Reading these two sections first will provide a foundation to understand the significance of the changes in the standard.

Annex A is an informative reference, which means that the information in the annex is similar to a note that provides clarifying information. It can be used to help organizations implement the standard and as a resource for demonstrating compliance to auditors.

It's also essential to read ISO 9000:2015—the normative reference for ISO 9001:2015—to help understand terminology. Chapter 3 provides details on ISO 9000:2015, including how it can help your organization.

Here are some of the key changes in ISO 9001:2015.

CHANGE: STRUCTURE

Because the new structure of ISO 9001:2015 is the most obvious change in the revision, it's important to understand the rationale for the change so that users can move on to the more substantive changes.

The structure of ISO 9001:2015 changed due to a decision by the ISO Technical Management Board to adopt a standardized format and common core text and terms for use in all new and revised ISO management system standards. This is to promote greater ease of use for organizations that want to integrate the requirements of multiple management system standards such as ISO 9001, ISO 14001, and ISO 50001. This standardized format is referred to as Annex SL, which is simply the alphanumeric indication of the index from the ISO Directives. Figure 2.1 compares the high-level clause titles of Annex SL in ISO 9001:2015 to the clause titles in ISO 9001:2008.

Figure 2.1	Comparison of Annex SL Clause Titles to ISO 9001:2008
Annex SL	**ISO 9001:2008**
4 Context of the organization	4 Quality management system
5 Leadership	5 Management responsibility
6 Planning	6 Resource management
7 Support	7 Product realization
8 Operation	8 Measurement, analysis, and improvement
9 Performance evaluation	
10 Improvement	

Understanding the change

Before getting too caught up in the structure of the revised standard, it's important to read subclause 0.4, Relationship with other management system standards, and annex A. Subclause 0.4 introduces the Annex SL high-level structure, explains the rationale of the structure, and highlights some of the changes in ISO 9001:2015. Specifically, it indicates that the structure relates to the framework developed by ISO to approve alignment among management system standards.

Subclause A.1 (located within annex A), Structure and terminology, provides details that should help organizations understand the requirements related to structure. Subclause A.1 specifically states that there is no requirement for organizations to adopt the ISO 9001:2015 structure in their own QMS nor do organizations have to change the terminology used in their QMS.

The text included in the annex should alleviate any concerns related to structure and required changes. With that said, organizations with an existing ISO 9001-based QMS should have already adopted the process approach in the structure of their QMS. Therefore, before making any structural changes to your organization's QMS, it's important to carefully consider the opportunities and issues associated with making such changes. Any change should add value. Making a change for the sake of aligning a QMS to an outside structure of any kind potentially adds unneeded cost and overhead.

If an organization wants to ensure that it has addressed any new requirements in ISO 9001:2015, it should develop a cross-reference of compliance methods such as implemented processes or documented procedures from whatever structure it's using to the requirements in the revised standard. A cross-reference of ISO 9001:2008 requirements to ISO 9001:2015's requirements is included in chapter 21. This cross-reference will help organizations understand the relationship of current requirements to requirements in ISO 9001:2015. This cross-reference is available to the public at no charge at *http://isotc.iso.org/livelink/livelink/open/tc176SC2public*.

Subclause 4.4, Quality management system and its processes, should also be considered when reviewing requirements related to the structure. Organizations that have taken a minimal approach to this requirement may need to make some changes in how they identify and control their processes. Organizations that have embraced the process approach will not only find that the transition to ISO 9001:2015 is simpler but also that the integration of any new requirements into their QMS is easier to accomplish.

PRODUCTS AND SERVICES

Ever since the first of edition of ISO 9001 was published, there has been feedback from some users that the standard is difficult to apply to all types of industries, specifically to the service sector. For that reason, the language in ISO 9001 was modified to make it easier to use across all sectors.

One way that ISO 9001:2015 has been made more generic is by replacing the word "product" with "products and services." Using "products and services" helps to emphasize that the standard can be applied to all types of organizations. In addition, some requirements have been specifically changed to emphasize this point. This includes subclause 7.1.5, Control of monitoring and measuring resources, which was made easier to apply to service industries by changing the words "monitoring and measuring equipment" to "monitoring and measuring resources" and incorporating requirements related to monitoring and measuring as applicable to the service sector.

INTERESTED PARTIES

Some of ISO 9001:2015's new requirements are practices that most organizations already do, but they may cause some discussion regarding implementation. This is partially due to the new terminology in ISO 9001:2015 related to "interested parties."

ISO 9001 has always been and remains a customer-focused standard. The high-level structure and common text that is required to be used by Annex SL uses the term "interested parties" instead of "customers." Specifically, subclauses 4.1, Understanding the organization and its context, and 4.2, Understanding the needs and expectations of interested parties, require you to focus on these aspects. These requirements, while new in the text of the standard, were implied in subclause 0.1, General, in ISO 9001:2008, which indicated that the QMS is influenced by the environment that the organization operates in, including changes and risks.

Understanding the change

To eliminate the potential for the term "interested parties" to be interpreted beyond the intent of ISO 9001:2015, subclause A.3, Understanding the needs and expectations of interested parties (located in annex A), explains subclauses 4.1 and 4.2. Specifically, ISO 9001:2015 doesn't require an organization to consider interested parties that aren't relevant to its QMS. Organizations will need to determine what is relevant for them based on whether the interested party has an effect on the organization's ability to meet customer, statutory, and/or regulatory requirements. Some organizations may choose to expand the interpretation of the requirement, but this is at their discretion and where it can be determined that such an application can add value. A list of examples of interested parties is included in ISO 9000:2015.

APPLICABILITY

When ISO 9001:2000 was published and ISO 9002 was eliminated, the concept of exclusions was introduced into the standard. Exclusions allowed an organization to exclude a requirement of clause 7 of the standard as long as it didn't affect the organization's ability to meet customer, statutory, and/or regulatory requirements or provide a product or service that conformed to such requirements.

With the introduction of the core Annex SL text, which includes a different structure, the standard has been made more generic. Therefore, it's easier to apply the standard's requirements. This change focuses ISO 9001:2015 on the *application* of the requirements and not on the *exclusion* of requirements. ISO 9001:2015 requires organizations to apply the requirements where they can.

Subclause 4.3, Determining the scope of the quality management system, still requires an organization to justify any instance where a requirement cannot be applied. However, it isn't limited to certain clauses of ISO 9001:2015 like it was in the previous two versions of the standard. The required justification for not applying a requirement of ISO 9001:2015 will assist with establishing the framework of an organization's QMS. This will be helpful not only to the organization but also to any third-party auditors who will be reviewing the organization's QMS.

Understanding the change

Subclause A.5, Applicability (located in annex A), outlines the new concept of "application not exclusion." It specifically addresses the idea that not all requirements have to be applied by an organization due to the nature of the product or service that it provides. Other influences might be the size of the organization, the management model it adopts, and/or its risks and opportunities.

Organizations that are already taking an exclusion to a requirement in their ISO 9001:2008-based QMS should be able to determine the requirement still no longer applies when they transition to ISO 9001:2015.

RISK-BASED THINKING

Another concept that has been integrated into ISO 9001:2015 is risk-based thinking. Although risk was *implied* in previous versions of ISO 9001, the word "risk" is now actually used in ISO 9001:2015. Using risk-based thinking allows an organization to determine the level of controls needed for certain requirements, thereby reducing some requirements that were seen as more prescriptive than others.

In alignment with risk-based thinking, ISO 9001:2015 doesn't use the term "preventive action." The language in the standard looks at how an organization determines the risks and opportunities that need to be addressed as part of an effective QMS. Subclause 6.1, Actions to address risks and opportunities, includes requirements to ensure that the QMS can achieve its intended outputs. It also addresses taking action appropriate to the potential effect of conformity of products and services and preventing the occurrence of potential issues.

Understanding the change

Subclause 6.1 includes a note that provides clarification of the options that can be used to address risks and opportunities, including the idea that risks and opportunities aren't always negative. The organization can take actions to avoid risks or actions to pursue an opportunity.

Subclause A.4, Risk-based thinking (located in annex A), emphasizes the point that there is no requirement to implement a specific, formal risk-management system. Instead, ISO 9001:2015 focuses on the potential risks and opportunities associated with the implementation of a specific requirement and the level of implementation required.

In addition, subclause 0.3.3, Risk-based thinking, includes the consideration of risks and the potential consequences for different types of organizations, which allows the application of requirements based on those consequences.

DOCUMENTED INFORMATION

Throughout the many versions of ISO 9001, the terms "documents" and "records" have been used. In ISO 9001:2015, these terms have been replaced with the term "documented information." In addition, in previous versions of ISO 9001 the requirements for documents and records were kept in separate clauses. They are now included in subclause 7.5, Documented information.

It's important to understand that this new terminology has been introduced because the way we control documented information today is vastly different than it was when ISO 9001 was first released. Despite this fact, there had been little change to the requirements in past revisions.

Understanding the change

Subclause A.1, Structure and terminology (located in annex A), identifies some of the biggest terminology changes in ISO 9001:2015. It states that although the terms have been changed, organizations aren't required to use the same terminology used by ISO 9001:2015 in their QMS. Furthermore, subclause A.6, Documented information (located in annex A), includes clarifying information related to when the term "documented information" is used. It states, "Where ISO 9001:2008 used specific terminology such as 'document' or 'documented procedures,' 'quality manual' or 'quality plan,' this edition of this International Standard defines requirements to 'maintain documented information.'

"Where ISO 9001:2008 used the term 'records' to denote documents needed to provide evidence of conformity with requirements, this is now expressed as a requirement to 'retain documented information.' "

The annex goes on to explain that when the word "information" is used without "documented," there is no requirement that the organization maintain documented information unless the organization determines it's necessary.

ORGANIZATIONAL KNOWLEDGE

Subclause 7.1.6, Organizational knowledge, requires organizations to determine what knowledge is necessary for the operation of their processes to meet product or service requirements. This is one of ISO 9001:2015's new requirements, but it's something that most organizations already have in place, even if informally.

This requirement is frequently confused with the requirements for employee competence. Organizational knowledge relates to the organization; competence is employee knowledge.

Understanding the change

Subclause A.7, Organizational knowledge (located in annex A), addresses this requirement. It specifically relates that the organization needs to safeguard against loss of knowledge through employee turnover. It also provides examples of methods for acquiring knowledge, such as benchmarking or sharing lessons learned.

CONTROL OF EXTERNALLY PROVIDED PRODUCTS AND SERVICES

This is another aspect of ISO 9001:2015 where the terminology has changed. In ISO 9001:2000, the term "vendor" was changed to "supplier." In ISO 9001:2015, the term "supplier" has been replaced with "external provider." This is because not all products or services are obtained through a traditional purchasing process. For example, some organizations receive parts or services from an associate company.

Understanding the change

Using the term "supplier" limited the organization's ability to see that there might be the need for controls for providers other than suppliers. With the understanding that the controls for a traditional "supplier" might be different than those for an associate company, subclause A.8, Control of externally provided processes, products, and services (located in annex A), provides clarification that the organization can take a risk-based approach to determine the type and extent of controls needed for each external provider based on the products and services to be provided.

In addition to this terminology change, additional terminology changes are included in subclause A.1, Structure and terminology (located in annex A). As with the previous examples outlined, there is no requirement that organizations transition to these terms. Organizations should use terms that best fit their needs regardless of their use in the standard.

ISO 9001:2015 introduces concepts that are familiar to organizations. However, some of these terms may have some nuances and specific steps that need to be incorporated into an organization's QMS.

Section II of this handbook reviews the requirements of ISO 9001:2015 clause by clause and provides keys to understanding the change as well as examples of how they can be implemented.

CHAPTER 3

ISO 9000:2015 Overview

Surprisingly, despite having a rather long history, it's still necessary to explain ISO 9000 and why it's important. ISO 9000 is the normative reference for ISO 9001 and many other management systems standards developed by the International Organization for Standardization (ISO)

In our usage, a *normative reference* is a document that's required for understanding or implementing a standard.

Unfortunately, the sales numbers and other evidence show that not nearly enough users of ISO standards familiarize themselves with ISO 9000. This chapter provides an overview of ISO 9000:2015. This overview of ISO 9000:2015 is *not* intended to replace the document, however. Users of ISO 9001:2015 are *strongly* encouraged to purchase, read, and refer to ISO 9000:2015 before, during, and after their ISO 9001:2015 implementation or transition effort.

BASIC FORMAT OF ISO 9000

ISO 9000:2015 consists of two primary clauses: Clause 2 lays out quality concepts and quality management principles that serve as fundamentals key to understanding and making use of ISO 9001:2015 and other management system standards. Clause 3 provides the specific terms and definitions key to understanding ISO 9001:2015. Additionally, there is an annex that gives the reader concept diagrams that are useful in understanding the context and relationships between terms. The terms and definitions in clause 3 are arranged in groupings of concepts.

2 FUNDAMENTAL CONCEPTS AND QUALITY MANAGEMENT PRINCIPLES

2.1 General

Keys to understanding

This opening section highlights the importance of understanding the fundamental concepts and principles within clause 2. Additionally, it presents the need for a deep understanding of a rapidly changing business environment and the importance of meeting those challenges and protecting the organization's reputation. It also introduces the concept of the influence of interested parties and their effect on the organization.

2.2 Fundamental concepts

- 2.2.1, Quality
- 2.2.2, Quality management system
- 2.2.3, Context of an organization
- 2.2.4, Interested parties

Keys to understanding

Subclause 2.2 discusses concepts that provide a fundamental understanding and baseline knowledge of quality and a quality management system (QMS). It's written at a very basic level.

Quality

An understanding of the concept of quality is key to developing and continually improving a QMS. The organization's quality culture is set by top management. However, culture isn't something that can simply be installed or implemented. It's the culmination of shared beliefs and behaviors that demonstrate the organization's commitment to quality and its effect on the organization's reputation.

Beyond the cultural aspects are the very straightforward requirements for the organization to ensure the quality of the products and services it provides. It's important to understand that quality isn't just about conformance to requirements; it's also about value and customer perception.

Quality management system

ISO 9000:2015 gives a basic description of what a QMS is and makes a clear link to the QMS and the organization's objectives. The basic components of the QMS are the processes and resources used to achieve objectives and provide value to customers and other relevant interested parties. It's essential to understand the interrelationship between processes and the role that top management plays in owning the processes and providing the needed resources.

ISO 9000:2015 also explores the QMS concept in terms of intended and unintended consequences in providing products and services. Although it's not explored in depth, it's something that many organizations deal with on a regular basis. The unintended consequences of a company's products or services can become fodder for newscasts. A QMS can help an organization understand, document, and mitigate the effects of these unintended consequences. At a minimum, it allows an organization to plan.

Context of an organization

One of the key points made by ISO 9000:2015 is that understanding the context of the organization is a *process*. It's not just something that is determined in a meeting and written on a flip chart. The organization uses this process to continually assess internal and external factors to strategically guide it. A clear and universal understanding of the context of the organization can provide consistent direction and influence the development of key artifacts such as vision, mission, policies, and objectives.

Interested parties

The customer is always the most important interested party in any organization. However, organizations must consider other interested parties. A complete and accurate understanding of interested parties is critical to the overall success and sustainability of the organization. If you expand the concept of interested parties to its broadest definition, it can apply to virtually anyone who has ever heard of the organization. ISO 9000:2015 directs you to focus on interested parties who are *relevant* to the QMS. A consideration of the results expected by relevant interested parties should drive the development of objectives and the overall sustainability of the organization.

2.2.5 Support

- 2.2.5.1, General
- 2.2.5.2, People
- 2.2.5.3, Competence
- 2.2.5.4, Awareness
- 2.2.5.5, Communication

Keys to understanding

The primary focus of subclause 2.2.5 is the support that must be planned for and provided by top management. In particular, the organization must provide support in the form of people and other resources. To achieve its objectives, top management supports the organization as it plans the attainment, development, and maintenance of resources. It's also more important than ever to consider the responsible disposal of certain resources.

People

Although it may sound cliché, it can never be overstated how important people are to any organization. Beyond the obvious necessity for people to perform work, the behaviors and capabilities of an organization's people directly relate to the levels of performance and quality achieved. It's crucial to ensure that all people within the organization are aligned and engaged with the organization's vision, mission, and objectives to meet the needs and expectations of their relevant interested parties.

Competence

One aspect of the organization having the right people with the right capabilities in place is to ensure a focus on understanding the required competencies to meet their needs. Organizations need to develop a plan to provide resources and opportunities to develop and enhance these competencies.

Awareness

Top management must always strive to ensure that employees are aware of their duties and roles within the QMS and how they affect the organization. This awareness is a key factor in providing leadership and employee engagement.

Communication

This subclause also addresses the need for active and thorough communication. Planned and thoughtful communication can help to drive satisfaction of employees and customers alike. Although there is no specific prescription for adequate communication, it's important to consider all relevant interested parties when planning internal and external communications.

2.3 Quality management principles

- 2.3.1, Customer focus
- 2.3.2, Leadership
- 2.3.3, Engagement of people
- 2.3.4, Process approach
- 2.3.5, Improvement
- 2.3.6, Evidence-based decision making
- 2.3.7, Relationship management

Keys to understanding

Quality management principles have always been a bedrock on which ISO 9001 has been based. They have also appeared in previous versions of ISO 9000 as well as in ISO 9004. Within the structure of ISO/TC 176 (the committee responsible for updating the ISO 9000 standard series), a team was developed to review, refresh, and revise the previous version of the eight quality management principles.

The team updated the quality management principles and combined two of them. The final revision of the quality management principles went through the normal comment and balloting process within ISO/TC 176. Upon approval in 2013, the quality management principles document (ISO/TC 176/SC 1/N 429) content was incorporated, word for word, into ISO 9000:2015. The structure for the incorporation of the quality management principles is as follows:

- *Statement*—The basic description of the intent of the specific principle.
- *Rationale*—The reason the user should consider the principle and its effect on the field of quality management.
- *Key benefits*—The key benefits the user may enjoy by the deployment and execution of the principle.
- *Possible actions*—Actions that may be taken by the organization to fully realize the effect of the principle.

Customer focus

One of the key elements of any QMS is to not only meet customer requirements but also to meet customer needs and expectations. No matter the product or service provided, all organizations have customers who help to define the organization's reason for existence. All customers evaluate an organization on the quality of its products or services. The continued success and sustainability of the organization ultimately depends on the satisfaction of its customers and other relevant interested parties.

Leadership

Excellence in leadership creates an environment in which all aspects of the QMS can be more efficient and effective. There are many aspects of top management's leadership role in ISO 9001:2015's requirements. This is no coincidence, as the drafters applied this important principle directly. The first of W. Edwards Deming's famous 14 points is creating a constancy of purpose. This is clearly the primary role of leadership in any organization.

Engagement of people

Clearly, the most important asset of any organization is its people. Consistently engaging them in contributing to the organization's shared vision, mission, and objectives is paramount to sustained performance. Engagement is more than simply involvement. Engagement implies a deeper level of culture and commitment toward shared values. However, this engagement cannot be taken for granted or neglected. High levels of engagement take consistent excellence in leadership.

Process approach

Although the process approach isn't a new feature within the quality management principles, it's a concept that is crucial for getting the most out of an ISO 9001:2015-based QMS. It's a key element within the structure and application of ISO 9001. A thorough understanding and ownership of the interrelated processes within the organization enables it to deliver value and the desired performance.

Improvement

Not only is improvement a quality management principle, but in many organizations continual improvement is also an integral philosophy or even department. The basic premise is that the organization should always seek to improve current systems, processes, and performance. Although the periods of improvement may vary from slow and steady to rapid, it should never have an end point. Improvement should be viewed as a journey—not just a series of destinations—to be truly transformational.

Evidence-based decision making

Another statement attributed to Deming is, "In God we trust, all others bring data." There is something attractive and even expedient about relying upon our legends and icons in the organization. We all hear about folks "going with their gut" and succeeding. Unfortunately, you don't hear about the many more stories in which it didn't payoff. Making decisions solely based upon the experience of team members isn't a likely recipe for long-term success. However, it should not be seen as a daunting enterprise to take the time to gather data during the decision-making process. Getting it right the first time will pay for itself in the long run in time and efficiency.

Relationship management

The last quality management principle within ISO 9000:2015 is related to the need to manage key relationships. The specific relationships are with those interested parties that are relevant to the QMS. With the ever-increasing linkages and interrelations of organizations, managing those relationships is a key to their mutual success. A particular relationship that all organizations must manage is that between a customer and its network of providers. The organization's value chain is like any other: It's only as strong as its weakest link. Therefore, true partnerships with providers always yield the best results.

2.4 Developing the QMS using fundamental concepts and principles

- 2.4.1, QMS model
- 2.4.2, Development of a QMS
- 2.4.3, QMS standards, other management systems, and excellence models

Keys to understanding

Subclause 2.4 of ISO 9000:2015 focuses on providing guidance on the development of a QMS, building on the fundamental concepts and quality management principles. It's written at a very basic level. Although it doesn't serve as a textbook or an exhaustive "how to," it does provides concepts that can foster further examination by the organization.

Consider the similarity of a QMS to a living organism. For the overall success (health) of a living organism, it must have multiple levels that all work together. When there is an interruption in the performance at any of the levels of an organism, it often results in a malady or even death. Within the QMS, unless all components of the system are working together effectively, the system may see a complete breakdown. At a minimum, it won't deliver the performance needed to satisfy relevant interested parties.

A secondary aspect of this analogy is to draw on the concept that an organism must adapt to its environment to survive and thrive. As a parallel, it's important for the QMS to have mechanisms to gain feedback from its relevant interested parties and respond with the appropriate improvement or innovative actions to be successful, or even maintain relevancy.

QMS model

ISO 9000:2015 breaks down the concept of developing a QMS into the following three levels of organization:

- *System.* The linked network of processes that are aligned to meet the needs and requirements of the relevant interested parties.
- *Processes.* Interrelated activities that convert the inputs to the process into the intended or unintended outputs of the process.
- *Activity.* The specific actions within a process that enhance performance or delivery of outputs.

QMS development

ISO 9000:2015 provides guidance on developing a formal QMS. When an organization embarks along this path, it probably already has quality management activities underway. Although they may be informal or not aligned to comply with any standard, these activities nonetheless may provide a starting point in building a QMS. The first activity is to understand the quality management practices and processes already in place.

When using ISO 9001:2015 as a framework to formalize the QMS, it may seem like there are many requirements and that the system must be fairly complex. One of the key goals of the drafters of ISO 9001:2015 was that the requirements be relevant to both manufacturing and service organizations, large and small. The QMS simply needs to meet the needs of the organization and satisfy the requirements of the relevant interested parties. Easy to say, but it takes some effort to actually accomplish. So, how does an organization move forward?

The development of the QMS isn't an event. It's not a singular meeting that takes place in an off-site location, facilitated by some external person who presents a well-crafted series of documents aligned with ISO 9001. It's a process that evolves and changes over time as the organization seeks to meet the needs of its changing environment. It requires dedicated and deliberate planning to achieve the intended results. The plan should consider the entire scope of the organization's processes and the standards and requirements that are to be met through deployment of the system.

As the organization begins to implement the plan, it's important to create points within the process that can be monitored, measured, and evaluated to ensure the plan is being met. If not, mitigating actions can be taken to minimize the effects of deviations from the plan. This may involve specific changes to the plan or require bringing additional resources to get the plan back on track. It's a good practice to identify the milestones within the plan so progress is clear.

Once the QMS is developed to meet the internal and external requirements of the organization, it's important to develop a process to consistently assess the extent to which the system is deployed, executed, and delivering the intended performance. Within the ISO 9000 family of documents, this takes the form of an auditing process. The process involves a plan to be developed to determine the scope and sampling plan for the process being examined. Evidence is then gathered that can be used by the auditor to make a judgment as to the extent to which the requirements of the process are being met. Then the most important part of any auditing process takes place. It's not the mere "gotcha" of a finding that something isn't done properly. It's a gift or opportunity to learn and make the system more robust. It's a series of improvement actions that are identified and implemented that are key to the audit process. Finally, for each action to solve an individual failure, there is an opportunity to apply the findings elsewhere to prevent other failures, thus multiplying the learning.

QMS standards, other management systems, and excellence models

The final part of clause 2 of ISO 9000:2015 provides guidance on the relationship between the ISO 9000 family of standards and other ISO management system standards. Regardless of the goal of the specific standard or the intended audience, there are common elements that all of the management system standards rely upon. In fact, it's with this premise that the ISO Technical Management Board (TMB) has developed a high-level structure that all management system standards developed by ISO must comply with. This structure is known as Annex SL. This document is intended to provide a commonality to all ISO management system standards, making it easier for organizations to align and integrate multiple management system standards.

Subclause 2.4.3 of ISO 9000:2015 provides guidance and a listing of the major management system standards that are most often associated and aligned with QMSs. The benefits are obvious to any organization in its ability to link and align the many operating systems, including the QMS.

3 TERMS AND DEFINITIONS

Keys to understanding

Although this is a rather large percentage of the materials contained within ISO 9000:2015, we won't attempt to summarize or pull key meanings out of the terms and definitions. In fact, providing meaning to words is the basis for any listing of terms and definitions, and frankly it's essential that all users of ISO 9001:2015 should know and utilize this clause. A couple of notes about this clause, though, may be relevant.

At first reading, there is a natural tendency to want to see the terms and definitions in a standard format. Most people prefer to see the terms and definitions in alphabetical order. In ISO 9000:2015, however, they are put into specific relative groups, or affinities. The goal behind this arrangement is that this clause isn't simply a list of definitions that can be found in the multitude of available dictionaries. Rather, it provides contextual definitions that support the very specific use of the words as they appear in the standards that use ISO 9000:2015 as a normative reference. Therefore, by providing these terms and definitions in relation to other terms, ISO 9000:2015 provides additional context as to the specific use and understanding of the terms. Of course, for those wanting a quick reference to a specific term, an alphabetical list is provided as the last section of ISO 9000:2015.

ANNEX A (INFORMATIVE) CONCEPT RELATIONSHIPS AND THEIR GRAPHICAL REPRESENTATION

The final element of ISO 9000:2015 is annex A. There are concept diagrams that are provided for the specific terms. These concept diagrams are another way for users to visualize in a graphical way the relationship between supporting terms. Users may find this graphical representation a more effective way of showing this relationship

IN CONCLUSION

A normative reference is a document that is ultimately required to achieve a thorough understanding of a standard. Therefore, it's crucial for users of ISO 9001:2015 who want a thorough and accurate understanding of the fundamental concepts, quality management principles, and vocabulary within ISO 9000:2015 to read it.

CHAPTER 4

ISO Standards Development Process

As a user of standards, you may wonder about the process for developing or revising them. Before considering the actual drafting process, the first step is to understand the rules and infrastructure within which ISO 9001:2015 was developed.

In this chapter we'll consider three phases of the revision process, including justification for the revision, the design specification that guided the drafting, and the drafting process itself.

JUSTIFICATION FOR REVISION OF ISO 9001

Management system standards are administered by a technical committee (TC), which is responsible for following the requirements for developing standards by following the ISO Directives. ISO/TC 176 develops and revises the ISO 9000 family of standards. The ISO Directives require ISO/TC 176 to conduct a systematic review of ISO 9001 within five years of publication. Some believe that the actual revision must take place within the five-year time period, but this isn't the case. If it was, the technical experts would have to immediately start revising ISO 9001 every time it's published to meet the five-year timetable.

The results of the systematic review will yield one of four decisions: withdraw, revise/amend, confirm, or confirm with error corrections. The systematic review of ISO 9001:2008 was conducted in 2011–2012. The feedback from the review indicated that the standard needed to be revised. This was due in large part to the fact that ISO 9001:2008 was a simple amendment to the ISO 9001:2000 standard. There hadn't been any significant changes to the standard in fifteen years. This, coupled with the changes in technology and the different ways in which organizations operate, provided a strong case for revision.

After a systematic review is conducted, the ISO Directives require the completion of a justification study. For the purposes of ISO 9001, this is typically completed by the ISO/TC 176/SC 2 secretariat with the participation of technical experts as necessary. Many times this will include the convener of the working group. The justification study considers a review of the market as well as feedback provided by participating countries on the systematic review.

DESIGN SPECIFICATION FOR THE REVISION

After the decision was made to revise the standard, the technical experts developed a design specification. The purpose of the design specification was to provide a framework to meet the needs of users and improve known issues.

The design specification was circulated to the voting members for approval. The voting process includes the opportunity for members to make comments, which must be considered before the final approval.

The design specification serves multiple purposes. It defines the scope of the revision project. It keeps the technical experts from deviating from the approved project specification. Finally, it's used by the task force in the working group assigned responsibility for verifying the final product to ensure that the output of drafters' work matches the defined inputs.

The working group began the actual revision process after the design specification was completed. To meet user needs, the editing focused on published sources of information. The inputs that were considered included:

- User needs:
  - ✓ The results of the "systematic review" that was completed on ISO 9001:2008 during 2011–2012 (document SC2/N1066)
  - ✓ Analysis of the results of the extensive worldwide ISO 9000 User Survey (document SC2/N1017)

- Other inputs include:
  - ✓ ISO/TC 176/SC 2 Vision and Mission (SC2/N1014)
  - ✓ ISO/TC 176/SC 2 Strategic Objective A.2.3 (2011)—SC2 portfolio of products for the next decade (SC2/N1016)
  - ✓ ISO/TC 176/SC 2/WG 18/TG1.19 Project Review Report (SC2/N845; WG24/N26)

- ✓ The work on developing *"Future Concepts for use in the work of ISO/TC 176/SC 2"* (SC2/N1013)
- ✓ The work of the ad hoc group that examined whether the requirements of ISO 9001 support subclause 1.1 (SC2/N789-1)
- ✓ Preliminary outputs from the joint SC1/SC2 task group on the revision to the Quality Management Principles
- ✓ The work of the ISO/TMB/TAG 13—JTCG (now formalized as Annex SL)
- ✓ The design specifications for ISO 9001:2000 and ISO 9001:2008, (SC2/N307 and SC2/N707-1), which identified users and user needs
- ✓ The comments received through the "systematic review," and on the "proposed actions" papers (SC2/N1068 and SC2/1075)

Although the design specification includes many different inputs, the focus on certain inputs provided a clear direction for the revision.

FUTURE CONCEPTS FOR USE IN THE WORK OF ISO/TC 176/SC 2

After ISO 9001:2008 was published, it was determined that there had been ideas that had been submitted that couldn't be considered because they went beyond the scope of an amendment. It was important to not only capture these ideas, but also to evaluate what the implications might be for incorporating them into a future revision of ISO 9001 or a related standard.

For this reason, task groups worked on analyzing some of these ideas. They were developed into a series of white papers that analyzed if the ideas should be incorporated into ISO 9001, if there was already existing information on the topics, and overall implications. These ideas included some of the new concepts that ended up in ISO 9001:2015, such as risk-based thinking and organizational knowledge.

These concepts were also included in the worldwide survey that was conducted in 2011, which provided user feedback on what users most wanted or least wanted to see in a revision to ISO 9001:2008.

All of this groundwork gave the technical experts a solid understanding of what needed to be accomplished when the revision process began.

Global user questionnaire/survey

In 2010–2011, ISO/TC 176 conducted a global survey that asked questions relating to everything from organizations' demographics to specific questions regarding clauses in ISO 9001 and future concepts to be considered in its next revision.

This data was considered during the drafting process. The organizational knowledge and risk-based thinking concepts had support in the survey and were incorporated into ISO 9001:2015.

Market justification study

The technical experts also considered the results of the market justification study. The report included information regarding relevant issues in the marketplace such as compatibility with other management system standards (e.g., ISO 14001) and the identification of interpretation issues that required clarification.

Interpretations process

Each of the sanctioned interpretations were considered during the editing process for ISO 9001:2008. Some of the interpretations couldn't be included in ISO 9001:2008 because they went beyond the scope of an amendment. However, they were kept and considered during the revision process. Consideration was also given to ensuring that changes based on an interpretation for ISO 9001:2008 were sustained wherever possible to ensure ongoing understanding by users.

Technical experts

One important additional input to the process is the technical experts' aggregated knowledge. This is the lifeblood of any technical committee. Although the technical experts represent a multitude of countries and associations (member bodies), they are indeed experts. Since revising ISO 9001 in 2008, they've learned new techniques, been exposed to new markets, and generally expanded their comprehension of quality management through daily work. Some experts retire and new candidates replace them, bringing along their own knowledge and unique perspectives. The ongoing exchange of ideas enriches all and contributes to the integrity of the standards that are ultimately produced.

DRAFTING PROCESS OF THE REVISION

As with most standards, the first version (or two) is referred to as a working draft (WD). Feedback at this stage on the drafting of the document is limited to the technical experts within the working group (WG), as WDs generally aren't circulated publicly. The WG is the cumulative umbrella for all the task groups (TGs) working on the project.

Work at the WD level can involve meetings as well as teleconferences and e-mails. Decisions are achieved through a consensus process. Considering that the technical experts hail from dozens of countries around the globe representing many different cultures, languages, and industries, this process is nothing short of extraordinary.

At the WD level, only the technical experts provide comments. When the WD reaches adequate maturity as determined by the task group with input from other WG members, it's released as a committee draft (CD). There can be multiple CDs depending on feedback from the voting members and the user community.

STANDARDS DEVELOPMENT PROCESS

CDs may be issued for comment only or for ballot. During the CD stage, participating countries also distribute the document for review by technical experts of their mirror committees. For the United States, it's the U.S. Technical Advisory Group to ISO/TC 176. The document can also be made available to the general public for comment.

Each country develops a consensus position on its comments and submits them to the secretariat of ISO/TC 176/SC 2 (the subcommittee that is responsible for the content of ISO 9001) for consideration.

A standard undergoing change can also be distributed as a CD for ballot. This means in addition to providing comments, each participating country also votes on the document.

Subsequent to the CD stage, the document goes through a succession of balloting and comment review. After CD, the document is published as a draft international standard (DIS). This document is released for public comments that are collected and submitted for review by the member bodies of ISO/TC 176.

After another round of drafting based on the feedback from the comments and voting, the document progresses to the final draft international standard (FDIS) phase. At this point, it's virtually ready for publication. The member bodies of ISO/TC 176 ballot for final approval of the document. After successfully passing this ballot, the document is prepared for final release through the editorial process within the Central Secretariat of ISO and released.

During the revision drafting process, face-to-face meetings are conducted to review comments. Each comment submitted is reviewed and dispositioned for either editorial or technical reasons. During the review of comments, some are quickly accepted because they meet the intent of the standard and are related to areas identified in the design specification as targets for clarification.

Although the standards development process may seem a bit complicated, it is deliberately formal to ensure that revisions and changes are not taken lightly. It's important to ensure that the market and users are thoroughly evaluated before starting. Once drafting begins, each draft is focused on advancing the maturity of the standard along with increasing the level of consensus to allow for easy adoption by participating countries at the time of final publication. Ultimately, the different drafts, the review of comments, and expert contributions all play a significant part in the standards development process

Part of this chapter originally appeared in The Insiders' Guide to ISO 9001:2008 *(Paton Professional, 2009), co-authors Lorri Hunt, Denise Robitaille, and Craig Williams.*

Chapter 5

Introduction and Annexes

One common mistake made by many users of ISO 9001 and other ISO management system standards is to jump directly to the standard's requirements and skip the rest of it. This results in missing valuable information and not understanding the context of the standard and fundamental concepts such as the process approach, risk-based thinking, and the plan-do-check-act (PDCA) cycle.

To have the best understanding possible, top management and process owners should read ISO 9000:2015 and the introduction and annexes of ISO 9001:2015 before reviewing the requirements in clauses 4 through 10.

An expectation of any organization using ISO 9001 as the foundation of its quality management system (QMS) is that everyone in the organization understands the intent of the process approach, risk-based thinking, and the PDCA cycle. These concepts shouldn't be seen in isolation but in conjunction.

ISO 9001:2015's introduction includes a list of the quality management principles, which are described in detail in ISO 9000:2015. Therefore, reading ISO 9000:2015 is needed to understand these principles and how they are a fundamental piece in ISO 9001:2015 and the organization's QMS.

In addition to the quality management principles, ISO 9000:2015 provides an explanation of the rationale for a QMS and how it can become an essential element for the organization's long-term success. It also includes the terminology used in ISO 9001:2015. Chapter 3 reviews ISO 9000:2015 in more depth and helps organizations understand its value to the QMS.

Annex A was developed to assist current users in understanding what's new in ISO 9001:2015. After reading ISO 9000:2015 and ISO 9001:2015's introduction, current users should review annex A to understand the changes in the new version.

Annex A includes information on:
- The new common structure (Annex SL) and terminology
- Reference to products and services
- Reasons for considering relevant interested parties
- The intent of the adoption of risk-based thinking
- The rationale of the expectation of the applicability of all the requirements
- The new approach to documented information
- A clarification of the requirements on organizational knowledge
- The new approach to external provision

Annex B includes a list of standards in the ISO/TC 176 portfolio to promote their use in understanding ISO 9001:2015's requirements. These standards provide guidance on the implementation of the requirements in ISO 9001:2015 such as training, use of statistical techniques, and customer satisfaction.

The bibliography provides a list of other standards and publications that can be useful during the implementation and maintenance of the QMS.

In summary, users should read ISO 9001:2015 in its entirety to clearly understand its requirements. It's also essential to read ISO 9000:2015 to have a better understanding of the rationale of a QMS and the key terms used in ISO 9001:2015.

CHAPTER 6

Process Approach and Risk-Based Thinking

Beginning with ISO 9001:2000, the standard has incorporated the process approach as the foundation of a quality management system (QMS). The expectation is that organizations adopting ISO 9001 will manage their operations on a structure based on processes.

These processes follow a logical sequence and interaction, and create a system that will produce intended results. In other words, a desired level of performance will be achieved. Understanding its performance level will lead the organization to establish improvement actions aimed at achieving its objectives and enhancing customer satisfaction.

ISO 9001:2015 is based on the process approach and incorporates the plan-do-check-act (PDCA) cycle and risk-based thinking as an integral part of an organization's QMS.

What's the difference between a process and a system? If we ask this question in any organization, we will likely get interesting responses.

According to ISO 9000:2015:
- A *system* is a set of interrelated or interacting elements.
- A *process* is a set of interrelated or interacting activities that use inputs to deliver an intended result.
- An *output* is a result of a process.

When using these definitions, we can see that in both cases an interaction or interrelation occurs. In this regard, a system can be a process and a process can be a system. So what's the difference?

The human respiratory system provides an example. What are the interacting elements in this system? We can say the nose, mouth, nasal cavity, larynx, pharynx, and lungs. It's easy to see that these elements are in constant interaction.

When reviewing the system from a process perspective, the main input is the air that we breathe. The intended result is oxygen delivered to the blood through the circulatory system. The system also takes carbon dioxide that results from breaking apart air molecules in the lungs and we exhale it and other particles. Through a set of activities that occurs in the interacting elements, this system is able to inhale air, produce oxygen, and exhale carbon dioxide.

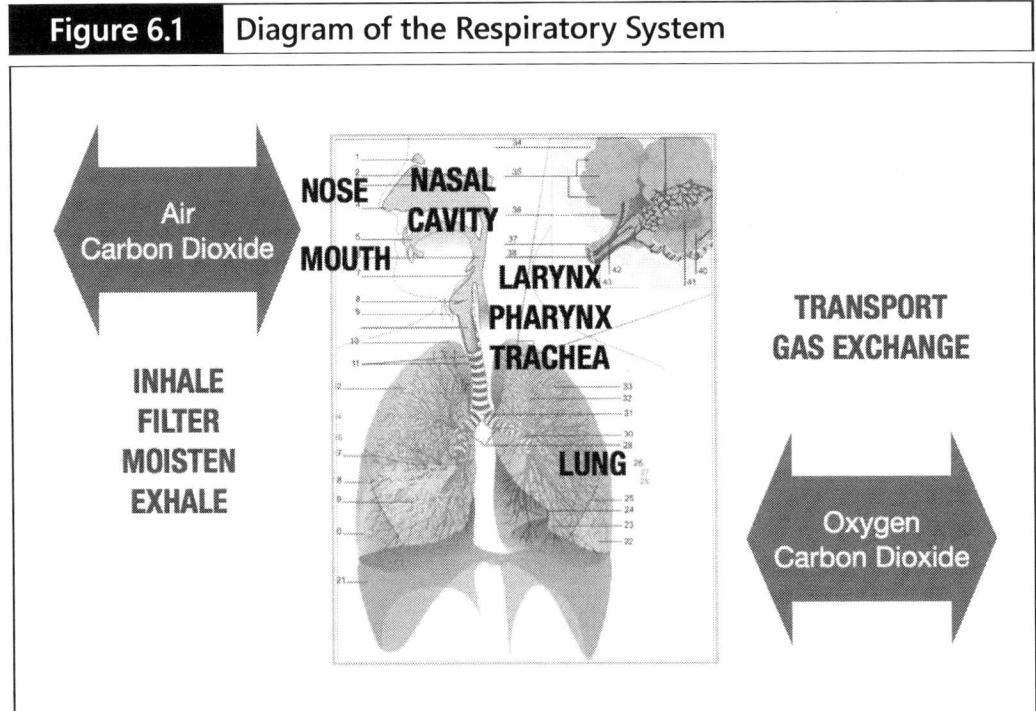

Figure 6.1 Diagram of the Respiratory System

Some examples of these activities are to inhale (air), to moisten (air), to transport (air to the lungs), to exchange (oxygen with carbon dioxide in the blood), and to exhale (carbon dioxide).

In the context of ISO 9001:2015, the elements of the QMS are the processes of the organization.

Another important aspect to consider is the relationship that exists between the output of a process and the objectives of the QMS that will be translated into the performance of the process in terms of effectiveness and efficiency.

According ISO 9000:2015:
- An *objective* is a result to be achieved.
- *Performance* is a measurable result.
- *Effectiveness* is the extent to which planned activities are realized and planned results are achieved.
- *Efficiency* is the relationship between the result achieved and the resources used.

One of the results of a planning process at a system or management level are the objectives of the QMS and the inherent risks and of the key inputs by its processes. These objectives will be based on certain level of effectiveness and efficiency that the organization is looking to achieve.

Some examples:
- Reduce the costs of operations by 5 percent in comparison to the previous year.
- Maintain an on-time delivery rate above 95 percent during the year.
- Respond within 24 hours to any customer request for information related to the service provision.

The operation, controls, measurement, and monitoring taking place at each process should be aligned with the determined objectives, risks, and opportunities. The organization should consider for which processes it will implement analysis-and-evaluation activities to determine the performance of the process, using the objectives, risks, and opportunities as a framework.

These processes should produce information, reports, or other indicators that show its performance level.

ISO 9001:2015 incorporates risk-based thinking, which becomes a key part of the process approach. This means that the people responsible for a process should be aware that things can go wrong with the outputs of the process that can jeopardize customer satisfaction.

Risk-based thinking should be seen as a code of conduct. Employees should have a robust knowledge of the process(es) they are responsible for or they participate in, and they should understand the consequences of anything that goes wrong. They should also treat opportunities in the same way.

According to ISO 9000:2015, *risk* is the effect of uncertainty. An *effect* is a deviation from the expected—positive or negative. Uncertainty is the state, even partial, of deficiency of information related to understanding or knowledge of an event, its consequence, or likelihood.

To better understand risk-based thinking, consider a baseball game where the two teams are tied. The home team is batting in the bottom of the ninth inning. Any run scored by the home team will end the game. Let's look at this situation from different perspectives. Fans of the home team know that there could be two effects.

Positive: The player hits the ball and reaches base or walks. Negative: The player is out.

On the other hand, for fans of the visiting team, there could be two effects. Positive: The player is out. Negative: The player hits the ball and reaches base or walks.

The same scenario will create the same positive and negative effects on the bench. The difference is the level of uncertainty. Managers, coaches, and players have more information about the pitcher and the batter. They have statistics and records. The coaches might choose to switch pitchers based on the known performance of the batter or a team might use a pinch hitter if the planned batter doesn't typically perform as well. When they use this knowledge and make decisions, they're taking actions to address risks.

When we relate this scenario to a business environment, organizations are frequently faced with risks and opportunities. An organization establishes its processes and considers risks and opportunities as it makes decisions. It uses data and information to make decisions about these processes. Sometimes it will determine it needs to take actions to address risk.

In summary, a risk will always have one or more effects as a potential result. These effects can be perceived as positive or negative. The level of knowledge of the effects and their consequences will determine the level of uncertainty.

ISO 9001:2015 requires that once the organization determines risks and opportunities, it needs to implement actions to address those risks and opportunities and evaluate their effectiveness. (See subclause 6.1.2.)

This means that the process owner or responsible person should ensure that all the outputs produced by the process are aligned with the intent of the objectives. Certain objectives will be more critical for certain processes. In these cases, the processes will be accountable for their achievement. Actions needed to ensure the process will contribute to the achievement of the objectives. They must also consider the inherent risks and opportunities.

Imagine that an organization has an objective based on productivity levels and another based on the number of permissible safety incidents. If the persons in the operational processes are only aware of the level of daily productivity to be achieved, the likelihood of having a safety incident is higher.

You might wonder what relationship a safety incident has to the quality of the outputs of this operational process. You might think that there is no relation. However, if people are injured while working, productivity may fall. This can create absenteeism, downtime, and a lack of motivation because the operations are performed under unsafe conditions.

Risk-based thinking and the process approach are aimed at ensuring the QMS will achieve its intended results and create good products and services, fulfillment of applicable requirements, satisfied customers, and continual improvement.

THE PDCA CYCLE

The QMS should be planned. The outputs of this planning are the objectives, risks and opportunities; a set of strategies or a business plan; the scope; and the QMS processes.

Using the strategies or business plan, each organization will implement actions to address risks and opportunities and achieve objectives and controls to ensure that processes are performed as planned. Processes need to produce information that demonstrates the performance achieved and the implementation of any improvement action.

The analysis and evaluation of the performance should be done at each process, as appropriate. This analysis and evaluation will facilitate decisions to ensure the achievement of the intended results at a system and process level.

If there are situations that put the process and its outputs in a nonconforming condition, corrections and corrective actions need to be implemented to prevent their recurrence.

According to ISO 9000:2015, continual improvement is a recurring activity to enhance performance. All the persons in the process need to be aware of the importance of implementing continual improvement efforts. Elements of the process such as infrastructure, awareness and competence of people, and documented information are subject to continual improvement.

In other words, the expectation should be that when problems occur, relevant persons in the process implement the necessary activities to treat nonconformities and implement correction and corrective actions. In addition, when everything is good, relevant persons in the process determine what actions can be implemented to enhance process performance.

These concepts: process approach, risk-based thinking, and the PDCA cycle, should be understood holistically.

Top management and process owners in the organization should have a thorough understanding of these concepts. The role of top management will be the promotion of the use of these concepts as required by subclause 5.1, Leadership and commitment. The role of process owners is to implement them.

Internal auditors will need to incorporate specific competencies when conducting audits to confirm that people involved in each process have a good understanding and awareness of these concepts to help ensure the expected performance of every process.

The concepts of process approach, risk-based thinking, and PDCA provide the foundation for the QMS. Establishing these pieces of your QMS prior to implementing any other requirements will help ensure that these philosophies are inherent in the QMS.

Section II

Clause-by-Clause Analysis

As the title suggests, this section provides a clause-by-clause analysis of ISO 9001:2015's requirements, keys to understanding those requirements, and guidance on transitioning to the new requirements.

CHAPTER 7

Clause 4—Context of the Organization

This section of the handbook includes a clause-by-clause review of the requirements an organization is responsible for implementing in a quality management system (QMS). The requirements are described in paraphrased text, the keys to understanding, and information for existing users on how to transition to the new requirements.

As a reminder, the handbook should be used in conjunction with ISO 9001:2015. The handbook also provides examples of implementation. It's important to note that in some cases best business practices have been included that go beyond the minimum requirements of the standard. These have been identified as such. It's also possible to demonstrate conformance using other methods.

4 CONTEXT OF THE ORGANIZATION

The requirements in clause 4, Context of the organization, form the foundation of the organization's QMS. Clause 4 drives the organization to determine the internal and external issues that could affect it. It also pushes the organization to seek an understanding of its relevant interested parties and related requirements. This provides the basis to develop the scope of the QMS and establish the processes needed for its effective operation.

The organization uses these processes to implement ISO 9001:2015's requirements and to establish the methods used to manage its QMS.

4.1 UNDERSTANDING THE ORGANIZATION AND ITS CONTEXT

- Determine the external and internal issues. Be sure that they are:
  - ✓ Relevant to the organization
  - ✓ Consistent with the strategic direction
  - ✓ Can affect the ability to achieve intended results

- Monitor and review information related to internal and external issues.

Keys to understanding

ISO 9000:2015 describes "context of the organization" as a combination of internal and external factors and conditions that have an effect on an organization's approach to its products, services, investments, and relevant interested parties. Business plans may also include this information. In short, it's the organization's business environment. The good news for most businesses is that they already do this, whether intentionally or not. When performed purposefully and formally, it becomes a source of alignment and provides a firm structure to build upon for the planning and execution aspects that follow.

When implementing this requirement, focus on external and internal issues that could significantly affect the organization's products and services or the performance and effectiveness of the QMS. For this reason, not every external and internal issue an organization identifies needs to be addressed and not every organization will have the same external and internal issues. The focus should be on those issues that could prevent the organization from achieving its intended results.

Figure 7.1 shows a partial list of potential external and internal issues; it does not include all possibilities.

Figure 7.1 Potential External and Internal Issues

External Issues	Internal Issues
Legal	Resources
Technological	Union negotiations
Competitive	Restructuring
Market	Values
Cultural	Culture
Social	Knowledge
Economic	Performance

Organizations can use many methods to determine external and internal issues. Larger organizations may have a strategic planning process in place or use a strengths-weaknesses-opportunities-threats (SWOT) analysis. Neither of these methods are required by ISO 9001:2015, but they can be used to meet the intent of the requirement.

After the organization determines the external and internal issues that could affect its processes, it should monitor and review information related to them. There is no requirement for documented information in this subclause. However, subclause 9.3, Management review, requires that external and internal issues be included as an input. For this reason, the intent of this subclause can be met through management review.

Typically, auditors verify that this requirement has been met by interviewing the leader of the organization and establishing the method used to identify external and internal issues. This can be followed up in management review. This method is probably more suitable for small- and medium-sized enterprises, but could be used for any size of organization.

Transition

This requirement is new in ISO 9001:2015. Although ISO 9001:2008 included some details in its introduction about an organization considering its environment, there were no specific requirements. Organizations must provide objective evidence that this requirement has been incorporated into the QMS.

4.2 UNDERSTANDING THE NEEDS AND EXPECTATIONS OF INTERESTED PARTIES

- The organization must:
  - ✓ Determine its relevant interested parties. (Relevant interested parties are those that have an effect or potential effect on the organization's ability to meet customer, statutory, and regulatory requirements.)
  - ✓ Determine requirements for relevant interested parties.
  - ✓ Monitor and review information about relevant interested parties and their requirements.

Keys to understanding

ISO 9000:2015 defines *interested party* as a person or organization that can affect, be affected by, or perceive themselves to be affected by a decision or activity.

Because the definition includes the consideration of relevant interested parties that "perceive" themselves to be affected, a caveat has been added to the requirement in ISO 9001:2015. To go beyond this caveat is to go beyond the scope of ISO 9001. The term "relevant" is the key to framing the scope. Relevant interested parties are only those that have an effect on the ability of the organization to provide a product or service that meets customer, statutory, and regulatory requirements. Annex A.3, Understanding the needs and expectations of relevant interested parties, further emphasizes the scope of ISO 9001:2015 by stating, "This International Standard is applicable where an organization needs to demonstrate its ability to consistently provide products and services that meet customer and applicable statutory and regulatory requirements and aims to enhance customer satisfaction."

Organizations typically know who their relevant interested parties are. However, if they aren't known, they can be determined via the strategic or business planning process. Even if they are known, it's useful to review your organization's relevant interested parties periodically. The relevant interested parties will vary based on what product or service your organization provides.

Examples include:
- Customers
- Partners
- Persons in the organization
- External providers
- Unions (if they influence employee competence)
- Regulatory agencies

Once the organization has determined its relevant interested parties, it needs to determine their requirements. Some requirements are based on the product being provided or the service being delivered; others might be customer specific. It should be noted that not all requirements the organization complies with are related to relevant interested parties. For example, an organization must comply with labor laws, but this isn't related to a requirement of an interested party.

Requirements are typically included in contracts, purchase orders, or other agreements with customers. If the organization and its customers are related to a specific industry, the regulatory requirements might be a directive of the product or service. Sources of requirements could include:
- Contracts
- Statutory and regulatory requirements (laws)
- Permits, licenses, or other forms of authorization
- Orders issued by regulatory agencies
- Relevant industry codes and standards

It's important to continually ensure that the requirements of the relevant interested parties are understood and met. Organizations may have departments or groups that manage these requirements for relevant interested parties. These could include:
- Customer service/customer contracts
- Legal department
- Compliance department

After an organization has determined its relevant interested parties and requirements, this information must be monitored and reviewed. Many different methods can be used to monitor the information, including reviewing the information during contract negotiation. It's also possible for specific departments or employees to monitor this information throughout the product lifecycle. Although not a requirement of ISO 9001:2015, organizations might include this topic in management review to ensure coverage. Smaller organizations might find this approach particularly helpful. Consideration should be given to the frequency with which this information is monitored and reviewed. Although documented information isn't required by the standard, the organization must be able to adequately demonstrate how this is handled by confirming the implementation of requirements.

Transition

In ISO 9001:2008, customer requirements were determined in subclause 7.2. Customer requirements related to design were incorporated in subclause 7.3, Design and development. ISO 9001:2015 expands the consideration of requirements to relevant interested parties. Organizations with a system that currently meets ISO 9001:2008 requirements will find the requirements they have considered in the past as good sources of information in determining relevant requirements.

4.3 DETERMINING THE SCOPE OF THE QUALITY MANAGEMENT SYSTEM

The organization shall:
- Determine the boundaries and applicability of the QMS.
- It shall consider:
    - ✓ External and internal issues (subclause 4.1)
    - ✓ Requirements of relevant interested parties (subclause 4.2)
    - ✓ Products and services of the organization

- Apply all the requirements of standard if they are determined to be applicable within the scope of the QMS.
- Make certain the scope is available and maintained as documented information. The scope shall state:
  - ✓ Types of products and services covered
  - ✓ Justification for any requirements determined not to be applicable. Only those requirements that don't affect the organization's ability to provide products and services that meet customer requirements can be determined not to be applicable.

Keys to understanding

The QMS scope must consider the external and internal issues of the organization that were determined in subclause 4.1, Context of the organization, the relevant interested parties, and their requirements established in subclause 4.2, Understanding the needs and expectations of interested parties, as well as the product and services provided by the organization. This is as simple as considering the effect of these items of interest as the scope is being developed.

There is no requirement to monitor and review the scope of the QMS, but a reasonable expectation is that this information would be reviewed when changes are made to any of the requirements that are considered to be a part of the scope.

Although the scope of the QMS isn't the scope of the certification, they are related. The scope needs to broad enough to include all the organization's products and services. The boundaries of the scope also relate to this. The boundaries can be specific geographic locations, certain departments, or product lines. If the organization chooses to only apply the requirements of ISO 9001:2015 to a specific product or service line and not the entire organization, this should be established and documented within the scope itself.

Once the scope of the QMS is determined, it shall be available and maintained as documented information. The organization can choose how this information is made available. Examples include providing the information in a specific document or posting it on a website. The documented information must include justification for when an organization chooses not to apply a requirement. However, it's important to note that an organization can't determine a requirement doesn't apply if it has the potential to effect its ability to provide a product or service that meets customer requirements. For example, an organization cannot determine that subclause 7.2, Competence, doesn't apply because not having competent persons working in the organization has a direct effect on the product or service being delivered.

Transition

The requirements for scope in ISO 9001:2015 are similar to ISO 9001:2008's requirements in subclause 4.2.2, Quality manual. Although there isn't a requirement for a quality manual in ISO 9001:2015, organizations can choose to retain a quality manual as a method for documenting the scope if it provides value.

ISO 9001:2015's subclause A.5, Applicability, also outlines the requirements for determining if a requirement is applicable to the organization. It makes a correlation between application of requirements in ISO 9001:2015 and exclusions in ISO 9001:2008.

The requirements for application of requirements are similar to the requirements for justifying any exclusions in the quality manual. Organizations can use current exclusions as a baseline for determining applicability. However, special emphasis should be placed on whether a product or service being provided by an external provider has previously been excluded.

Organizations cannot exclude products and services obtained from external providers. This is because they affect the organization's ability to provide products and services that meet requirements. Consideration should be given to what controls are in place for these external providers.

4.4 QUALITY MANAGEMENT SYSTEM AND ITS PROCESSES

Subclause 4.4.1

- The organization shall establish, implement, maintain, and continually improve the QMS in accordance with ISO 9001:2015, including:
  - ✓ Processes needed
  - ✓ Interaction of processes

- The organization shall determine:
  - ✓ The processes needed and their application throughout the organization
  - ✓ Inputs required and outputs expected from the processes
  - ✓ Sequence and interaction of processes
  - ✓ Criteria, methods/measurements, and related performance indicators necessary for effective operation and control
  - ✓ Resources needed and their availability
  - ✓ Assignment of responsibilities and authorities for processes

- The organization shall also:
  - ✓ Address risks and opportunities according to subclause 6.1

- ✓ Evaluate processes
- ✓ Implement needed changes to ensure processes achieve intended results
- ✓ Improve processes and the QMS

Subclause 4.4.2

- The organization shall:
  - ✓ Maintain documented information that supports the operation of processes
  - ✓ Retain documented information sufficient to provide confidence that processes are completed as planned

Keys to understanding

The process approach is the foundation of the organization's QMS. Even a minimal approach using this foundational concept has the potential to strengthen a QMS that struggles with the overall requirements of ISO 9001:2015.

The first step in implementing the process approach is to determine the processes needed. This can be done by making a list of all the processes. For example, some organizations write each process on a Post-It note so they can organize the processes. It's important to consider the level in which you identify processes based on the additional requirements that are placed on these processes. Identifying the process at a higher level may make it easier to manage on an ongoing basis. For example, determining manufacturing processes at their highest levels vs. different manufacturing subprocesses such as welding, heat treating, or plating. In this scenario, the organization could establish an additional requirement for subclause 4.4 at the process level instead of the subprocess level.

Some organizations may already have key processes established and identified and this is a good place to start when implementing this requirement.

Once the processes have been determined, the organization has to determine the inputs and expected outputs from these processes. This should be considered with the requirement to determine the sequence and interaction of the processes. Although there is no requirement to do so, some organizations depict the sequence in a diagram or develop a business model that illustrates the hierarchy of the processes. Other organizations may demonstrate this requirement by referencing procedures that are developed as documented information.

It's important to note that while ISO 9001:2015 subclause 0.3, Process approach, provides illustrations of a sequence interaction as well as an illustration of the ISO 9001:2015 clauses in a plan-do-check-act (PDCA) model, these models are provided only as examples. Each organization needs to establish the sequence and interactions of its processes based upon its context and the needs of its relevant stakeholders.

These models will vary based on the size of the organization as well as the products and services it provides.

There are a variety of methods organizations can use to determine if their processes are effective. The first step is to establish the criteria. This could be accomplished by establishing a specific level of performance for the process, such as a goal. Because the methods to be used also include performance indicators that would be a measurable result, it's reasonable to consider whether these criteria should be linked to the quality objectives, which require a measurable result.

Although not a requirement of ISO 9001:2015, many organizations determine key process indicators, which are indicators established for a certain portion of their processes that provide information on the performance of the process.

It's also possible for an organization to use internal audits as a method for monitoring the performance of the process. Internal audits are a structured method of determining that the requirements of the organization and ISO 9001 have been effectively implemented. The output of internal audits provides information that indicates whether processes meet requirements.

Organizations should also consider the needed resources for the processes and their availability. There are several requirements in ISO 9001:2015 that relate to ensuring that resources are available. These include subclause 7.1, Resources, and subclause 9.3, Management review. All types of resources, not just people, should be considered.

Figure 7.2 illustrates different resources and considerations for those resources.

Organizations also need to assign the responsibilities and authorities for processes. Although there isn't a requirement that this information be maintained as documented information, compliance can be achieved by owners assigned to the processes in a business model or through organization charts. In smaller organizations, this assignment may be made more informally. In this scenario, employees must be able to consistently provide information through interviews on who owns specific processes.

Regardless of the method of compliance, the purpose of this requirement is to ensure that the process is maintained. For this reason, many organizations develop and train process owners on these responsibilities. This includes making sure that any changes in processes are properly implemented and that employees are provided training and awareness of the change. Process owners are also frequently assigned responsibility for maintaining documented information such as procedures. In this situation, the process owner would also be responsible for incorporating any changes in the documented procedures.

Figure 7.2 — Resources and Considerations

People—Internal auditors	The organization needs to ensure that it has internal auditors who are competent and that they are given the time to perform the audits.
Infrastructure	The organization needs to ensure that it has the proper resources, such as buildings, equipment, and transportation to support the processes.
Environment	The organization needs to ensure that any special environment that may be required for a process is available. For example, this might include clean rooms or certain environments for technical process requirements.
Monitoring and measuring resources	The organization needs to determine the monitoring and measuring resources to demonstrate that requirements have been met. Consideration should be given to the number of monitoring and measuring resources that are available. For example, if a set of calipers is sent out for calibration, back-up sets need to be available for use.
Organizational knowledge	It is important for an organization to determine the information that is held by individuals or groups and to develop a repository or methodology to share this information with others. Management of organizational knowledge as a shared resource protects the organization from losses upon separation of any individual and assures a common understanding of information.

Organizations must also address the risks and opportunities related to processes. Subclause 6.1 addresses risks and opportunities for the organization. Organizations must consider whether a process requires any type of change to address the risks and opportunities. For example, an organization may determine that there is a risk that an external provider won't be able to provide enough raw materials for a specific product. Based on this risk, the organization might need to address in its supplier management process the identification of alternative or back-up external providers. Conversely, there may be opportunities to have one external provider

Clause 4—Context of the Organization

combine subprocesses conducted by multiple suppliers, thereby reducing complexity or reducing problems related to the quality of the product.

The focus of determining processes is to ensure that they are achieving the intended results. Language in ISO 9001:2015 focuses on this to ensure that not only does an organization have a QMS that meets requirements, but that the product or service that the organization is providing also meets the requirements. There are a multitude of instances where an organization that has achieved ISO 9001 certification still has product quality problems. It's also possible to have an external provider that provides a product to an organization that doesn't meet requirements.

For this reason, organizations need to constantly evaluate their processes. This evaluation should be based on the criteria and methods that have been established. Subclause 9.1.3, Analysis and evaluation, requires organizations to analyze and evaluate data. Organizations can link the data that is evaluated in subclause 9.1.3 with the need to evaluate processes in subclause 4.4. Based on the evaluation, a decision will need to be made whether a change to a process is needed. Not every incident where a process isn't performing as intended will result in a change. Organizations will need to consider the potential effect to the organization if the intended result isn't achieved.

Not only is it important that organizations achieve the intended results, but also that QMS processes be improved. Organizations should incorporate the requirements of clause 10 related to improvement when implementing this subclause.

Organizations will have established the methods to monitor, measure, and analyze processes. If the organization is achieving its intended results, the process should be reviewed to determine if improvement is necessary. The organization might determine that improvement isn't necessary in some cases. There are often scenarios where the process could be improved, yet to achieve the desired results, the cost of improvement is more than the improvement is worth.

The organization is also responsible for determining the necessary documented information. ISO 9001:2015 is less prescriptive than previous versions of the standard when it comes to the need to maintain or retain documented information. The standard provides the flexibility in the requirements in subclause 4.4.2 for determining what documented information is necessary. Although there may not be specific documented information requirements in individual clauses of the standard, subclause 4.4.2 requires the organization to determine the needed documented information. Therefore, the requirements in subclause 4.4.2 aren't specific to demonstrating compliance to the implementation of processes through the provision of documented information. The documented information determined for processes should support the effective operation of processes as well as provide objective evidence that applicable requirements have been met, the expected results are achieved, and the activities are carried out as planned.

For example, an organization may have determined "management" to be one of its processes. Although there are requirements to retain documented information for management review and maintaining information related to quality policy, there aren't specific documented information requirements for context of the organization or relevant interested parties. An organization could determine that it requires documented information to show that these processes have been implemented. However, this is dependent on the needs of the organization.

It's reasonable to assume that smaller organizations would have less documented information than larger organizations. Regardless, they would still be responsible for showing how processes are effective.

Transition

The requirements in subclause 4.4 relate to ISO 9001:2008, subclause 4.1. Although the requirements are similar, there are more prescriptive requirements than in previous versions. Organizations that have taken a minimal approach to the process approach will find that additional actions are needed to achieve compliance. Organizations should specifically consider the requirements related to determining the inputs and outputs for processes, determining performance indicators for the processes, addressing risks and opportunities, assigning responsibilities and authorities, managing change to the processes, and determining necessary documented information.

Chapter 8

Clause 5—Leadership

Leadership is one of the cornerstones of any organization's quality management system (QMS). It's also one of the clauses of the standard that certification bodies use as a gauge of how well the QMS is functioning. A third-party auditor can determine if top management is engaged by whether it holds management reviews or makes time available during audits.

Lack of top management support of the QMS is a key indicator of the failure of the organization's QMS. A QMS will not be successful if it is treated solely as a quality initiative or if it does not receive top management support and the resources necessary for success.

ISO 9001:2015 leadership requirements focus the role of top management in engaging, directing, promoting, and supporting the personnel involved in the QMS as well as the QMS itself.

Top management might choose to delegate some of the responsibility for the QMS, but it must use caution and ensure that if responsibilities are delegated, top management is still actively engaged in the QMS.

5.1 LEADERSHIP AND COMMITMENT

5.1.1 General

Top management must:
- Demonstrate leadership and commitment to the QMS
- Be accountable for the effectiveness of the QMS
- Ensure that the quality policy and quality objectives are established

- Integrate the QMS processes into the business processes
- Promote the process approach and risk-based thinking
- Make resources available
- Communicate the importance of the QMS
- Ensure the QMS is achieving intended results
- Direct activities related to the QMS
- Promote improvement
- Support relevant management in their roles related to demonstrating leadership

Keys to understanding

Who is top management?

ISO 9000:2015 defines *top management* as the "person or group of people who direct and control an organization at the highest level." Therefore, a key aspect for an organization to consider based on this definition is who directs and controls the organization. Who is making key decisions aimed at achieving the intended results and ensuring that customer and relevant interested parties will be satisfied?

Some organizations refer to top management using different terms such as "senior leadership team," "steering committee," or by titles such as CEO, general director, or plant manager. If this is the case, the organization may wish to keep this term to refer to top management.

The first thing to consider in ensuring that requirements for top management have been met is the objective evidence that the requirements have been effectively implemented. These requirements emphasize that top management can demonstrate its commitment. There are no documented information requirements to provide this demonstration, so it's achieved by other means. Based on the requirement, different types of objective evidence might demonstrate top management's commitment.

Typically, this can be demonstrated by the actions of the top management team as well as participation in management-related activities in the QMS. In most cases, a common sense approach is probably already in place in your organization. In other cases, the leadership and commitment of certain requirements relate to other clauses of the standard.

Some of the requirements in this subclause can be delegated to others. However, in this situation, top management is responsible for ensuring that necessary actions are taken.

Top management is required to be accountable for the QMS and its effectiveness. Demonstrating that top management is engaged in this activity can be accomplished by its involvement when the QMS is not meeting requirements. This could include active involvement in problem solving or ensuring that required actions are taken. Accountability is one requirement that cannot be delegated because it requires the ownership of top management.

Quality policy

Subclause 5.2 identifies the requirements for establishing the quality policy. Top management needs to be involved in this activity and must ensure that the quality policy aligns with the context and the strategic direction of the organization. For that reason, top management may wish to use an existing vision or mission statement.

Quality objectives

Subclause 6.2 identifies the requirements for establishing quality objectives. This subclause requires that top management be involved in establishing the quality objectives for the organization. The organization may choose to use existing company goals or measures as its quality objectives. Using top management's regular meetings or management reviews to establish and review the objectives provides a simple means of providing objective evidence that this requirement has been met.

Top management is responsible for ensuring that QMS requirements are integrated into business processes. There is sometimes a tendency to separate the QMS from day-to-day activities. For example, the organization may have an annual leadership meeting where the status of the performance of the organization is discussed but has a separate management review to address the required inputs. ISO 9001:2015's requirements should be incorporated into the business processes, which simply means that the organization should not have "ISO processes" that are separate from the way it actually conducts business.

Process approach/risk-based thinking

Subclause 4.4 requires the determination of processes and actions related to these processes where subclause 6.1 includes the determination of risks and opportunities. These two subclauses are the basis of the process approach and risk-based thinking. The QMS processes will implement the actions needed to address the determined risks and opportunities.

The process approach requires that the organization manage its QMS through processes and their interactions. Although not a requirement of the standard, leadership could demonstrate support of the process approach by:

- Conducting regular review activities based on QMS processes
- Requiring that internal audits be conducted by process and not departments
- Developing and controlling documented information, including documented procedures, according to processes and not department-specific activities

Risk-based thinking is not risk management. Risk-based thinking is simply the consideration of risks and opportunities when making decisions related to the QMS. It's common sense, and most organizations do this on a routine basis. Risk-based thinking comes into play when organizations are trying to achieve intended results. For example, the organization may be able to achieve improvement if it makes a change to a process, but there is also a certain amount of risk that the result might not be achieved.

Providing resources

Subclause 7.1 specifically addresses providing resources for the QMS. Top management must ensure the availability of resources needed for the operation of an effective QMS. Objective evidence of this might include demonstrating that personnel critical to the QMS are in place and that they are competent. This could include process owners, internal auditors, or QMS coordinators. Resources could also apply to infrastructure and the environment needed for the operation of QMS processes. For example, top management authorizes the purchase of capital equipment needed for a production facility or the infrastructure needed to provide customer service such as a telephone system in a call center.

Communication

Subclause 7.4 identifies requirements for both internal and external communication. This communication is focused on top management providing information related to the importance of an effective QMS as well as conforming to its requirements. This communication can be accomplished through employee meetings, daily meetings, the company intranet, or newsletters. Top management should make it clear that when the organization does not conform to the QMS requirements, customer satisfaction may suffer.

Achieve intended results

Leadership is responsible for ensuring that the organization is achieving its intended results. This can be confirmed by the review of quality objectives or performance metrics that show how the organization is doing according to established goals. Based on the results of this review and situations where the organization is not achieving goals, top management will need to demonstrate that actions such as corrective actions or other relevant improvement actions are being taken. The organization's management review process should also allow for demonstration of this particular management commitment action.

Subclause 9.3 identifies the requirements for conducting a management review of the QMS. Top management needs to be involved with the management review process. This includes attending management review meetings and taking any necessary actions as a result.

This subclause also requires top management to be involved in how employees contribute to the QMS. This can be addressed in how top management communicates with the organization and how actions are taken related to the QMS. It can be demonstrated by top management having an understanding of the QMS as well as by providing the time for personnel to participate in internal audits or providing training to employees on areas of improvement.

It's not necessary for top management to be involved in every decision related to the QMS, but support for those decisions is important. It's equally important to support the leadership team.

In some organizations, there may be multiple levels of leadership. When this is the case, it's important that top management support all levels of leadership in their specific areas of responsibility.

Improvement is important to the quality management system.

Top management's role in promoting improvement can easily be demonstrated by supporting improvement programs such as corrective action or problem solving, Six Sigma, *kaizen* events, or employee suggestion programs. Top management participation in improvement teams can also demonstrate commitment.

Transition

This subclause was addressed in ISO 9001:2008, subclause 5.1, Management commitment. The requirements in ISO 9001:2015 are more prescriptive and will require review of the new requirements by the leadership team. Although members of the top management team don't necessarily have to be trained on ISO 9001:2015, they should have an understanding of the standard's requirements.

A simple approach to this is to have the top management team read ISO 9001:2015 in its entirety. It's difficult to ensure that top management is engaged in the QMS if they don't understand its requirements.

5.1.2 Customer focus

Top management shall:
- Demonstrate leadership and commitment.
- Consistently meet customer and applicable statutory and regulatory requirements.
- Address risks and opportunities that could affect products and services.
- Maintain a focus on customer satisfaction.

Keys to understanding

The role of top management in customer focus may not always be a day-to-day activity. More often, their role may be one of ensuring that processes are in place that consistently maintain a focus on the customer.

Some organizations may have a customer service department or a specific employee assigned to coordinate customer issues. Other organizations don't have any one individual or department assigned. Regardless of the approach, the organization should use the requirements in subclause 8.2 to determine customer requirements and subclause 9.1.2 to address customer satisfaction.

However, it's the responsibility of top management to convey the customer focus message throughout the organization. The focus on customers can be demonstrated by the methods used by the organization to address the specific requirements. These include:

- Ensuring that customer, statutory, and regulatory requirements are considered when entering orders
- Considering any potential customer issues when determining the risks and opportunities for the organization (see subclause 6.1)
- Reviewing customer satisfaction information for areas where the organization can make improvements to enhance satisfaction

Customer focus can also be determined by how quickly customer complaints are addressed. Although the goal should be to prevent customer complaints by addressing the associated risks and opportunities, when they do occur, the organization should take timely action to contain and correct the issue.

This can be accomplished by responding with corrective action documentation as well as conducting meetings to communicate actions taken.

Transition

The requirements for customer focus were previously addressed in ISO 9001:2008, subclause 5.2. Although the requirements are very similar, ISO 9001:2015 includes consideration of the risks and opportunities related to products and services delivered to the customer as well as how these risks and opportunities have the potential for enhancing customer satisfaction.

These concepts, while new, may require organizations to make some slight adjustments to their customer interfacing processes.

5.2 POLICY

5.2.1 Establishing the quality policy

Top management shall establish a quality policy that is:
- Implemented and maintained
- Appropriate to the context of the organization including its strategic direction
- A framework for setting quality objectives
- Committed to satisfying applicable requirements
- Committed to continual improvement

Keys to understanding

Top management is responsible for establishing the quality policy. It is also responsible for implementing and maintaining the policy after it is established. Many organizations have an existing vision or mission statement that expresses the organization's purpose. If the organization chooses to use an existing statement, it's important to remember that it needs to meet some minimum requirements. Therefore, it may be necessary to modify the statement to meet the intent of this subclause.

Subclause 5.2.1 can be interpreted to require specific words in the quality policy, such as "meeting customer requirements" or "continual improvement." To avoid this common error, the requirements in this subclause should be used as an input in a process or activity led by top management that results in the statement of the quality policy. It is important to note that inputs—such as the organization's mission statement, vision statement, or values of the organization—can be used if they exist.

When a higher level quality policy is established that does not include the specific language in this subclause, the organization must communicate the intent of these requirements. Employees would then be responsible for communicating the quality policy in a manner that addresses these requirements.

The quality policy must be appropriate to the organization. In simple terms, it should be relevant to the organization. Many large corporations establish a theme. Wherever possible, top management should consider how to make this theme its quality policy because it reflects the strategic direction of the organization. Although there is no requirement for an organization to review its quality policy, the quality policy needs to be in line with the strategic direction of the organization. If the context of the organization (see subclause 4.1) changes, the quality policy should be reviewed for its ongoing suitability.

The quality policy must also provide a framework to establish and review quality objectives. For this reason, the organization should use measurable statements. For example, it's difficult to measure that an organization will be "the best" in a certain field unless it participates in some type of independent survey or analysis program. An example would be an automobile company that can determine where its vehicles rank compared to its competitors.

Transition

The requirements for the quality policy were previously addressed in ISO 9001:2008, subclause 5.3, Quality policy. During the transition, organizations will need to consider whether the quality policy is appropriate to the context of the organization and its strategic direction.

5.2.2 Communicating the quality policy

The quality policy should be:
- Available and maintained as documented information
- Communicated throughout the organization
- Available to relevant interested parties, as appropriate

Keys to understanding

After top management has established its quality policy, it needs to be made available. This can be done in a variety of methods. Different types of organizations will find that different methods work best for them. For example, smaller organizations may be able to post the quality policy in different strategic areas of the organization while larger organizations may find that this approach is not as helpful since it is difficult to maintain multiple postings in different areas and ensure they are current when changes are made.

Other methods for making the quality policy available include:
- Employee orientation

- Posters strategically located throughout the organization
- Direct communication (e-mail or memorandum) to employees
- Laminated cards worn with employee's badge
- A section of the organization's website or intranet

The quality policy must be communicated and understood by the employees. By making the quality policy available and communicating it to employees, the organization has achieved the first step of conformity. However, it's also necessary that employees be able to communicate the policy. Employees must be able to answer the questions: "What is the quality policy? How do you support it?" It's not necessary that employees memorize the quality policy, but they should know where to find it and be able to describe what it means to them. This addresses the need for the quality policy to be applied. Employees can also demonstrate their knowledge of the quality policy by doing their job as planned, following documented procedures or work instructions, stopping work when they cannot complete the task as defined, or identifying areas for improvement in their work area.

The quality policy also must be maintained as documented information. Although there is no requirement that an organization review its quality policy, the fact that the quality policy needs to be maintained as documented information is an indication that the document would be reviewed and updated as needed. If the strategic direction of the organization (see subclause 4.1) changes, the quality policy must be reviewed for its ongoing suitability.

The quality policy also needs to be available to relevant interested parties. This will vary from organization to organization. Some organizations might determine that making the quality policy available upon request is sufficient. Others might have customer or regulatory requirements that require the quality policy to be available. This could also be done on request or available on a company website.

Transition

The requirements in subclause 5.2 are similar to the requirements in ISO 9001:2008, subclause 5.3, Quality policy. There is a new requirement for organizations to make the quality policy available to relevant interested parties. This will need to be addressed in the gap analysis.

5.3 ORGANIZATIONAL ROLES, RESPONSIBILITIES, AND AUTHORITIES

- Top management shall ensure relevant roles and authorities are:

- ✓ Assigned
- ✓ Communicated
- ✓ Understood

- Specific responsibilities to be assigned include:
  - ✓ Confirming that the QMS conforms to requirements of ISO 9001:2015
  - ✓ Ensuring that processes are delivering their intended outputs
  - ✓ Reporting on the performance of the QMS
  - ✓ Reporting opportunities for improvement (subclause 10.1)
  - ✓ Promoting customer focus
  - ✓ Maintaining the integrity of the QMS when changes are planned

Keys to understanding

The top management team is responsible for defining responsibilities and authorities within the organization. The responsibilities can be assigned to one or more persons. However, the responsibilities need to be clearly communicated to employees so that they know who to contact if questions arise. For smaller organizations, one person is usually assigned responsibility.

There is no requirement for this information to be maintained as documented information. It's up to the organization to determine the best methods for managing this. Relevant roles and responsibilities can be defined in organization charts, job descriptions, or other means through defining responsibilities in any documented procedures the organization determines to be necessary or communication tools such as employee meetings.

Subclause 5.3 lists several requirements related to the responsibilities and authorities that top management must assign. One of these requirements relates to ensuring the QMS meets all the requirements within ISO 9001:2015. This is typically met by assigning a person responsibility for the overall QMS. Although this person is frequently someone in a quality role, it can be assigned to any person within the organization regardless of the person's job function. Some organizations where ISO 9001 is perceived to be a quality initiative will actually find that assigning the responsibility to a person in another part of the organization will broaden the understanding of the standard.

Responsibility for ensuring that processes are delivering outputs is necessary. This is related to the need for an organization to achieve its intended results. Subclause 5.1.1 identifies this as one of the areas in which top management must demonstrate commitment. Organizations should consider whether this is the responsibility of one member or multiple members of top management. One way to handle this would be to assign this responsibility to all members of the top management team, but assign one person with overall responsibility of coordinating this activity.

Responsibility for reporting on the performance of the QMS also needs to be assigned. This includes opportunities for improvement as determined in subclause 10.1.

Subclause 9.3, Management review, as its name implies, includes the requirements for top management to review the QMS. Some organizations choose to assign this responsibility to one person, while others assign the reporting of the different inputs in management review to the role most closely associated with a specific input. This role doesn't necessarily need to be a member of top management, but it should be performed by someone who is engaged in top management meetings. When reporting on opportunities for improvement, the note in subclause 10.1 can provide clarification on what types of improvement might be considered. Examples include correction, corrective action, continual improvement, breakthrough change, innovation, and reorganization. Not all of these will be appropriate for all organizations nor is an opportunity for improvement necessary if the performance of the QMS doesn't indicate that improvement is needed.

When assigning the responsibility for customer focus, top management should consider the requirements in subclause 5.1.2, Customer focus. The role of top management in maintaining customer focus may not always be a day-to-day activity. However, there should be assurances that employees are taking action to meet customer requirements. Many organizations adopt a "customer comes first" philosophy. In this environment, there is typically someone who is assigned responsibility for ensuring that customer needs and expectations are being met.

Top management is also responsible for maintaining the integrity of the QMS when changes are being made. Subclause 6.3, Planning of changes, addresses the requirements for how to actually make the changes. Subclause 9.3, Management review, also addresses the management of change in the QMS. This requirement provides the philosophy that when the organization is making changes, it's not necessary that the QMS be perfect but only that the integrity of the system be maintained. The review of subclause 6.3 will outline methods in which the integrity of the system is maintained.

The responsibilities for this should be assigned in the organization. Again, this could be assigned to one person or multiple persons in the organization. It's reasonable that this responsibility would be assigned to the person responsible for implementing the change unless the organization has a specific department or person who coordinates these efforts in the organization.

Transition

The requirements for responsibilities and authorities were addressed in ISO 9001:2008 subclauses 5.5.1, Responsibility and authority, and 5.5.2, Management representative. The responsibility for maintaining the integrity of the QMS were addressed in ISO 9001:2008, subclause 5.4.2, Quality management system planning.

ISO 9001:2015 no longer has a specific role in the QMS called "management representative," but includes all of the same responsibilities and authorities to be assigned, among others. Organizations may continue to use the role of management representative if it adds value. If the organization eliminates this position, it needs to ensure that the assigned responsibilities and authorities are clearly understood.

There is one slight change in the responsibilities and authorities related to processes. In the ISO 9001:2008, top management responsibilities included ensuring that processes were established, implemented, and maintained. ISO 9001:2015 requires that the responsibility and authority be assigned to ensure that processes are delivering their intended outputs (see subclause 4.4 (e)).

Finally, ISO 9001:2008 required that there was a promotion of awareness of customer requirements. ISO 9001:2015 has broadened this to be a promotion of customer focus, which goes beyond requirements.

Although the general requirements remain the same, organizations will need to consider the subtle changes in wording to ensure that requirements are being met.

CHAPTER 9

Clause 6—Planning

This clause focuses on the quality management system (QMS) requirements that ensure plans are determined and objectives are established to achieve them. ISO 9001:2015 includes the concept of risk-based thinking. Risk-based thinking is directly connected to planning activities and doesn't require a formal risk management system or plan. Most organizations perform risk-based thinking without even using the word "risk."

For example, there may be an opportunity to do work with a new customer. However, to do this work would require the organization to purchase new equipment at a significant cost. The customer won't sign the contract until the equipment is purchased and the organization has no guarantee that the customer will sign the contract at all. The organization must make a decision based on the risks and potential opportunities that this new work will bring.

The planning clause also focuses on the organization avoiding potential pitfalls by taking actions to address them before they happen.

6.1 ACTIONS TO ADDRESS RISKS AND OPPORTUNITIES

Subclause 6.1.1

- Planning for the QMS shall consider:
  - ✓ Issues determined in subclause 4.1
  - ✓ Requirements determined in subclause 4.2

- The organization must determine the risks and opportunities to:

- ✓ Provide assurance that intended results can be achieved.
- ✓ Enhance desirable effects.
- ✓ Prevent or reduce undesired effects.
- ✓ Achieve improvement.

Keys to understanding

Prior to addressing planning actions, the organization needs to identify its internal and external issues (see subclause 4.1) and the requirements of relevant interested parties (see subclause 4.2). Both of these activities provide information that the organization needs to determine the risks and opportunities associated with its operations.

There isn't a requirement that an action be put in place for every issue or every relevant requirement, only that these inputs are to be considered. There also isn't a requirement that any kind of prioritization be conducted when addressing risks and opportunities. That said, it's reasonable that organizations would adopt such a review as a best practice to determine necessary actions.

There are different tools and methodologies that can be used to accomplish this. In some organizations, these methods may already be in place.

If an organization chooses not to implement a structured process to determine the actions it will take for risks and opportunities, it still needs to provide information about what rationale was used to demonstrate conformance to the requirements.

When reviewing the issues and relevant requirements, organizations should not only consider the potential risks but also the opportunities. This could include actions that improve an already successful process such as strategic planning or business planning. This would meet the intent of the requirement to improve the organization or enhance something that's already achieving intended results.

Transition

Transition guidance for subclause 6.1.1 is combined with the transition guidance for subclause 6.1.2.

Subclause 6.1.2

- The organization shall plan:
  - ✓ Actions to address risks and opportunities
  - ✓ How to integrate and implement actions into the organization's processes
  - ✓ How to evaluate the effectiveness of actions
  - ✓ How actions taken should be proportionate to the potential effects

Keys to understanding

Once the organization has determined its risks and opportunities, actions need to be planned to address them. Based on the potential effect of the risk or opportunity, organizations may take different types of actions. Organizations should carefully consider any actions necessary in regard to risks and opportunities. These actions should be based on potential effects to the organization. In simple terms, the organization shouldn't put an expensive or resource-intensive plan in place to address risks and opportunities if the potential effect is minimal. Similar to corrective actions, organizations need to evaluate the effectiveness of the actions taken.

There is no requirement for documented information in this subclause. However, actions to address risks and opportunities are a required input into management review (see subclause 9.3). Because the output of management review is documented information that must be retained, it's reasonable to use this method for tracking actions to address risks and opportunities.

If an organization conducts management review infrequently, consideration should be given to how the organization will ensure that actions to address risks and opportunities are effective. For example, an annual management review may not be frequent enough to ensure that actions taken on risks and opportunities are not only effective but that they are being completed in a timely manner.

As part of the requirements in subclause 4.4, Quality management system and its processes, the organization is to consider risks and opportunities. Specific actions or controls to address these risks and opportunities should be defined and implemented. Measurement and monitoring activities should consider how effective these actions or controls are and produce specific information that demonstrates the level of performance achieved (e.g., reports, performance indicators).

Organizations may want to consider using a tool such as a rolling action item list that's regularly updated or including the actions on risks and opportunities with other actions that are being tracked.

Transition

The requirements related to planning and actions to address risks and opportunities were previously addressed in multiple clauses of ISO 9001:2008. They include subclause 5.4, Planning, and subclause 8.5.3, Preventive action.

ISO 9001:2015 no longer uses the term "preventive action." However, this concept has been incorporated into the planning clause. The concept of preventive action has always been focused on preventing the potential cause of a nonconformity. Because it followed corrective action, many organizations considered preventive action as the action of preventing something that has been identified as a nonconformity through corrective action from happening again.

For this reason, while some organizations may be able to leverage some of the activities of their preventive action process to transition to the requirements in ISO 9001:2015, others may find that they have to make modifications to their system or implement something entirely different.

Organizations will also have to confirm that any risk-based approaches they use will meet the intent of this requirement. Specifically, organizations need to ensure that internal and external issues (see subclause 4.1) and the requirements of relevant interested parties (see subclause 4.2) have been considered.

6.2 QUALITY OBJECTIVES AND PLANNING TO ACHIEVE THEM

Subclause 6.2.1

- The organization shall stablish objectives at relevant functions, levels, and processes that are:
  - ✓ Consistent with the quality policy
  - ✓ Measurable
  - ✓ Meet applicable requirements
  - ✓ Relevant to product and services meeting conformity requirements
  - ✓ Relevant to enhancing customer satisfaction
  - ✓ Monitored
  - ✓ Communicated
  - ✓ Updated as appropriate

- The organization shall maintain documented information

Keys to understanding

Quality objectives must be established by top management according to the requirements for subclause 5.1.1, Management commitment. Quality objectives need to be established at relevant functions and levels within the organization. This doesn't mean that there is necessarily going to be a quality objective for every person in the organization, but it's common that objectives are relevant to most employees. The organization should also consider whether quality objectives should be established for processes.

Subclause 4.4, Quality management system and its processes, requires that the organization determine the criteria and method, including performance indicators that demonstrate that processes are effective. The organization should consider this requirement as quality objectives are established to relate the two requirements in an effort to streamline the methods used to demonstrate compliance to this requirement.

Although the term "quality objective" is used in ISO 9001:2015, it's not meant to indicate that these objectives are stand-alone or unrelated to the overall performance of the QMS. In many cases, the organization can use its existing goals or metrics to meet the intent of this requirement while taking into account the specific requirements for quality objectives.

These objectives must meet certain criteria to meet the intent of ISO 9001:2015. The quality objectives must be consistent with the quality policy. Subclause 5.2, Policy, indicates that the quality policy provides a framework for developing the quality objectives. When establishing quality objectives, the best practice of developing specific, measurable, attainable, realistic, and timely (SMART) goals can assist the organization with meeting the intent of ISO 9001:2015. This approach is more relatable to top management and meets the intent of the requirement.

Quality objectives must be updated as appropriate and maintained as documented information. Many organizations establish objectives at a certain time of the year. These objectives, also known as company goals, are either confirmed or updated at this time. In some cases, the goal may be adjusted based on current information. For example, an organization that frequently achieves its target may have the goal adjusted higher. An organization that's struggling with meeting the objective may have it confirmed or lowered, keeping in mind that objectives should be attainable.

The documented information can be maintained in different ways. An organization may have a company dashboard or intranet that includes organizational performance, including quality objectives and the QMS. Some organizations choose to post the quality objectives in areas where daily meetings are held to brief management and employees on the performance of the organization. Another option is to maintain the quality objectives in the organization's strategic plan. The methods used to maintain the quality objectives as documented information can also be used to communicate the objectives to employees. However, just because information about objectives has been posted or made available, employees may not necessarily be aware of or understand the relevance to their jobs.

Quality objectives must be measurable, which typically means some kind of quantitative measure. It's typically not possible to measure an organization being the "best" or "premiere" of something unless there are systems in place that compare the organization's products to those of its competitors.

In certain services, objectives can be based on qualitative aspects such as courtesy and respect, among others. It's important to define how these qualitative aspects will be measured. Sometimes surveys or interviews are used. A degree or value is assigned for the relevant qualitative aspect.

The established quality objectives also need to consider any applicable requirements of the organization. These could include those related to the requirements of a relevant interested party, including regulatory agencies.

Quality objectives should enhance customer satisfaction. For this reason, many organizations identify an objective that relates to on-time delivery or even the number of quality escapes/defects that reach the customer. Service organizations may establish objectives related to wait times or the number of complaints. Once the quality objectives are established, they must be monitored. Quality objectives are one of the inputs to management review (see subclause 9.3), but management review may not be conducted frequently enough to take action if objectives aren't being met. Other methods of reviewing quality objectives could be reviewing the meetings held by management, including daily reviews, monthly operations reviews, or weekly staff meetings.

Transition

This requirement was previously addressed in ISO 9001:2008, subclause 5.4.1, Quality objectives. The requirements in ISO 9001:2015 are much more prescriptive than those in ISO 9001:2008, which only required that the objectives be set at relevant functions and levels, be measurable, and consistent with the quality policy.

Although the requirements in ISO 9001:2015 are broader than the previous version, most organizations have methods that will address these requirements. The organization should leverage these existing methods for reviewing the performance of the organization to achieve compliance.

Subclause 6.2.2

- When planning, the organization needs to consider:
    - ✓ How plans will achieve quality objectives
    - ✓ What the organization must do
    - ✓ What resources are needed
    - ✓ Who is responsible
    - ✓ When it is to be completed
    - ✓ How the results will be evaluated

Keys to understanding

Quality objectives need to be specific. Although the requirements for establishing quality objectives include requirements for maintaining documented information, there isn't a specific documented information requirement included in this subclause.

Organizations may wish to incorporate some specific language in the objective to demonstrate that the requirement is included. For example, an organization might have a quality objective that states, "Improve on-time delivery by 5 percent by the end of the calendar year." The location for the daily performance briefing in the organization might identify who the owner of the quality objective is, keeping in mind this could be a person, a department, or a process. In this scenario, the organization would still need to determine what resources are needed and how the results are to be evaluated.

Some examples:
- Response time not to exceed 24 hours for any request of information related to the service
- No complaints will be allowed due to a lack of courtesy or respect when providing the service
- Reduce operation costs by 5 percent vs. previous year.

Transition

ISO 9001:2008 included requirements for establishing quality objectives, but it didn't include specific requirements for how to plan the achievement of the objectives. This is a new requirement and organizations will need to confirm that existing quality objectives include the actions, resources, responsibility, completion, and evaluation for establishing and monitoring objectives.

6.3 PLANNING OF CHANGES

- Determine the need for changes to the QMS
- Carry out changes according to plans
- Consider:
    - ✓ The purpose of the change and any potential consequences
    - ✓ How to maintain the integrity of the QMS
    - ✓ Resources needed to make the change

- Allocate the necessary responsibilities and authorities

Keys to understanding

There are different types of changes in the QMS. Changes in subclause 6.3 are specific to the overall QMS, while changes in subclause 8.3.6 are related to changes in design, and changes in subclause 8.5.6 are related to changes to provide the product or deliver the service. There is no requirement in ISO 9001:2015 that an organization must be perfect. It does require organizations to manage any change that could affect the QMS. This subclause provides the flexibility to manage change within the organization to ensure the integrity of the system is sustained.

What does this mean for the organization? When an organization is planning a change that could potentially affect the QMS, the key is to manage the change in a way that ensures it's monitored and corrects or improves the actions being taken. This can be done by establishing a plan that indicates required actions and countermeasures to mitigate any potential effect. This plan should also include the resources to manage the change and make sure the necessary responsibilities and authorities are known.

This subclause doesn't require documented information, but as the organization should do with any of the requirements of ISO 9001:2015, a determination should be made whether any documented information is needed according to the requirements in subclause 4.4. For example, an organization might determine it doesn't need to maintain documented information on changes considered, but might determine the need to maintain documented information for a specific change. It might also determine that a plan is needed to monitor the change.

Transition

This requirement was addressed in ISO 9001:2008, subclause 5.4.2, Quality management system planning. The new requirement's intent is basically the same but goes beyond maintaining the integrity of the QMS to include the consideration of resources and assignment of responsibilities and authorities.

Chapter 10

Clause 7—Support

Clause 7, Support, includes requirements that are indirectly related to the quality management system (QMS). Providing the resources needed to ensure that products are provided and services delivered in a manner that not only meets customer requirements but also enhances the customer's confidence in the QMS is essential.

Clause 7 includes resource requirements for people, infrastructure, environment for the operation of processes, monitoring and measuring resources, and organizational knowledge. Because employees play a critical role in the success of the QMS, this clause also includes requirements for competence, awareness, and communication. Employees need to not only be competent to do their jobs but also understand how they contribute to the overall effectiveness of the QMS.

7.1 RESOURCES

7.1.1 General

- Determine and provide resources to establish, implement, maintain, and continually improve the QMS.
- Consider the capabilities of and constraints on existing internal resources.
- Determine resources needed from external providers.

Keys to understanding

This general subclause is an introduction to the potential resources that an organization may need to provision to maintain its QMS and processes. These resources can include people, infrastructure, environment for the process to operate, monitoring and measuring resources, and organizational knowledge.

Each of these subclauses has detailed requirements in additional subclauses. Subclause 7.1.1's goal is to focus the organization on the resources it needs to maintain the QMS and what internal resources are available. This includes what the resources are capable of and any constraints associated with the resources.

It's very important that the determination of the people, infrastructure, environment for the operation, monitoring and measuring resources, and organizational knowledge occur within each QMS process. One of the responsibilities of the process owner or responsible person is to ensure these determination activities are implemented.

When an organization determines that it has constraints on internal resources, consideration can be given to obtaining the resource from an external provider. This could include the need to hire employees (full-time or temporary) or obtaining new equipment to produce more parts.

When an organization determines that it doesn't have specific capabilities (e.g., knowledge of a new business application or equipment or parts that require a production clean room) in its internal resources, consideration can be given to obtaining these resources and implementing them or obtaining the resource from an external provider.

When an organization chooses to obtain resources from an external provider, the requirements in subclause 8.4, Control of externally provided processes, products, and services, shall be followed.

Transition

The requirements in subclause 7.1.1 are similar to the requirements in ISO 9001:2008, subclause 6.1, Provision of resources. ISO 9001:2015 includes additional requirements that link internal resources and potential limitations with resources resulting in a determination that resources will need to be outsourced.

Organizations that currently conform to ISO 9001:2008 most likely already have processes in place that address this requirement. However, some adjustments may be needed to an organization's QMS to ensure that when resources are discussed in management review or at other times, this requirement is addressed.

7.1.2 People

- Determine and provide the persons for:
  - ✓ Implementation of the QMS
  - ✓ Operation and control of its processes

Keys to understanding

Subclause 7.1.2 requires that the organization provide the persons necessary to have an effective QMS. It can be implemented in conjunction with subclause 9.3, Management review, which requires that needed resources be determined.

The organization should consider whether human resources need to be acquired through hiring new or temporary employees if it's determined that the current workload cannot be supported with the existing resource level.

Transition

This requirement doesn't have a specific correlation with ISO 9001:2008. However, it's somewhat related to the requirements in subclause 6.1, Provision of resources. This subclause was added to include all of the resource types that an organization should consider including people, infrastructure, environment, and monitoring and measuring resources. The subclause is generic in nature and shouldn't require an organization to make a change to its existing QMS.

7.1.3 Infrastructure

- Provide and maintain the infrastructure needed for the organization to:
  - ✓ Achieve conformity of products and services.
  - ✓ Support operation of its processes.

- Note: Examples can include buildings, equipment, transportation, and information and technology.

Keys to understanding

Infrastructure includes those needs that an organization has to provide product or deliver services that meet customer requirements. Although a manufacturing organization needs an infrastructure that has suitable equipment and buildings, a service organization might have infrastructure needs focused on information and technology.

Infrastructure needs are considered frequently and don't require any documented information. However, organizations need to ensure that they have sufficient infrastructure in place to effectively and efficiently deliver products and services.

Frequently infrastructure needs require large capital investments, which is why these activities may not always be timely. When capital funding is needed but the acquisition isn't yet approved, the organization may want to consider demonstrating that a plan is in place.

Examples of changes in the organization that could affect infrastructure include:
- Moving to a smaller manufacturing facility. Can product can still be produced to meet schedules?
- Procuring new purchasing software. Is software compatible with existing systems?
- Does the organization need to purchase new equipment or software to build product or deliver a service to customer requirements?

Because infrastructure addresses equipment, the preventive maintenance of equipment is considered under this subclause. For organizations to meet requirements, the equipment must be in working order. This includes the development of schedules to maintain the equipment. These schedules can be based on a specific time interval or on the amount of use (e.g., number of hours).

Not all of the infrastructure areas are needed by every organization. The organization needs to consider those that are applicable to their business. For example, an organization that provides services where employees work remotely from home may want to require that certain infrastructure needs are met (e.g., high-speed internet connection, land line telephone, laptop with certain memory) but would most likely not need to consider the building requirements.

Transition

This requirement was previously addressed in ISO 9001:2008, subclause 6.3, Infrastructure. The ISO 9001:2015 requirement is similar, but now more specifically requires that the infrastructure support the operation of its processes. In addition, the examples that were previously included in the text of the standard are now included as a note. Notes provide clarification to understanding the requirement, but they do not include requirements themselves. Organizations that meet the intent of this requirement in their existing system should conform to the new requirement. However, they should ensure that the infrastructure also considers the operation of the organization's processes, specifically those related to service processes.

7.1.4 Environment for the operation of processes

- Provide and maintain the environment needed for the organization to:
  - ✓ Achieve conformity of products and services.
  - ✓ Operate processes.

- Examples include social, psychological, and physical factors that differ based on the product or service provided.

Keys to understanding

When the word "environment" is used in the context of ISO 9001:2015, it is related to the environment for the operation of processes, not environmental issues such as pollution. This correct use of the term is critical for an organization to correctly apply the requirement. The environment for the organization is determined by the product it provides or the services it delivers. Some organizations have very specific needs for the environment for processes; other organizations may find that the requirement has minimal application.

Organizations need to review the processes they have in place to determine any environmental issues that could affect processes.

Manufacturing organizations typically focus on engineering or manufacturing requirements for the product. Manufacturing examples include:
- Product that must be built in a clean room environment
- Product that must be built in a controlled temperature or within a certain level of humidity
- Product that must be stored at a certain temperature
- Ear protection or noise control provided to manufacturing areas with loud equipment

Because service organizations rely heavily on employees, they often incorporate physical, social, and psychological factors that relate to the job. Service examples include:
- Noise control in areas where employees are working in a call center
- Icy conditions for a security guard that walks the perimeters of buildings
- A catering organization that considers workload or stressful situations that may occur when a team is setting up a banquet for hundreds of people

Transition

This requirement was previously addressed in ISO 9001:2008, subclause 6.4, Work environment. The requirement is similar to the previous requirement; however, the language has been changed to make it easier to understand and apply to service organizations. Manufacturing organizations will generally not need to make any changes. Service organizations should review the notes that have been provided to determine if the clarification requires a change to the existing QMS.

7.1.5 Monitoring and measuring resources

7.1.5.1 General

- Determine and provide the resources needed for valid/reliable results when verifying that products and services meet requirements.
- Resources provided shall be:
  - ✓ Suitable for the type of activities
  - ✓ Maintained for fitness of purpose

- Retain appropriate documented information
- Evidence of fitness for purpose

Keys to understanding

Subclause 8.1, Operational planning and control, includes in its controls the availability and use of suitable monitoring and measuring resources. Subclause 7.1.5.1 focuses on determining what monitoring and measuring resources are needed and ensuring that they are capable of providing results that help an organization verify that products and services meet requirements.

This subclause applies to those monitoring and measuring resources that have an effect on the conformity of product and service requirements. This means that it's possible that an organization might have some types of monitoring and measuring resources that aren't used for conformity purposes. This could be a set of scales that are used to weigh items or a tape measure used as a reference and not for acceptance to criteria.

The first step is to ensure that the resource is suitable for the type of monitoring and measuring activity. This means that if an organization needs to obtain a certain measurement, the resource that is being used is capable of doing it. For example, an organization that produces chemical solutions might have a requirement that chemicals incorporated into the solution must be weighted at plus or minus one pound. If the scale being used to measure the chemicals is only capable of providing weights in two-pound increments, the scale would not be suitable for use.

The resource also needs to be maintained to ensure that it's fit for the purpose to which it is assigned. This could be maintenance on the equipment or, in the case of a service, it could include performance monitoring. For instance, an organization that provides a service of grading standardized tests might find that one of the persons performing the grading isn't falling within the grading pattern. Follow-up reviews could ensure that the person is following the grading scheme correctly.

The organization is responsible for retaining appropriate documented information specific to the fitness of purpose for the resource. This could be a calibration certificate that indicates that the resource has passed or failed calibration. In the case of a resource that's damaged, such as a piece of equipment, the documented information might indicate the repairs that have been completed as well as consideration of its ability to fulfill its original purpose. The requirement for documented information would include any results found in subclause 7.1.5.2, Measurement and traceability, where measuring equipment is found not to be fit for its original purpose.

Another example is a hotel that has pictures or layouts of the rooms, restaurant, or any other public area. The people performing housekeeping duties will use the diagram as a resource to verify that every item (remote control, towels, toiletries, room service menu) is in its place after cleaning the room. A similar activity may happen after the catering team completes the setup on a room for a training session or banquet.

7.1.5.2 Measurement traceability

- Where measurement traceability is:
  - ✓ A requirement
  - ✓ Considered essential for validity of measurement results

- Measuring equipment shall be:
  - ✓ Verified or calibrated or both
  - ✓ Specified intervals/prior to use
  - ✓ Traceable standard
  - ✓ Retain basis for calibration when no standards exist
  - ✓ Identified
  - ✓ Safeguard from adjustments

- Determine if previous results have been adversely affected when measuring equipment is found unfit.
- Take appropriate action.

Keys to understanding

Subclause 7.1.5.2 specifies steps that an organization with monitoring and measuring resources needs to take to ensure that the resource provides the confidence needed for valid results.

The organization must first calibrate or verify the resource at a specified interval. This interval might be established by the manufacturer of a piece of equipment, by the number of hours that a piece of equipment is used, or could be a weekly review of process if the calibrated resource is a person.

Some organizations might choose not to calibrate each piece of equipment but verify it prior to use. This is completed by having a standard such as a gage block in a manufacturing area where the accuracy of a set of calipers can be confirmed prior to use. In this scenario, employees need to be trained on this process.

The calibration of monitoring and measuring resources needs to be traceable to a standard. If there isn't a standard, the organization must maintain what was used to conduct the calibration or verification. This could be a documented procedure that lists the steps taken to complete the calibration or verification.

Some organizations outsource calibration activities. In this scenario, the requirements provided to the external provider need to identify the calibration standard that is to be used.

Regardless of whether calibration is conducted internally or externally, this information is to be retained as documented information. It's typically included on the calibration certificate. When a database is used in lieu of a calibration certificate, the database should include the standard used.

The monitoring and measuring resource is also required to have identification. This is to determine its status. Some organizations will include a calibration label that provides the identification of the equipment as well as a date on which the calibration expires. Another method is to identify the equipment with a serial or other unique number. In this case, the status can be determined by comparing the unique number to documented information. However, this method minimizes employees' ability to determine if equipment is current and relies heavily on ensuring only equipment with valid calibration is available.

Identification of a resource used in academics could be a grading standard used to grade tests or an employee number for the person who is doing the grading.

The last control is safeguarding resources from adjustment. This includes adjustments made during maintenance. For example, if a thermocouple used to monitor temperature is found to be malfunctioning and maintenance either repairs or replaces it, the calibration of the device must be confirmed and, when determined necessary, recalibrated.

Equipment must be protected from damage and deterioration during handling, maintenance, and storage. How measuring equipment is stored can affect its performance. Organizations may protect equipment by storing it on specific shelves or allowing only trained employees to move it. It's also important to emphasize to employees that if calibrated equipment is possibly damaged, it can invalidate the results. Therefore, if equipment is dropped or possibly damaged, it should be reviewed to ensure it's still fit for purpose.

At times, a resource may be found not to conform to requirements. In this scenario, the organization is responsible for assessing and reviewing the validity of previous measuring results. This review will provide an indication of the appropriate action the organization needs to take related to the resource.

For example, if a piece of equipment that confirms a specific tolerance is found to be out of calibration, the organization might be required to recall specific products. The organization could also determine that the out-of-tolerance condition is so small that no additional action is required. This analysis would need to be retained as documented information

Transition

The requirements in subclause 7.1.5 were previously addressed in ISO 9001:2008, subclause 7.6, Monitoring and measuring equipment. The requirements have been moved to clause 7 in ISO 9001:2015 to better emphasize that this is the control of the resource. The requirements for implementing monitoring and measuring are addressed in clause 8.

The term "monitoring and measuring resources" replaces "monitoring and measuring equipment." This is to transition to language that relates to both equipment and resources that are applicable in service organizations. The revision also includes the phrase "fitness for their purpose." ISO 9001:2008 required that monitoring and measuring are completed. The new language is more in line with language that is used when managing monitoring and measuring resources.

Organizations that meet the intent of the ISO 9001:2008 should find the transition fairly simple. Due to changes being made to make this requirement easier to apply to service organizations, these organizations should carefully review the requirements to determine if changes are needed based on a better understanding of the requirements.

7.1.6 Organizational knowledge

- Determine the necessary knowledge for:
  - ✓ Operation of processes
  - ✓ Conformity of products and services

- Knowledge shall be maintained and made available (as necessary).
- Consider knowledge when addressing changes in the organization.
  ✓ Need to acquire knowledge

- Note: Organizational knowledge can be:
  ✓ Knowledge specific to the organization
  ✓ Gained by experience
  ✓ Information that is used and shared to achieve the organization's objectives
  ✓ Gathered from external sources

Keys to understanding

Organizational knowledge is something that every organization manages whether consciously or not. It could be defined in different ways, but for the purpose of ISO 9001 it is the knowledge that is specific to the organization generally gained by experience. It's used and shared to achieve the organization's objectives.

It's important to recognize that "specific" means something unique and not in the public domain. For example, an organization may have employees who understand and apply technical specifications or standards (e.g., ASTM, DIN, etc.) used on specific activities such as maintenance or inspection. If the employee with this specific knowledge leaves the organization, the organization needs to consider if it can find someone with the required knowledge and experience. On the other hand, if these technical specifications or standards are part of the intellectual property of the organization, the transfer of the knowledge and experience should be considered.

The introduction of this concept brings with it questions about how this requirement differs from the requirement of subclause 7.2, Competence. The best way to differentiate between the two concepts is to consider that competence is defined in ISO 9000:2015 as the ability to apply knowledge and skills to achieve intended results. Organizational knowledge would just be one aspect of achieving competence. It's the overall knowledge of the organization and not always specific to employees.

The requirements in this subclause are specific in stating that knowledge shall be maintained and made available to the extent necessary. This provides the organization the option of determining the different processes where knowledge is needed. Indications that an organization might be lacking needed knowledge include having only one person knowledgeable about a job, a lack of information about the conclusions of a project, or not enough knowledge about new technology.

There are specific ways to obtain needed knowledge. This could be done by going to a technical conference or including it in documented information such as procedures or standardized work. Some organizations choose to take photographs or shoot video of certain processes that are performed infrequently for reference at a later time.

Knowledge can also be obtained by transferring it from one organization to another. For example, a sister plant might transfer the production of a part from one organization to another. The plant that is acquiring the production line might go to the sister plant to learn the process.

Although competence and organizational knowledge aren't synonymous, cross-training can provide a level of organizational knowledge. Having an employee learn how to do a unique skill of another person, for example. This knowledge would be preserved if one of them were to leave the organization.

There is no specific documented information requirement for organizational knowledge. This is similar to management commitment where there are many requirements that must be met to meet the intent of the requirement, but no specific documented information that would be verified. For the purposes of organizational knowledge, this could be demonstrated through organizations having established methods for managing knowledge, providing consistent answers during audits, and the auditor confirming that methods are being adhered to.

Transition

This requirement wasn't included in ISO 9001:2008. Organizations will have to ensure that they are managing organizational knowledge. In most cases, methods will be in place that are doing this. They could include conducting lessons learned at the completion of a project, going to a sister plant to observe how a process works when the process is being transferred, or succession planning that ensures that knowledge is transferred from one person to another.

7.2 COMPETENCE

- Determine competence based on the appropriate education, training, or experience.
  - ✓ Persons doing work under the organization's control

- Take actions to acquire necessary competence.
  - ✓ Evaluate the effectiveness of actions taken.

- Retain documented information.
- Note: Actions related to acquiring the necessary competence include:
  - ✓ Training

- ✓ Mentoring
- ✓ Reassignment of employees
- ✓ Hiring temporary employees

Keys to understanding

Subclause 7.2 is focused on ensuring that whoever does work for the organization has the competence needed to support the QMS. The term "person of the organization" is specifically used to indicate that work may be performed by an employee, temporary employee, or contractor. Each of these types of person must have the necessary competence.

An organization first needs to determine what method(s) it will use to identify competence. Organizations can determine competence by job position or individual employee. Competence requirements could also be stated in a purchase order when obtaining a resource externally.

The organization may consider the competence determination based on the different roles and processes a person participates in. If job descriptions are used to establish competence, they should indicate which processes the person will perform and what and the specific competence required. For example, a quality engineer will require a specific level of competence when he or she is supporting the activities for controlling a nonconforming output in production. If the engineer will conduct inspection as part of receiving activities, he or she will also need to be competent in this area.

When an organization identifies competence by job position, it frequently uses job descriptions—if they exist—to identify what qualifications the employee must possess. The organization will compare the job description to the individual employee to determine competence. It's also important to remember when determining competence by job position, that some employees have special assignments or job duties. Competence for these special assignments also needs to be established. For example, a buyer that is assigned additional responsibilities as an internal auditor would need to meet the competence requirements of the buyer position and have the additional training required for internal auditors.

It's important to remember that job descriptions aren't a requirement of the standard but an existing tool that many organizations use. However, if job descriptions are going to be used to determine what requirements are needed, the organization must ensure that they are controlled according to the requirements in subclause 7.5, Documented information. Job descriptions also need to be reviewed to ensure that they don't include ambiguous requirements (e.g., "equivalent experience") or confusing requirements (e.g., carry 50 pounds and climb a ladder).

When competence is determined by the individual employee, a list of the necessary education, training, and experience needs to be identified for each person who has an effect on the performance and effectiveness of the QMS. Performance of the QMS can be affected directly (e.g., manufacturing worker or customer service agent) or indirectly (e.g., purchasing agent or order entry).

This method is frequently used in smaller organizations or organizations that don't have formal job descriptions in place. They might use the description of job duties that was listed in a job posting to analyze competence.

After the organization has determined the required experience, education, and training, it must review the persons of the organization to determine if they are competent. This review can be conducted as a stand-alone activity or in conjunction with the organization's performance review system.

If it's determined that an employee doesn't meet competence requirements, the organization will need to take action. This can be achieved by many different methods. Although many organizations focus on completing this action through training, other methods such as mentoring, reassigning the person to another position where he or she meets the competence requirements, or hiring or contracting competent persons can also be used.

If the person is determined not to meet the competence requirements, a plan may be put into place that provides details of how the person will achieve competence. It might also include restrictions of what work may be performed. For example, a police officer who has been injured in the line of duty may be determined not fit to work in the field but approved for desk work. Other examples include an employee doing the work under the supervision of another employee or leader in the area where the work is being performed.

When an organization takes actions for a person of the organization to achieve competence, these actions need to be evaluated for effectiveness. Without the consideration of effectiveness, the organization runs the risk of persons not being able to adequately perform their jobs or expending resources on a method to achieve competence that isn't working.

Although some organizations test employees to ascertain this competence, testing at the time the training is provided might not be an indication of long-term effectiveness. For this reason, supplemental methods should be used to evaluate whether employees have achieved competence and whether actions taken are effective.

These methods could include a supervisor monitoring the performance of the employee and performance reviews. The organization can also use its internal audit process to ensure that competence needs are being achieved. By monitoring the work of the persons of the organization during internal audits, it can be determined if the employees are following procedures or meeting competence requirements.

To provide objective evidence that persons of the organization have been determined to be competent, the organization will need to retain documented information of training, experience, and education. This includes documented information for temporary employees or contractors. In some cases, the documented information may be retained by the temporary agency or outsourced company. However, this information must be available upon request by the organization.

Examples of documented information that the organization could require include:

- Training records (formal/informal)
- Certifications (e.g., soldering/welding)
- Resumes
- Diplomas
- Experience (past or current)
- Special training
- Medical records
- Licenses (e.g., driver's, nursing)

Where the organization hasn't had a QMS that requires documented information to be retained, there may not be objective evidence available from past training or competence. In this scenario, an organization can choose to "grandfather" its existing employees based on past performance. The organization chooses a date after which employees must meet competence requirements. Some requirements, such as specific license or regulatory requirements, cannot be grandfathered due to legal implications.

The documented information related to the competence of the persons of the organization should be readily accessible, especially in a production environment where employees are frequently moved from one department to another based on workload. A matrix posted in the work area that indicates who has training in which areas is often used in this situation. This helps ensure that employees are placed in the areas where they are competent.

Transition

This subclause is similar to the requirements in ISO 9001:2008, subclause 6.2, Competence, training, and awareness. The requirements for awareness are now in a stand-alone subclause 7.3, Awareness. The word "training" has been removed from the title to emphasize that this subclause is focused on competence and not just the method of training to achieve competence. A note has been added to clarify this and provide examples. Most organizations will meet the intent of this requirement. However, this is an opportunity to determine if the organization has been too narrow in its approach for how it ensures the competence of the persons doing work under its control. There could be opportunities to use an approach that is more flexible and not driven by training.

7.3 AWARENESS

- Persons under the control of the organization need to be aware of:
  ✓ Quality policy
  ✓ Quality objectives
  ✓ Contributions to the effectiveness of QMS
    - Benefits of improved performance

  ✓ Implications of not conforming to the QMS

Keys to understanding

The subclause for awareness is simple: Persons under the control of the organization must know how they contribute to its success. Without this information, they may not understand why they are required to do something, which could lead to being disengaged from the QMS.

This requirement applies to full-time employees, temporary employees, and contractors. The awareness of these persons is critical to the fundamentals of the QMS. For this reason, there should be a level of awareness as to how they contribute to the objectives of the organization. This understanding should be based on the relevance of the objectives to the person.

If an organization has an objective of on-time delivery, employees should be aware of how they contribute to that objective. They also need to understand what it means if the objective isn't met. For example, not meeting on-time delivery could result in customer dissatisfaction and a loss of orders.

Top management is responsible for promoting the process approach, risk-based thinking, and improvement. Another responsibility of top management is engaging, directing, and supporting persons to contribute to the effectiveness of the QMS. This promotion and interaction of top management with the persons in the organization will likely result in an enhanced awareness at all levels.

Persons doing work at each process should be aware of how their regular activities contribute to the control of inherent risks and opportunities and the achievement of intended results. Based on the performance of the process, persons should be aware of their relevance to the implementation of an improvement activity such as correction or corrective action.

The persons of the organization also need to be aware of the quality policy. Most organizations make the quality policy available to employees. However, the employees need to relate what the quality policy means to them. This could be the actions employees take such as complying with documented information requirements or stopping work to ask the supervisor for clarification when they don't understand a specific required action.

The persons of the organization also need to understand what can happen if the QMS isn't followed. Rework, scrap, and loss of business are all examples of an organization not achieving its intended results. When considering the implications of nonconformances, the organization needs to remember that these implications aren't meant to indicate that a level of punishment is needed for persons in the QMS. The requirement is simply reflecting the need for understanding what happens when requirements aren't followed. Relating this to the success of the organization can help minimize concerns.

Many organizations have standard communication with employees on many of these topics. This can be a daily start-up meeting, quarterly review with all employees with top management sharing performance information, or posted metrics in highly visible areas such as break rooms. Subclause 7.4, Communication, includes details on how communication makes the persons of the organization more aware.

Transition

This requirement was addressed in ISO 9001:2008, subclause 6.2.2. It has been expanded to include awareness of the quality policy in addition to objectives. Although ISO 9001:2008 focused on awareness of how the persons of the organization contributed to the achievement of the quality objectives, ISO 9001:2015 includes a requirement that they have an awareness of how they contribute to the effectiveness of the QMS as well as what it means when the QMS does not meet requirements. The organization should emphasize this point during the transition along with examples to employees to help them understand the requirement. Organizations will need to emphasize this type of awareness and ensure that the persons of the organization can relate in their own language their understanding of the requirement and how they contribute to the QMS.

7.4 COMMUNICATION

- Determine the need for internal and external communication relevant to the QMS.
    - ✓ What?

- ✓ When?
- ✓ With whom?
- ✓ How?
- ✓ Who provides communication?

Keys to understanding

Communication is an important aspect of every organization and helps ensure the persons of the organization have an understanding of the QMS that helps meet the intent of subclause 7.3, Awareness. This requirement includes both internal and external communication. Internal communication would be that which is provided to the persons of the organization. External communication could include communication with relevant interested parties such as customers, regulatory agencies, and external providers. Customer communication is specifically addressed in subclause 8.2.1, Customer communication.

Most organizations have one or more existing communication tools. Typically, these tools are based on the size of the organization. Smaller organizations may be able to use more informal tools; larger organizations may need to rely on more formal communication methods. The key is to define the method(s) that works best for your organization. They can include:

- Website
- Newsletters, e-mails, memos, quarterly or annual reports
- All-hands meetings
- Staff meetings
- Scorecards
- Posted metrics
- Videos or video conferencing
- Teleconferences

Once top management determines how they will communicate with the organization, they will need to determine what information to communicate. Management may determine that not all employees need the same information based on their effect on the QMS. In addition, some organizations may find that some of the information may be sensitive. For example, data regarding the effectiveness of the QMS could provide an advantage to competitors if the information were to become known. In this case, the organization may want to provide a higher level review of information and omit any sensitive data.

External communication would typically be directed to relevant interested parties such as external providers, regulatory bodies, and customers. This communication would in most cases be related to either performance of the external provider or how to ensure that the needs and expectations of customers are being met. Many organizations establish a meeting frequency (e.g., weekly or monthly) to communicate with key external providers to ensure that the product being provided or service delivered doesn't have an effect on the organization.

ISO 9001:2015 includes specific requirements for establishing what the organization communicates, and when, how, and with whom it communicates, but it doesn't require a formal communication plan. However, an organization could choose to develop one as part of meeting the intent of the requirement.

Transition

The requirements in subclause 7.4 were addressed in ISO 9001:2008, subclause 5.5.3, Internal communication. It has been expanded to also include external communication. However, because external communication was addressed in subclause 7.2.3, Customer communication, the only consideration most organizations will need to make in the transition process is the communication with external providers and other relevant interested parties.

In most cases, the organization will have methods in place that accomplish this, as it's a typical part of most business operations. A review should be conducted to ensure that the level of communication is sufficient.

7.5 DOCUMENTED INFORMATION

7.5.1 General

- The QMS must include:
  - ✓ Documented information required by ISO 9001:2015
  - ✓ Documented information determined necessary by the organization

- Note: The extent of documented information may differ based on:
  - ✓ Size of organization
  - ✓ Complexity of processes
  - ✓ Competence of persons

Keys to understanding

Documented information is defined in ISO 9000:2015 as information required to be controlled and maintained by an organization and the medium on which it's contained. The intent of ISO 9001:2015 is that the organization focus on controlling the information and not just implementing controls for the medium (e.g., procedures) that contains the information.

Since the first edition of ISO 9001 in 1987, the focus in the standard was on the creation of documented procedures describing in detail how the requirements were fulfilled. ISO 9001:2000 provided a more flexible approach for organizations. Subclause 4.2.1(d) in ISO 9001:2008 required the QMS to include documents, including records, determined by the organization to be necessary to ensure the effective planning, operation, and control of its processes.

The intent of this requirement is consistent with subclause 4.4.2, which provides a more flexible approach. There are still several requirements where ISO 9001:2015 requires documented information to be maintained and retained. In addition to these requirements, the organization will need to maintain or retain documented information to ensure an effective control of the processes and to demonstrate that performance is achieving intended results. Therefore, documented information is a critical component of the QMS.

The organization should also consider that the processes that are determined may have different types of information that is used on a regular basis such as information kept on a calendar, notebook, or website. When determining the controls for more "informal" information, the organization should consider whether it is critical to support the control of processes, provide objective evidence that a requirement has been carried out, meet a specific documented information requirement in this standard or others, or to meet customer or statutory and regulatory requirements. If these criteria are not met, then the information would not need to follow the requirements in subclause 7.5

There are two types of documented information that require control.

Documented information that is required by ISO 9001:2015

This type of documented information is referred to as documented information that needs to be maintained and retained.

Documented information that is to be maintained is typically information that requires review and is updated on a periodic basis (e.g., quality policy, scope of the QMS).

The list in figure 10.1 includes requirements where the organization is to maintain documented information in ISO 9001:2015.

Figure 10.1	Clauses Requiring Documented Information to Be Maintained
4.3 Determining the scope of the quality management system	
4.4.2 Quality management system and its processes	
5.2.2 Communicating the quality policy	
6.2.1 Quality objectives and planning to achieve them	
8.1 Operational planning and control	

Documented information that is to be retained is used to provide objective evidence that a requirement has been fulfilled (e.g., design reviews or competence). It's typically what organizations call records.

Figure 10.2 includes requirements where the organization is to retain documented information. If a requirement has been determined not to be applicable, then the requirement for retaining the documented information would also not apply.

Figure 10.2	Clauses Requiring Documented Information to Be Retained
4.4.2 Quality management system and its processes	
7.1.5.1 General	
7.1.5.2 Measurement traceability	
7.2 Competence	
8.1 Operational planning and control	
8.2.3.2 Review of requirements for products and services	
8.2.4 Changes to requirements for products and services	
8.3.3 Design and development inputs	
8.3.4 Design and development controls	
8.3.5 Design and development outputs	
8.3.6 Design and development changes	
8.4.1 General	
8.5.2 Identification and traceability	
8.5.3 Property belonging to customers or external providers	
8.5.6 Control of changes	
8.6 Release of products and services	
8.7 Control of nonconforming outputs	

Documented information that the organization determines to be necessary

This relates to any type of documented information that is determined to be needed by the organization and is not required by any clause of the standard.

The requirement directly relates to subclause 4.4.2, which includes requirements for documented information and allows the organization to make decisions on what documented information is needed. In this context, subclause 4.4.2 applies to any type of documented information required by ISO 9001:2015 and determined as necessary for the organization.

Process owners should consider the requirements of subclauses 4.4 and 7.5.1 together. For example, the process owner of the design and development process will identify that the standard has several requirements for maintaining and retaining documented information in subclause 8.3, which would be one of the relevant clauses applicable to the process. However, the process owner may determine that there is additional documented information that is relevant to the process that's not required by the standard (e.g., drawings or design of experiment results). In this case, the organization would establish additional documented information requirements.

During the review of the current documented information that is maintained and retained in each process, process owners may also identify documented information that isn't required by the standard but provides value and is relevant for the operation of the process and will still need to be controlled. On the other hand, it's possible that identified documented information doesn't provide any value and isn't relevant to the operation of the process. Therefore, it can be eliminated.

Criteria can be established that helps the processes to determine when documented information is necessary. This criteria is usually linked to documented information that is maintained. The note in subclause 7.5.1 helps an organization to establish this criteria. It includes:

- What is the size of the organization?
- What is the complexity of the processes?
- What is the competence of the personnel performing the tasks associated with the processes?

Once the process owners determine the two types of documented information that are necessary for the operation of its processes, controls according to subclauses 7.5.2 and 7.5.3 will need to be implemented.

Documented information will vary from one organization to another. Organizations need to focus on their specific needs.

7.5.2 Creating and updating

- Documented information shall include appropriate:

- ✓ Identification
- ✓ Format
- ✓ Review/approval for suitability and adequacy

Keys to understanding

When an organization establishes a QMS, it often focuses on one type of information: documented procedures. In reality, there are many types of documented information that must be controlled. This includes any type of document that the organization determines to be necessary to control processes as well as documented information (e.g., records) that demonstrate the performance and effectiveness of the QMS. Documented information types include but are not limited to drawings, procedures, forms, specifications, and work directions. It also includes documented evidence that demonstrates fulfillment of a requirement (e.g., records)

When creating and updating documented information, the organization should put in controls to ensure that documented information is identified. Identification can be through a number, date, author, or title. Organizations should keep in mind that identification is to assist with finding documented information; when changing titles and other information the traceability of the documented information could become lost.

The organization also needs to establish the format for documented information. This format should be based on the needs of the organization. Format can include but is not limited to the following:

- *Language.* Consideration should be given as to whether the organization is global and where the documented information will be accessed by persons speaking multiple languages.
- *Software.* Specific software tool or a specific version of a software package.
- *Graphics.* Flowcharts or other tools to relay documented information.
- *Media.* Paper or electronic.

Documented information must be reviewed to ensure it's suitable and adequate. Organizations should also establish who has the authority to approve documented information. Although many organizations will choose to require multiple approvals, ISO 9001:2015 does not prescribe the level of approval needed. Organizations that use fewer approval levels will find that the cycle time to release documented information is reduced. However, in some situations this isn't possible based on the documented information that is being provided or because of specific customer or regulatory requirements.

Approval does not require a handwritten signature. Approval can be granted through software process flows and access rights to the electronic system in which the documented information resides.

When it comes to reviewing documented information, many organizations implement a system in which some types of documented information are reviewed for adequacy on a predetermined frequency level. If an organization doesn't want to set a predetermined frequency, it can have document owners review documented information when changes are made to processes.

7.5.3 Control of documented information

Subclause 7.5.3.1

- Documented information shall be controlled.
  - ✓ Available/suitable for use
  - ✓ Adequately protected

Keys to understanding

Documented information must be controlled. There are two aspects to controlling documented information. It first needs to be available and suitable for use, but it also needs to be protected.

When ensuring documented information is suitable for use, consideration should be given to ensuring that the correct documented information has been made available. This can be done by only making the current version available through the organization's system for controlling documented information. If an organization uses electronic documented information, it needs to consider how persons of the organization will access it. If not every person is granted access to a computer where the documented information is stored, there is a risk of the person not having the necessary documented information.

Consideration should also be given to employees who work in the field, such as service technicians. They might not be able to access documented information electronically if the organization they provide service to limits internet access. In this case, the organization would need to determine how this information would be made available (e.g., hard-copy manuals).

Organizations also need to ensure that the proper controls are in place for protecting information that could be confidential. This might be specific company proprietary information about a new technology or be specific to the performance of an employee. Restrictions can be put on this type of documented information through access that is granted and provisioning of passwords.

Organizations that use electronic documents must remember that they need to retain previous versions of documented information for historical purposes. Therefore, an electronic archive is necessary. Electronic documented information must also be protected from loss of integrity. This could include the ability of any person to change documented information without authorization or approval or the ability to overwrite a released version with a draft.

Subclause 7.5.3.2

- Control of documented information shall address:
    - ✓ Distribution, access, retrieval, use
    - ✓ Storage/preservation/legibility
    - ✓ Change control
    - ✓ Retention and disposition

- External documented information (for the QMS) shall be identified and controlled.
- Retained documented information shall not be altered.
- Note: Access can include permission to view or view and change.

When establishing controls for documented information, organizations must consider how the documented information will be distributed, accessed, and retrieved.

In some cases, distribution of documented information may be through work order packages that are provided to operators in manufacturing areas, while in other situations the documented information may simply be distributed in an electronic system with persons being responsible for retrieving the information.

Access to documented information may be related to who has permission to see it. For example, documented information related to the specific analysis of an employee's competence might only be accessible by the employee and the employee's manager.

When an organization sets up its system for providing documented information, it must keep in mind that the system needs to allow for retrieval. This can relate to how the documented information is numbered, filed, or stored. For this reason, a standard structure is often used for storing documented information so that all persons of the organizations know where to retrieve it.

Consideration must be given to data recovery in the case of "crashed" systems as well as long-term storage. This could include offsite storage for hard-copy documented information. Many organizations implement a mechanism for ensuring that documented information can be retrieved. This could include requesting the offsite storage site retrieve a certain number of specified documents periodically to determine the ability to locate the needed documented information in a timely manner.

The organization must consider where and how documented information is stored. This can include identifying a central location within the organization or at employees' workstations.

Documented information should be stored in a way that protects it from potential destruction. The organization needs to consider issues such as fire, water, and other environmental conditions that could affect the documented information. The protection for hard-copy documented information might include locked or fireproof cabinets. Protection for electronic documented information would include the backup of documented information and the methods to ensure the backups are protected, such as offsite storage or remote backups.

Protection of documented information should also consider ongoing legibility. Some documented information in hard-copy format might lose its legibility due to the media being used. For example, documented information recorded in erasable ink or pencil can deteriorate over time and therefore become illegible. Corrections made to documents by obliterating the information through cross out or using Wite-Out can also make the document illegible. In this case, a simple pen-and-ink change with a line through, initial, and date helps maintain the legibility of the document.

Legibility can also apply to electronic documented information. For example, if an organization transitions to a new method for maintaining its documented information but does not maintain an older version of software, it's possible that previous versions of documents may not be legible in the new system.

Changes to documented information must be controlled. This includes the version of the documented information. Typically, when a new version of documented information is created, the change to the existing documented information is noted. This helps users understand what was changed. This could include a change log on a drawing or document. It could also be highlighted text in a documented procedure.

Organizations need to remember that documented information used to provide evidence of conformity to a specific requirement—also known as records—are not *revised* but *corrected*. For this reason, the organization needs to ensure that documented information used for these purposes cannot be unintentionally changed. This would include documented information such as design reviews. If it's determined that there is a correction needed to the information after the design review has been approved, there would be a need to complete a supporting document such as an addendum or a pen-and-ink correction made. In some cases, this would require an additional approval.

Organizations need to determine how long documented information will be retained. If an organization has a formal records management program, these retention times will already be established by a corporate headquarters or the legal office. If the organization doesn't have a formal records management program, it's important that it set guidelines to ensure consistency.

If an organization doesn't have an established records management system, it will frequently set a generic retention time during the initial implementation. Many organizations set a period of five to seven years. However, when developing records retention times, the following might be considered:
- Regulatory requirements
- Product liability or other legal issues (e.g., safety training)
- Expected lifetime of the product
- Customer or contract requirements

The organization must also identify how documented information is dispositioned. This might include how it's destroyed or archived when the retention time has expired. For example, an organization determines that documented information is to be retained for five years and then destroyed. At the end of the five years, the documented information is either destroyed if hard copy or deleted if electronic.

Many organizations use external documented information for the operation of its processes. This documented information requires identification as appropriate. It must also be controlled. This requirement can at times be difficult to implement because some of the external documented information may be received from an organization that hasn't implemented a QMS and may not use identifiers. If this is the case, the organization shall identify the means that it will use to control these documents. This could be adding a unique identification number.

Transition

The requirements in this series of subclauses were addressed in ISO 9001:2008, subclauses 4.2.3, Control of documents, and 4.2.4, Control of records. The main change is that the requirements for these two types of documented information have been blended into one subclause. This is because many times the lines between a traditional "document" and "record" are blurred.

Organizations that have an existing ISO 9001 system will generally meet the intent of the requirements and little change should be required. There is also no need to transition to the language of documented information as outlined in annex A.1. Organizations will need to make sure that documented information that is to be retained (e.g., records) has retention times and dispositions assigned. There will also need to be caution applied in ensuring that this documented information is not revised but corrected when a change is needed.

Chapter 11

Clause 8—Operation

Once an organization has a clear picture of its objectives, their inherent opportunities and risks, and what resources are in place and needed to support the organization, it needs to deploy its operations to transform the needs and expectations of customers and other relevant interested parties into a product or service that satisfies their needs.

Clause 8 of ISO 9001:2015 frames the operations of any organization in the way it generally interacts with its customers: from the initial engagement until the release of the product and service, including the control of changes and, if applicable, post-delivery activities.

One key premise this clause aims to achieve is the need to maintain operations that are planned and controlled. Organizations need to ensure that they effectively plan and control operations. ISO 9001:2015 provides the basis for achieving this feat.

Clause 8 is the largest in ISO 9001:2015. It begins with the requirements applicable to the planning of the operation (subclause 8.1) and continues with the engagement of current or potential customers (subclause 8.2), before the production or service provision (subclause 8.5). It also sets out the requirements for design and development (subclause 8.3) and external provision (subclause 8.4). Once the product or service is ready to deliver to the customer, it establishes the requirements for release (subclause 8.6) and the control of nonconforming outputs (subclause 8.7).

8.1 OPERATIONAL PLANNING AND CONTROL

- Plan, implement, and control the processes determined in subclause 4.4.

- ✓ Meet requirements for providing products and delivering services.
- ✓ Implement actions for addressing risks and opportunities determined in clause 6.

- Determine requirements for products and services.
- Establish criteria.
  - ✓ Processes
  - ✓ Acceptance for product and service

- Determine resources needed.
  - ✓ Meet product and service requirements.

- Implement the controls needed for processes.
- Determine the documented information to maintain and retain to ensure:
  - ✓ Processes carried out as planned
  - ✓ Product and services conform to requirements

- Output of this planning is suitable to the organization.
- Control planned changes, review consequences of unintended changes, and take action to mitigate any adverse effects.
- Control outsourced processes (see subclause 8.4).

Keys to understanding

The application of this subclause will vary depending on the nature of an organization's operations. The planning process should be performed using a cross-functional approach with persons from the different disciplines assigned responsibility for the processes. They should be directly involved in the operations to ensure the best understanding of the requirements and operation activities.

In subclause 4.4, the quality management system (QMS) processes are determined. In this subclause, the processes related to the operations are described in more detail, including any process or part that will be outsourced.

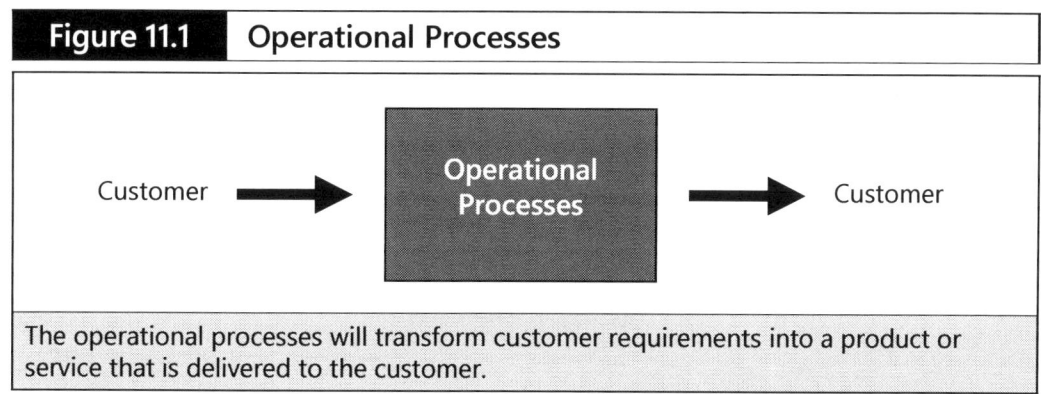

Figure 11.1 Operational Processes

The operational processes will transform customer requirements into a product or service that is delivered to the customer.

There should be clearly defined responsibilities and authorities for the operational planning process that can be performed at regular intervals based on the nature and complexity of the organization when a new product or service needs to be provided or a major change is implemented.

During the planning process the organization should determine the requirements for the products and services and establish the criteria for the processes and products and services to determine acceptance. This can be completed by the development of drawings that indicate acceptance criteria for products or a performance level for a service.

The organization also needs to determine the resources it needs to provide the product or deliver the service. These resource needs might be determined by the part of the organization that will be involved in the provision of the product or service. These resource needs are often determined and approved by management.

The organization must also determine the documented information it needs to maintain and retain. ISO 9001:2015 includes specific documented information requirements, but the organization must determine what specific documented information it might need to demonstrate that products and services meet requirements and that processes have been completed according to plans. Organizations may choose to specify documented information to retain such as first/last piece inspection or customer wait times.

The organization might also choose to do this by maintaining documented information that can be used as a reference during operations. This documentation becomes the foundation for the implementation of the operation processes.

The results of this planning may be in different forms. The form determined might relate to the complexity of the work. Quality plans or control plans are examples of documents that are normally produced where the requirements in this clause are included in the plan in addition to other relevant information, such as customer, statutory, or regulatory requirements.

ISO 10005—an ISO/TC 176 standard—provides guidance on quality plans and can be used as a reference. However, there's no requirement in ISO 9001:2015 to use this guidance document. Specific methodologies may be also considered, such as advanced product quality planning (APQP), which is used in the automotive industry, or other project management techniques.

A service industry such as a restaurant might provide a special event such as a birthday or company party. In this scenario, the owner of the restaurant needs to establish a plan for the event. Activities will be identified that must be performed before, during, and after the event. This includes things such as the menu, room setup, how the event will be separated from regular customers, and how parking needs will be addressed.

The owner of the restaurant can create a plan for this event with clear responsibilities and timings. He or she can also determine that documented information about the event can be retained for planning future events.

When controlling the processes determined in subclause 4.4, the organization must also consider processes that are outsourced. Typically, these controls are managed through subclause 8.4 when the process is provided by an external provider. However, these outsourced processes must also include the controls included in this subclause.

Transition

The intent of this subclause was addressed in ISO 9001:2008, subclause 7.1. Organizations may need to make some adjustments. This includes the more comprehensive requirements related to implementing, planning, and controlling the processes determined in subclause 4.4 and ensuring that actions identified in clause 6—specifically those related to risks and opportunities—are addressed.

8.2 REQUIREMENTS FOR PRODUCTS AND SERVICES

8.2.1 Customer communication

- Customer communication shall include:
  - ✓ Information about the products and services
  - ✓ How the organization will handle questions, including those related to orders and changes
  - ✓ Receiving customer feedback (including complaints)
  - ✓ How customer property will be controlled
  - ✓ Relevant contingency plans

Keys to understanding

ISO 9001:2015 recognizes the importance of establishing the communication process that an organization needs to promote and provide its products and services.

In today's world, the way organizations interact with their customers relies on more efficient ways of communication. The use of online applications for introducing and promoting products and services is growing. Online stores, where the customer can review and confirm an order without any interface with a marketing or salesperson, are a reality.

Organizations need to establish the methods they will use to communicate with customers. These methods should be known to the customer to provide for better communication. Different methods may be used based on the topic or customer preference. For instance, an organization may make information related to its products and services available on a public website or catalog. Salespeople might also hold meetings with customers.

Questions from customers related to contracts or orders may be managed through a customer representative or a single point of contact. This group may also be responsible for obtaining customer feedback through surveys and receiving customer complaints. These complaints could be specific to the product or service or related to an action. Customer complaints should be handled according to the requirements of subclause 10.2.1, Nonconformity and corrective action.

The organization is also responsible for communicating about customer property. This could be managed through reports on a specified frequency such as an inventory.

The organization is also responsible for communication related to contingency actions. This could include communication to the customer about what will happen if a production facility is shut down due to weather or if there's a breach in the security of customer data.

Transition

This subclause is consistent with the requirements in ISO 9001:2008, subclause 7.2.3. Although many of the requirements are consistent with the previous version, there is a new requirement related to communicating to customers about customer property. This requirement is consistent with previous requirements for customer property, so most organizations will only need to make minimal changes. There is also a new requirement related to communicating to the customer regarding any relevant contingency plans. Organizations will need to ensure this requirement is addressed.

8.2.2 Determining the requirements for products and services

- Determine requirements for products and services, including:
  - ✓ Applicable statutory and regulatory requirements
  - ✓ Requirements considered necessary by the organization

- Ensure claims for the products and services can be met.

Keys to understanding

ISO 9001:2015 focuses on two aspects of determining requirements for products and services. In one scenario, the specific requirements for the product or service are defined by the organization itself because it's a standard offering by the organization. In the second scenario, the customer provides specific requirements for the product or service that differ or are unique from the standard offering. Subclause 8.2.2 establishes requirements for the standard offering of products and services by the organization.

The organization will use its customer communication process to make this definition available to the customer. Consistency between what's explained by the salesperson and the online information is important to ensure customer expectations are met.

The organization will first determine the requirements for products and services. This can be done by developing a catalog or website where orders can be entered directly. These products and services are required to meet statutory or regulatory requirements. For example, if the organization provides a medical device, it is responsible for meeting the requirements for the regulatory agency in the country in which the device is being manufactured and distributed.

When the organization is establishing its list of products and services to be offered, it's also responsible for ensuring that it can fulfill the claims it's offering. If the organization claims that the product is faster than that of its competitors, there must be a way to prove this.

Because this subclause is focused on predetermined requirements for a product or service, organizations must ensure that any change in product or service characteristics is addressed by informing or training salespeople about the change and updating online information.

Development and maintenance of the website needs to be considered as part of the QMS. It can be a subprocess of any sales or marketing process. In some cases, this process is provided by an external provider (a supplier or a sister company).

Many organizations have a sales or customer service person who interacts with customers on the phone. They explain the characteristics, benefits, and value of a product or service, including all post-delivery activities (e.g., installation or service). Some information describing the characteristics of the product or service may be shown on the organization's website or literature. The customer has the option to place an order with the salesperson or online.

For certain products and services, a human interface in the sales process is vital, but the support of a comprehensive website can supplement this.

Whether the product or service is offered by a person, online, or a combination of both, the organization must ensure that it has the capability to fulfill any applicable requirement it has defined as part of its QMS.

Transition

This subclause 8.2.2 was partially addressed in ISO 9001:2008, subclause 7.2.1. However, it has been restructured to show that not every determination of requirements for a product or service goes through an extensive process of negotiation with the customer. In some cases, the customer simply chooses a product or service where the requirements have been previously established.

Organizations may want to review their processes for establishing requirements for products and services to determine if changes in requirements provide flexibility that the organization does not currently have.

8.2.3 Review of the requirements for products and services

Subclause 8.2.3.1

- Organizations shall:
  - ✓ Ensure that requirements for products and services can be met.
  - ✓ Review requirements before agreeing to provide them to the customer.

- Requirements need to include:
  - ✓ Customer-specific requirements for delivery and post-delivery
  - ✓ Customer requirements that are not stated but known by the organization
  - ✓ Requirements specified by the organization
  - ✓ Statutory and regulatory requirements applicable to specific product or service
  - ✓ Review and resolution of differing requirements
  - ✓ Confirm customer requirements before acceptance, including when the customer doesn't provide documented information.

Subclause 8.2.3.2

- Retain documented information on the results of review and any new requirements.

Keys to understanding

The main intent of this subclause is to ensure that the organization has the ability to meet requirements offered to its customers and when the acquisition of the product or service is confirmed by the customer, it has the capacity to satisfy the applicable requirements.

The need to conduct a review before committing to supply products and services to the customer is still a requirement in ISO 9001:2015.

The next step after the requirements have been determined is to review them. There are specific considerations the organization will want to make before committing to supplying a product based on the defined requirements. The organization should ensure that the correct person is reviewing the requirements. For example, an organization might choose to have a technical person review the technical requirements through a quote and have an order entry person enter the requirements.

The organization needs to review capability, capacity, and resources, including labor and equipment, to ensure that it can meet its commitments. Consideration should be given to whether the customer request meets the organization's guidelines for lead times and the current workload.

If the organization cannot meet the established times, it should offer an alternative date in its communication with the customer.

In reviewing the requirements for the specific product or service the customer is requesting, the organization should review requested delivery methods. This could be overnight air, a specific carrier, or delivery on a specific date. The order might also include post-delivery requirements. For the service industry, this might include delivery of an order at a specific time. For example, a customer might request room service at a specific time and indicate during the request that they would also like room service to pick up the table service at a specific time.

Organizations also need to consider which requirements are necessary for the intended use. These could include a requirement that improves the product or standard requirements that the organization uses in each proposal it develops. For example, an organization may know that a certain electronic product is going to be used in Europe. The requirements don't include the voltage, but the organization realizes this needs to be confirmed to meet customer requirements.

Requirements specified by the organization should also be considered. In this scenario, requirements for the product or service have been previously established in subclause 8.2.2, so it's reasonable that these would be the requirements for review by the customer.

Statutory and regulatory requirements have also been established in subclause 8.2.2. This subclause requires an additional review in consideration of the customer requirements.

If either the customer or organization has made changes to the original requirements, both parties need to review and agree on the changes prior to approval. This can be done by submitting a customer acknowledgment document to the customer.

At times, the customer may not provide a documented statement of requirements. This is common in small organizations or organizations where the customer has a high level of confidence in the organization. In these situations, the organization shall ensure that it has confirmed the requirements prior to acceptance. This can be handled by documenting a telephone conversation and providing written follow-up to the customer via e-mail or through a customer acknowledgment document. It can also be confirmed by repeating the order to the customer over the telephone and providing a sales order number.

Many organizations are migrating to the use of online sales. In this case, the review of requirements is managed through the review of the catalog according to subclause 8.2.2. This would focus on the confirmation by the customer when completing an online order. This review process would occur before the publication of the product or service description (e.g., catalog). When catalogs or online information is used, the organization may review this information on a periodic basis or when a change is made to ensure it still accurately describes the products and services.

When completing the review process for an online order, a website may have a screen where the customer will see the details of the order and provide payment information. The customer will review all the details and click on the specific button for accepting the order.

Transition

Subclause 8.2.3 was addressed in ISO 9001:2008, subclause 7.2.2. Most organizations will meet the intent of the new requirements. However, organizations should review the requirements in subclause 8.2.2 and this subclause to determine if any change to minimize bureaucracy for reviewing customer requirements can be incorporated into the QMS.

8.2.4 Changes to requirements for products and services

- Ensure that relevant document information is changed.

- Ensure relevant persons are made aware of change.
- Include changes to products and services

Keys to understanding

The actions that an organization performs to address changes to the requirements for products and services will depend on customer interaction. In some cases, the need for change happens during the review process. In other cases, it occurs after the order has been confirmed.

When a change is made, the organization needs to ensure that relevant documented information is changed. This could include the order itself, work orders released to the production floor, or changes needed to drawings. Relevant persons being informed could be the production worker on the floor or the engineering person who needs to make a change to a drawing.

For the service environment, this could include letting a restaurant worker know that a change is requested on an order. The restaurant worker would then need to notify the kitchen personnel as quickly as possible to ensure the order meets customer requirements.

These days, customers are accustomed to a great deal of flexibility in their transactions with businesses. For this reason, some organizations may put limits on the number and type of changes they allow customers to make after confirmation is made. This could include a penalty fee for making a change to the order. For example, airlines and hotels provide policies for canceling or changing a reservation.

Transition

Subclause 8.2.4 was addressed in ISO 9001:2008, subclause 7.2.2. However, this requirement is now a stand-alone requirement that emphasizes the importance of managing changes to requirements. Most organizations will meet the intent of this requirement.

8.3 DESIGN AND DEVELOPMENT OF PRODUCTS AND SERVICES

8.3.1 General

- Establish, implement, and maintain a design and development process as appropriate to ensure products can be provided or services delivered.

Keys to understanding

One of the purposes of subclause 8.3 is for organizations to consider a design and development process in their QMS. Some organizations may determine that this requirement isn't applicable because they aren't conducting design and development activities. It's also possible that some or all of the requirements may not apply. In these cases, a justification must be prepared and included as part of the scope of the QMS according to subclause 4.3.

The requirements and structure of subclause 8.3 were established for consistency with the way a design and development process operates.

Plan-inputs-controls-outputs-change control

When establishing the design and development process, organizations need to consider different aspects of the organization. For example, an organization needs to consider whether it obtains the design from a customer or an associate/headquarters organization. In this scenario, the organization may determine that only some of the activities of the process apply, such as design and development controls (subclause 8.3.5) and design and development changes (subclause 8.3.6).

Transition

The determination of requirements for processes was addressed in ISO 9001:2008, subclause 4.1. Although this requirement is more specific in establishing a design and development process in subclause 8.3 itself, there would have been a reasonable expectation that a design and development process would have been previously established.

The nature of the more prescriptive requirement is a reminder for organizations to carefully review the information related to design and development. Organizations that have excluded this subclause may find some adjustments are needed to indicate how design and development information is controlled at their organization.

8.3.2 Design and development planning

- Determine the stages and controls for design and development by considering:
  - ✓ Nature, duration, complexity
  - ✓ Process stages, including reviews
  - ✓ Design and development verification and validation
  - ✓ Responsibilities and authorities
  - ✓ Internal and external resource needs

- ✓ Control of interfaces
- ✓ Involvement of customers and users
- ✓ Requirements for providing products and services
- ✓ Expected controls of the design and development from customers and relevant interested parties
- ✓ Identification of needed documented information

Keys to understanding

Design and development planning is not a one-size-fits-all process. With that said, many organizations treat it as such and don't consider the flexibility that ISO 9001:2015 allows. Guidelines for different types of design and development projects are helpful for incorporating this flexibility. For more complex projects, it's reasonable to have multiple meetings from cross-functional areas of the organization, representing different disciplines.

The requirements in subclause 8.3.2 outline these steps and help tailor projects. Some organizations have established stages where criteria have already been determined for these planning activities. In this situation, the organization needs to ensure that its established system meets the criteria of ISO 9001:2015. It should also consider sector or industry mandates for using specific methodologies.

In determining the stages, the organization may choose to use the requirements in subclause 6.1, Actions to address risks and opportunities. The inclusion of risk-based thinking in these activities will help organizations to understand the level of control needed for the type of design and development activity being performed.

When determining the different stages, the organization needs to consider how long the design and development activity will last, the type of activity it is (e.g., new product development or product change), and the complexity of the activity. It's reasonable that a simple design and development activity based on an existing design might not include certain stages such as validation. Some organizations use established stages or they develop a check sheet with criteria that indicates the consideration of the certain parameters for needed stages. These criteria help to provide supporting evidence to demonstrate why certain types of documented information might not be available for a specific design and development activity.

Planning needs to consider the stages that the design and development activity goes through. This includes design reviews and verification and validation activities. Planning typically indicates what actions must be completed prior to conducting these activities.

In addition to these stages, the organization should also establish who has what responsibilities and authorities. This could be a list of team members and specific assignments for these individuals. For example, it might include the software engineer as being responsible for developing cases for testing or the product engineer for developing draft drawings.

Design and development planning also needs to include what internal and external resources are needed. This might include the consideration of an outside resource for a heat treating process.

It's important to remember that interfaces can also be relevant to the persons who have been assigned responsibility and authority for a design and development activity. These are frequently persons internal to the organization.

The organization also needs to consider the level of involvement from the customer and users. In instances where the organization is building a product for a specific customer based on customized requirements, it's common that the customer participates in certain stages of the design and development process, such as reviews and validation.

The planning activity needs to consider the requirements for providing the product or delivering the service. This can be related to the output of the design and development process (e.g., specification, drawing, or training curriculum).

Planning also needs to include any controls that are deemed necessary by a customer or relevant interested party. It's possible that a customer might choose to waive some of the controls, but it's important to remember that the planning should indicate this. It might also be necessary to include certain methodologies based on regulatory agency requirements, which would be considered a relevant interested party.

Planning must include any documented information necessary to demonstrate that the design and development requirements have been met. Specific requirements in subclause 8.3, Design and development of products and services, identify documented information requirements in specific subclauses. The planning activity is specific to the project and should include for each specific project the indications that the requirements have been met. These could include a verification report, drawing, or specification.

Transition

Subclause 8.3.2 was addressed in ISO 9001:2008, subclause 7.3.1. Some new requirements are included in ISO 9001:2015 that provide the flexibility to tailor design and development activities. Organizations will find that most of these activities are in place. New to subclause 8.3.2 is the consideration of the complexity of the design and development activity, internal and external resource needs, the need for involving the customer, requirements for providing product or delivery service, and the determination of documented information to demonstrate that requirements have been met.

8.3.3 Design and development inputs

- Determine requirements for design and development, including:
  - ✓ Functional and performance requirements
  - ✓ Information from previous similar design and development activities
  - ✓ Statutory and regulatory requirements
  - ✓ Standards or codes of practice
  - ✓ Potential consequences of failure due to the nature of the products and services

- Inputs shall be adequate, complete, and unambiguous.
- Resolve conflicting inputs.
- Retain documented information.

Keys to understanding

The intent of this subclause is for the organization to identify any requirements that are essential for the design and development activity to meet its intended use.

This subclause includes the types of things to consider, but all of the considerations may not be relative to the type of design and development project being conducted. The requirements might also be influenced by the nature or type of project. The organization should consider that in some sectors, the types of inputs may be mandated. These inputs are frequently determined through meetings with those who are responsible for the project.

Examples of inputs might include:

- Requests for proposal specifications
- Customer descriptions
- Regulatory (industry, state, or federal) codes and standards
- Specifications for components and parts
- Good manufacturing practices
- Commonly accepted engineering practices
- Customer contract

During the planning of design and development, the organization identified stages when reviews would be conducted. One of the stages should be when the design and development inputs would be reviewed. This review includes the consideration of complete and unambiguous inputs. In the simplest of terms, the inputs must be understood to confirm that the product or service meets requirements.

ISO 9001:2015 also requires the organization to retain any relevant documented information. This documented information was determined in the planning stage, but could include:

- Records or minutes of meetings
- Relevant information used to consider inputs (e.g., lessons learned from previous projects, manufacturer specifications, and operation manuals).

Transition

Subclause 8.3.3 was addressed in ISO 9001:2008, subclause 7.3.2. Some new requirements are included in ISO 9001:2015. However, these new requirements were implied in ISO 9001:2008, which required the organization to include requirements it determined necessary. These include standards or codes of practice and potential consequences of failure. ISO 9001:2015 includes a specific documented information requirement for design and development inputs. This documented information would have typically been covered in design and development review in the past (ISO 9001:2008, subclause 7.3.4).

8.3.4 Design and development controls

- Apply controls to the design and development process to ensure:
  - ✓ Results to achieve are defined.
  - ✓ Reviews are conducted.
  - ✓ Verification activities—outputs meet inputs
  - ✓ Validation activities—resulting products and services meet requirements or intended use
  - ✓ Necessary actions are taken during activities.
  - ✓ Documented information is retained.

- Note: Reviews, verification, and validation can be conducted separately or together.

Keys to understanding

Subclause 8.3.4 focuses on the controls that are part of the design and development process to ensure that results are being achieved. The planning stage of the project determines when specific controls (e.g., review, verification, and validation) will be conducted. Based on the planning and the complexity of the project, these review, verification, and validation activities will vary.

In certain cases, the participation of external providers, customers, or final users will be needed. In certain sectors, customers approve the results of the verification and validation activities. When considering less complex projects, reviews may be less formal and could be as simple as the sign-off of a drawing or documenting actions in an engineering notebook.

For more complex projects, review meetings can take place on a more frequent basis and should include ongoing resolution of actions taken on problems identified during the review, including verification and validation activities. Organizations that have implemented a stage gate review process typically have criteria established related to these controls. These gate reviews are conducted with a group that has been assigned responsibility for approving the criteria. Even if an organization doesn't have a stage gate process, this is a good practice to help determine what actions are needed to resolve any problems.

Retaining documented information is a requirement for the controls. This could include:
- Meeting minutes or presentations
- Checklists used for verification
- Test results
- Personnel qualification records

Transition

The requirements in subclause 8.3.4 were addressed in ISO 9001:2008, subclauses 7.3.4, 7.3.5, and 7.3.6. These subclauses included redundant requirements. They also gave the impression that review, verification, and validation were separate activities and couldn't be conducted together. ISO 9001:2015 simplifies these requirements, eliminates the redundancies between the subclauses, and provides a format to facilitate the understanding of the design and development requirements to service organizations. It also aligns subclause 8.3.4 with that of one of the main intents of clause 8, Operations, which is control.

There is a specific requirement that the intended results to be achieved are defined. In the past, this requirement was more related to the ability of the design and development to meet requirements. Achieving the intended results is more focused on the design and development inputs meeting the outputs. Organizations that meet the intent of ISO 9001:2008 should meet the intent of the new requirements.

8.3.5 Design and development outputs

- Design and development outputs shall:
  ✓ Meet the input requirements
  ✓ Be adequate for the processes that follow
  ✓ Include or reference monitoring and measuring requirements, as appropriate
  ✓ Include acceptance criteria

✓ Specify what's essential for the product to meet its intended purpose and safe and proper provision.

- Retain documented information.

Keys to understanding

When an organization implements effective design and development review, verification, and validation activities, this will result in outputs that need to be verified. Based on the nature and complexity of the design and development project, the outputs will vary.

Not only does the organization need to confirm that the outputs meet the input, the organization must also ensure that the outputs are adequate for the subsequent processes that provision the products and service. Subsequent processes include the provision of externally provided processes, products, and services (subclause 8.4) or the production and service provision requirements (8.5). This could be in the form of specifications for equipment that needs to be purchased or work instructions used in manufacturing. The organization may also want to consider details regarding preservation of the product such as packaging.

Outputs for a service organization might include check sheets, flowcharts, or prepared documents/plans.

The outputs need to include the appropriate monitoring or measuring requirements. This could include dimensions and tolerances on a drawing or the use of recording or monitoring on a customer service call. The output needs to indicate the acceptance criteria, which is the criteria that allow the product to be provided or the service to be delivered. It could be a specific test, a visual review, or a qualification process for the persons doing the work.

In addition to the required monitoring and measuring, the organization needs to specify any characteristic for the product that ensures that the product is used or the service delivered safely. A lawnmower might include a "kill" switch that turns the device off if the handle is released. For a service organization such as a bank, there could be a provision that requires two persons to open the vault to protect employees.

The organization is required to retain documented information on design and development outputs. This documented information is determined during the planning stage (subclause 8.3.1) and could be the same documented information retained as part of design and development controls. Examples include the results of validation activities where the project team is confirming that the outputs meet the inputs and might include redlined drawings for updates or the actual drawings themselves.

Transition

Subclause 8.3.5 is consistent with ISO 9001:2008, subclause 7.3.3. Organizations that met the requirement in ISO 9001:2008 should be able to transition with minimal, if any, changes to their QMS. Although ISO 9001:2008 referenced purchasing, production, and service provision when considering the adequacy of needed information, ISO 9001:2015 is more generic and refers to subsequent processes.

In addition, although ISO 9001:2008 required documented information (e.g., records) for design and development verification, the specific requirements for design and development outputs did not include the need for documented information. This requirement is more specific and should be considered during an organization's transition.

There is also a slight change in the language regarding safe and proper provision. This was previously safe and proper use. The word "provision" is used to make the requirement more generic and applicable to both products and services.

8.3.6 Design and development changes

- Identify, review, and control changes to the extent necessary (during or after design and development).
- Ensure no adverse effect on requirements.
- Retain documented information on:
  - ✓ Changes
  - ✓ Reviews
  - ✓ Who authorized the change
  - ✓ Actions taken to prevent adverse effects

Keys to understanding

One of the most important pieces of design and development is controlling changes. The change in subclause 8.3.6 is specific to design and development while the change in subclause 8.5.6, Control of changes, is specific to operations. Changes made in subclause 8.5.6 could result in subsequent design and development changes.

There are two types of changes. There is the type of change that occurs during the initial design and development process. This could be a change that occurs as a result of design review, verification, or validation. For this type of change, the authorization required is typically the team and the documented information that needs to be retained would be either meeting minutes or a revised document or specification.

The other type of change is when the product has already been provided or the service has already been delivered. This type of change requires structure around managing the change. Many times this type of change is processed through an engineering change request. This request could be made by an employee, a customer, or the person responsible for the design.

This change is reviewed and, whenever it's necessary, the effect or potential effect of the change is considered. For example, if the change is being made to correct a known defect, the organization will need to consider whether any actions are required to notify existing customers.

When there is a minimal effect, changes may not require the same level of control as a change that has a more significant effect. The engineering change request frequently turns into the actual change. This change must be authorized by a person with the authority to make it. Organizations with best practices in place will not only require that authorization, but will also require an authorization from any effected departments. This could mean that an authorization (e.g., approval) is required from the purchasing organization when a change is made to a drawing that results in a change of raw materials to be procured.

Information on the change must be retained as documented information. This could include specific forms that process the change, meeting minutes, or a database that tracks design and development changes. It must include the authorization or approval of changes.

Transition

Subclause 8.3.6 was addressed in ISO 9001:2008, subclause 7.3.7, and maintains the same intent. Although ISO 9001:2008 indicated that the change needs to be approved, ISO 9001:2015 includes the authorization of the changes.

8.4 CONTROL OF EXTERNALLY PROVIDED PROCESSES, PRODUCTS AND SERVICES

8.4.1 General

- Ensure externally provided processes, products, and services conform to requirements.
- Determine the controls when:
  - ✓ Products and services from external providers are intended for use by the organization in providing products or delivering services
  - ✓ Products and services are to be provided directly to the customer(s)

✓ A process or part of a process is provided by an external provider

- Determine and apply criteria for the evaluation, selection, monitoring of performance, and reevaluation of external providers.
- Retain documented information, including necessary actions.

Keys to understanding

There are providers that are frequently called suppliers, providers that we outsource a process to such as heat treating or engineering services, or a provider that is a "sister" or "parent" company. Because "sister" or "parent" organizations aren't typically referred to as suppliers, the more generic term of "external provider" is used to ensure the application of requirements to all types of external providers and not just suppliers. The purpose of this subclause is to ensure that processes, products, or services that are obtained from an external provider conform to the requirements that the organization specifies. In today's world, organizations obtain processes, products, or services from different types of external providers.

The organization must determine the controls that will be used for processes, products, or services that it obtains externally. Subclause 8.4.2 specifically addresses the type and extent of control to be applied to external providers. In addition, although this subclause doesn't specifically provide a link to subclause 6.1 where actions to address risks and opportunities are determined, the risk-based thinking aspects of these requirements will be helpful in determining the level of control needed.

This subclause also emphasizes that when the organization is determining its controls, it needs to consider all of the different types of external providers. This could include a provider where a customer purchases an item from the organization but it's directly shipped to the customer. In the service industry, it could be when an organization procures a service such as auditing and the auditing company uses the services of a contractor to fulfill the auditing activity.

In addition to different types of external providers, there are also different types of products and services that will be obtained from the external provider. The organization must determine the criteria it will use for evaluation, selection, monitoring of performance, and reevaluation of external providers.

Organizations may find the need to have different criteria based on the process, product, or service. For example, an organization would have different criteria for a provider that provides toilet paper and one that provides parts that will be used in the final product or a service such as calibrating equipment.

Once the criteria are established, the organization is responsible for evaluating and selecting the provider based on these criteria. This means that if the organization establishes a criterion of completing a questionnaire, this must be retained as documented information.

Organizations can use a variety of methods to select and evaluate providers, but the results must be appropriate to the process, product, or service that's being provided. Examples include:
- Supplier audits conducted by the organization
- Product quality history
- Reviewing previous performance in supplying similar products (including services)
- On-time delivery
- QMS status
- Debarred list—used frequently in government. If a supplier is on this list, the organization cannot use it.

For an organization seeking ISO 9001:2015 certification, there could be a situation in which there are existing external providers with no detailed information regarding the criteria on how they were selected. In this situation, a decision may be made to "grandfather" the provider based on past performance. The organization would need to establish a date for when the providers are considered grandfathered. From this date forward, the providers would be required to follow the newly established criteria and be reevaluated as defined.

When the external provider is specified (e.g., selected by the customer or predetermined, such as a "sister" company), the organization may not be using established criteria, but it is still responsible for the ongoing monitoring of performance and reevaluation.

The performance of external providers must be monitored. This should be conducted based on established criteria. Because many organizations have many external providers, they establish criteria for a certain number of providers to be monitored. This could be the "top 10" suppliers according to purchase dollars. However, this scenario might not always apply. The general rule should be that if the external provider has the ability to affect your ability to meet customer requirements, the performance for that provider should be monitored.

The criteria should include the frequency of the monitoring. Organizations typically implement a minimum of monthly or quarterly reviews. Monitoring performance at a less frequent interval doesn't allow the organization to determine if actions are needed and make necessary corrections. Because the performance of the external provider can affect the organizations ability to meet its objectives, it's critical that these reviews be timely.

The organization must also establish the criteria for reevaluation. Many organizations also establish a planned interval to conduct the reevaluation. Some organizations establish criteria that indicates that the monitoring of performance is inclusive of reevaluation. However, if performance is being monitored for only a percentage of external providers, the organization may determine that a planned interval is necessary for the remaining external providers.

For some external providers where processes, products, or services are obtained infrequently, an annual reevaluation may not be necessary. In this scenario, it may make sense to reevaluate the provider at the time the process, product, or service is needed. The key is to establish flexibility in your QMS.

The organization is responsible for retaining documented information on the selection, evaluation, monitoring of performance, and reevaluation based on the established criteria. This could include audit reports and corrective actions or a copy of the external provider's ISO 9001 certificate.

Transition

Sublause 8.4 is similar to requirements included in ISO 9001:2008, subclauses 4.1, 7.4.1, and 7.4.2. In addition to products and services, this subclause also includes the concept of processes that are obtained from an external provider. This was addressed in ISO 9001:2008, subclause 4.1. Many organizations indicated they fulfilled the requirements of this subclause through the purchasing requirements. However, when the process was being obtained from a "sister" or "parent" company, the purchasing process isn't always used. Recognizing this inconsistency, ISO 9001:2015 transitioned from the use of the concept of purchasing and supplier to "external provision" and "external provider." This rationale is further explained in ISO 9001:2015, annex A.8.

Subclause 8.4 is also more specific in that it addresses products and services that are provided directly to the customer on behalf of the organization.

Some organizations will find that they've already incorporated the requirements for all types of external providers. Other organizations may find that some adjustment is needed to the QMS. Specifically, organizations may need to establish how they monitor the performance for "sister" or "parent" organizations and whether they consider that performance based on established criteria such as quality issues or on-time delivery. In either scenario, there is no requirement that the organization transition to the new language in the standard (see annex A.1) or adopt the term "provider."

8.4.2 Type and extent of control

- Ensure externally provided processes, products, and services don't affect the organization's ability to provide products and services to customer.

- Ensure that external processes remain within control of QMS.
- Define:
  - ✓ Controls for external provider
  - ✓ Controls for output

- Consider:
  - ✓ Effect of process, product, or service
  - ✓ Ability to meet requirements
  - ✓ Effectiveness of controls by provider

- Determine verification to ensure products and services meet requirements.

Keys to understanding

Although organizations have outsourced processes, products, and services, they must maintain control to ensure that what is being provided doesn't affect the conformity of products and services.

Because there are different levels of processes, products, and services that are provided and not all of them will affect the conformity of products and services, ISO 9001:2015 gives the organization the flexibility to define the type and grade of control based on the effect of these providers to the organization's ability to consistently deliver conforming products and services.

The organization can determine what specific controls are to be implemented to an external provider. These controls may vary depending on the nature of the process, product, or service and the applicable requirements. These requirements could be customer requirements or applicable statutory and regulatory requirements.

- *Control of processes.* The organization must control processes through its QMS. For example, in a heat treating process performed by an outsourced provider, controls can be related to validation activities, personnel qualification, and tests. It's still the responsibility of the organization to determine what these controls are to ensure they meet the intent of requirements. It's reasonable to consult with the external provider, but ultimately the organization is still responsible.
- *Control of external provider and its resulting output.* The organization also needs to establish the controls for an external provider and the process, product, or service it provides. In the case of a raw material, the controls can be implemented in the incoming quality or receiving process through inspection activities, submission of laboratory test reports (internal or external), or second-party audits. If the service provided is the maintenance of the IT infrastructure, the controls can be related to the personnel qualification or supervision of the maintenance activity.

It's possible that controls could vary for different external providers. The organization can determine what controls the external provider has in place (e.g., inspection, certificate of analysis). It might consider the effectiveness of these controls. For example, an organization might initially put into place a receiving inspection activity for an external provider. If the external provider has a certain number of receipts with no issues, it might be determined that this step is no longer necessary. The organization might reinstitute a receiving inspection step if quality issues are later identified.

Transition

The intent of subclause 8.4.2 was addressed in ISO 9001:2008, subclauses 4.1, 7.4.1, and 7.4.3. Subclause 8.4.2 now includes consideration of the effectiveness of the controls in place for an external provider. Organizations implementing ISO 9001:2015 should review what controls are currently in place and evaluate their effectiveness. A need for change, adjustments, or consideration of other controls may result from this evaluation. The organization should specifically look at controls for external providers such as "sister" or "parent" organizations.

8.4.3 Information for external providers

- Ensure the adequacy of requirements prior to sending to the external provider.
- Communication to external provider shall include requirements such as:
  - ✓ Processes, products, and services
  - ✓ Approval of:
    - Products and services
    - Any specific methods, processes, or equipment that need to be used
    - Release

  - ✓ Required competence/qualification
  - ✓ Required interactions
  - ✓ Control and monitoring that the organization will use to determine performance
  - ✓ Verification and validation to be performed at external provider's premises.

Keys to understanding

This subclause focuses on providing information to the external provider and communicating about expectations, required controls, and the expected performance for the provided process, product, or service. The organization can specify the requirements for the implementation of these controls in policies or agreements with the external provider.

The organization is responsible for ensuring that the information communicated to external providers is adequate. This might include a purchase order or confirmation letter that includes information from the external provider's catalog, a request for a quote, or a previously provided quote. In the situation where the external provider is a "sister" plant, it's common that purchase orders aren't used. Many times the information is an order release in the organization's enterprise resource planning system.

In addition to these considerations, the information for the external provider also needs to include specific requirements such as personnel qualifications, liability and confidentiality considerations, specific legal or regulatory requirements (e.g., use of safety equipment), or information security. For example, an organization might specify that the persons performing the process must be trained in a certain type of software development or be a certified welder.

When an external provider provides a service or a process, the organization should establish an agreement that covers all the relevant aspects to be considered during the provision of the service or the externally provided process.

It's up to the organization to determine how this communication will take place and what documented information will be needed. All the applicable requirements need to be complete, clear, and address any potential issues. The organization and the external provider should agree upon what is being requested. This includes any agreements for delivery (e.g., required date) and any necessary steps that the external provider needs to complete for release, such as inspection, test reports, or review of an established process prior to delivery of a service.

Depending on what is externally provided, the exchange of information between the parties can differ. The established interaction could be a meeting held at regular dates and times and appointing a primary contact for each the organization and the external provider. Communication methods may be different between a traditional external provider and an external provider that is a "sister" plant. However, it's still a requirement that these types of external providers meet the established criteria.

The organization must establish communication related to the controls for the external provider as determined in subclause 8.4.2 as well as how the external provider's performance will be evaluated. This might include requirements for percentage of on-time deliveries, expectations for quality, or response time for a service. The organization will need to determine how it will communicate the external provider's performance (e.g., monthly or quarterly) and provide it information on what will be required if performance expectations aren't met.

The purchasing information provided to the external provider also needs to include any requirements for when the organization will conduct the verification or validation on the external provider's premises. This could be due to the size of a product, time constraints, or where the product or service is originally confirmed, such as a production part approval process (PPAP).

Some organizations may decide to establish a policy or manual applicable to all their external providers. In certain cases, organizations can include specific requirements that external providers must fulfill. There is no specific requirement for documented information in this subclause. However, there is a management review input to review the performance of external providers. Because the results of management review must be retained as documented information, it's reasonable to assume that there will be some level of documented information related to the performance of external providers.

Transition

Subclause 8.4.3 includes requirements covered in ISO 9001:2008, subclause 7.4.2. ISO 9001:2015 is more specific with the types of purchasing information and expands the requirement to include communication for monitoring performance. Most organizations already monitor provider performance. However, consideration should be given to how this is being communicated. A key aspect to be considered in the transition is how the communication is implemented. Organizations should ensure that the information exchanged is consistent with the nature of what is externally provided.

8.5 PRODUCTION AND SERVICE PROVISION

8.5.1 Control of production and service provision

- Provide product and deliver services under controlled conditions.
- Control conditions, as applicable.
    - ✓ Availability of documented information
        - Characteristics of the products and services
        - Activities to be performed
        - Results to be achieved

    - ✓ Suitable monitoring and measuring resources
        - Availability of use

    - ✓ Implementation of monitoring and measurement
        - Appropriate stages
        - Confirm that criteria have been met

- ✓ Suitable infrastructure/environment for the operations of processes
- ✓ Assignment of competent persons
  - Qualifications

- ✓ Validation and revalidation of processes
  - Those where the resulting output cannot be verified through subsequent monitoring and measurement

- ✓ The implementation of actions to prevent human error
- ✓ Release, delivery, and post-delivery activities

Keys to understanding

Based on the results of the planning activities conducted in subclause 8.1, a set of conditions to control the product and service provision should be determined and implemented.

Controls should be in place for the complete cycle of production and service provision, including applicable post-delivery activities. Therefore, a clear determination of the processes needed for production and service provision is the first step. The organization's processes have been determined according to the requirements in subclause 4.4. This subclause focuses on implementing the controls needed for these processes to achieve customer satisfaction and conformity with all applicable requirements as well as the effective treatment of determined risks and opportunities.

The application of the list of controlled conditions included in this subclause will depend on the nature and complexity of the production and service provision processes. The operational planning, design and development, and external provision processes also have a key interface with the controls needed for the production and service provision.

The organization needs to have documented information that describes the characteristics of the product. This information can come from customer orders or design and development by the organization or customer. It can be a drawing, specification, or information in a work order. Some organizations may use standardized work to deliver this documented information. The level of documented information directly relates to the needed controls. It could be based on the level of competence of the persons doing the work or the complexity of the job. More complex processes and less competent persons would be an indicator for the need for stronger controls.

The documented information should also indicate what results are to be achieved. This could be a service delivered in a certain amount of time (e.g., your food order is delivered in 10 minutes or it's free).

The organization needs to ensure that monitoring and measuring resources are available and are used when required. These type of resources could include gages or calibrated equipment. In the service industry, this could be a specific method used to grade a test or deliver a service. Additional controls for identifying requirements for monitoring and measuring resources are included in subclause 7.1.5, Monitoring and measuring resources.

The organization is responsible for implementing monitoring and measurement processes for the products it provides and the services that are delivered. Frequently, this is inspection, but in some cases verification of work by the person building the product or delivering the service can be considered monitoring. A service industry example is a call center that has a person who monitors the performance of the person providing the service by listening to telephone calls.

When considering the controls for implementing monitoring and measurement activities, the organization needs to ensure that acceptance criteria have been met. These acceptance criteria might be on an inspection check sheet or a control plan.

The organization also needs to consider the infrastructure (subclause 7.1.3) and the environment for the operation of its processes (subclause 7.1.4).

When the organization is considering the controls needed for infrastructure, it will want to review the suitability of equipment. Controls might include equipment checks at the beginning of the shift or preventive maintenance programs. Service delivery might focus more on controls such as the infrastructure needed to provide customer service from an employee's home (e.g., computer and telephone requirements).

When considering the environment necessary for the operation of processes, the organization may need to make sure controls for temperature and lighting are in place for a product that relies on them. Service environment considerations might include the amount of ambient noise in an area where the service is reviewing tests.

The organization also needs to ensure that the persons performing the work are competent and, when necessary, qualified. Subclause 7.2 addresses specific requirements for determining competence. The controlled condition is to ensure that competent persons are assigned. For this reason, organizations frequently maintain a matrix of competence in a production area. Some processes such as welding might also require the person to be qualified. In this case, controls should address the assignment of these persons to specific work based on qualifications.

Depending on the nature of its operations and the processes of the organization, it might have processes for which output cannot be verified by subsequent monitoring or measurement. These processes are frequently called "special processes." These processes require validation. According to ISO 9000:2015, validation is the confirmation, through the provision of objective evidence, that requirements for a specific intended use or application have been met. If an organization doesn't implement a validation activity for any special processes existing in its operations, the risk of nonconforming outputs or customer complaints rises.

Examples of manufacturing processes that fall into this category include nondestructive testing or painting. This requirement can also apply to organizations that provide services. Examples would include validating a process to ensure the persons of the organization follow the process (e.g., emergency or disaster planning). The organization validates that if employees follow their established procedures, the emergency response to a disaster will go as planned.

The organization is responsible for defining the criteria for reviewing and approving the process. The criteria could include acceptable performance for the process as well as who is authorized to approve it.

After the equipment and qualifications of personnel are identified, the organization must also identify any specific methods or procedures to be followed. For example, a welder may be required to perform the weld in a certain position or an employee who works in a customer service organization is required to follow a procedure for how he or she interacts with customers.

The organization must also consider the applicable revalidation. Processes may need to be revalidated based on results related to exercising the process. The organization may also wish to establish a regular frequency for revalidating the process, such as every two years or when a change is made.

The organization also needs to implement controls to prevent human error. This requirement considers the fact that people can make mistakes. Controls might include the use of a fixture to help ensure the product is built correctly or creating a work environment for a person providing a service that limits distractions. Some organizations have incorporated standing workstations for employees who spend a lot of time at their desks because they find that this keeps them more aware and less prone to errors.

The organization must also consider the controls for how the product will be released or the service delivered as well as any post-delivery activities such as maintenance or warranty. It's up to the organization to determine these controls based on customer, statutory, or regulatory requirements.

Controlled conditions can be summarized in the following areas:
- Human resources (e.g., competence and required qualification, other human factors)
- Physical resources (e.g., for monitoring and measuring, infrastructure and environment for the operation of the processes, necessary documented information)
- Methods (e.g., for monitoring, measuring, inspection, verification and validation, preservation, and identification)

In the case of a retail store, most of the listed controlled conditions are applicable. As part of its regular operations, the company will need to implement:
- Methods for preserving the products in its warehouses and during release, delivery, and post-delivery activities
- Methods for monitoring, measuring, and inspection
- Controls and maintenance of all the infrastructure, including measuring and monitoring resources and controls of the environment needed for the operations (e.g., illumination, ventilation, ergonomics, workload, and safe and secure conditions)
- Inventory controls and specific methods (e.g., FIFO, flow of products)
- Specific activities for ensuring competent persons are doing the work and specific controls to prevent human error
- Documented information describing the operations (e.g., work instructions, visual aids, layouts), used as reference (e.g., product specifications), and kept as evidence of the implementation of all the activities (e.g., inspection checklists, information systems for order handling and inventory control)

Transition

This subclause includes requirements addressed in ISO 9001:2008, subclauses 7.5.1 and 7.5.2. The requirements have been expanded to include controls needed for the infrastructure and environment for the operation of processes. Because these are existing requirements in ISO 9001:2008, organizations will simply need to confirm that controls are in place.

Subclause 8.5.1 also includes implementation of actions to prevent human error. Organizations will need to consider this new requirement during the transition.

Because the requirements for validation of processes for providing a product or service are now included in this subclause, organizations should review whether the merging of these two sets of requirements indicates a need for change in controls based on a better understanding of the requirements.

Organizations can also use this opportunity to review how the current controls in their operations are performing and evaluate if any change or adjustment is needed.

8.5.2 Identification and traceability

- Use suitable means to identify outputs, when necessary.
- Identify the status of outputs.
    - ✓ Monitoring and measurement requirements

- Control unique identification.

✓ Where traceability is a requirement

- Retain documented information.

Keys to understanding

Output is defined in ISO 9000:2015 as "result of a process." In the context of this subclause we are considering tangible outputs, including relevant information when determining the requirements for identification and traceability.

ISO 9001:2015 doesn't require a specific way of identifying the outputs throughout the production and service provision. The method and type of identification will depend on different aspects:
- Nature of the outputs
- Applicable requirements (e.g., customer, legal, and regulatory)
- Technical specifications or standards
- Intended use of the identification (e.g., control of nonconforming outputs, labeling)

Normally, the identification will occur when there is a release activity where a verification or inspection is in place. Identification can also apply to raw materials and identification of subassemblies. The identification should indicate the status of the output (e.g., conforming, suspicious or unknown, nonconforming, or obsolete). Some organizations apply the identification with a color-coding or marks. It's also possible to designate status by location (e.g., a specific shelf).

Where there is a requirement to trace outputs, the organization should ensure that relevant documented information about each identified output is retained and available. In manufacturing organizations, traceability is typically maintained through lot numbers. An example of traceability in a service organization could be a report number or a customer complaint number.

Transition

This subclause is consistent with the requirements in ISO 9001:2008, subclause 7.5.3. The intent remains unchanged in ISO 9001:2015. ISO 9001:2015 uses the term "output" where ISO 9001:2008 used the term "product realization." This is to make the requirements easier to understand for the service industry.

Service organizations should review the new language to determine if it results in a change in how it understands the requirements and if it requires a change to the QMS.

8.5.3 Property belonging to customers or external providers

- Exercise care over customer property or external provider property.
  - ✓ Under the organization's control
  - ✓ Used by organization

- Identify, verify, protect, and safeguard property.
  - ✓ Use
  - ✓ Incorporated into product or service

- Report lost, damaged, or unsuitable for use property to the customer or external provider.
  - ✓ Retain documented information.

- Note: Property can include intellectual property, personal data, materials, components, and tools and equipment.

Keys to understanding

Subclause 8.5.3 addresses external property provided by either a customer or external provider that will be incorporated in the product (e.g., a component, packaging), used for transporting the product (e.g., pallets, containers), or used for processing the product or providing the service (e.g., technical and personal data or tools). When considering property provided by an external provider, it could be a piece of equipment used to dispense packaging material. The external provider provides the equipment at no charge, but the organization purchases the materials used in the equipment.

It's important to remember that customer property shouldn't be confused with purchasing property on behalf of the customer. For example, if a customer requests that you use a specific supplier to purchase product and you use the organization's own money for this purchase, it's not customer property. Organizations that are prime contractors for a specific customer, such as a government entity, will find that they have a significant amount of customer property.

The contracts, purchase orders, or any documented information used to confirm the transactions of the organization with their customers or external provider should include a section for the control of external property.

When there isn't any external property to be controlled, these requirements won't be applicable under the scope of the QMS. However, because this situation can change, the organization should keep a vigilant watch on this requirement and incorporate any changes.

This subclause also relates to other requirements in subclause 7.5. The organization needs to consider requirements for identification in subclause 8.5.2 and preservation in subclause 8.5.5. If the external property is documented information, the requirements in subclause 7.5 should be also considered.

The organization must also communicate with the customer or the external provider when a problem exists with their property. This includes if the property is lost, damaged, or otherwise found unsuitable for use. For example, a fixture that is provided by the customer is good for a certain amount of uses. Once the organization reaches this number of uses, the customer should be contacted.

External property that is damaged or found to be unsuitable would need to meet the requirements in subclause 8.7, Control of nonconforming outputs. It's also possible that the nonconformity would require corrective action. In this case, the requirements in subclause 10.2 would need to be applied. Retaining relevant documented information is vital for supporting any improvement action.

If there is a statutory or regulatory requirement on the protection of personal data, the organization should implement activities to protect its customers' or external providers' data, such as contact information or legal documentation.

In addition, if an organization provides services for installation or maintenance, it should exercise care with the product that belongs to the customer that requires maintenance or needs to be installed. The maintenance activities can be provided at the customer's premises or at the facilities of the organization.

Transition

Subclause 8.5.3 was addressed in ISO 9001:2008, subclause 7.5.4. ISO 9001:2015 maintains the intent of the requirement, but extends it to include property belonging to external providers. Special attention should be given to this part of the requirement. Organizations should review whether they have this type of property and take appropriate action.

8.5.4 Preservation

- Preserve outputs during production and service provision.
    - ✓ To the extent necessary
    - ✓ Ensure conformity to requirements

- Note: Examples of preservation include identification, handling, contamination control, packaging, storage, transmission, transportation, and protection.

Keys to understanding

Preservation is one of the controls the organization should consider during operational planning and the design and development process. The conformity requirements and the specific characteristics of the product or service are the key inputs in determining the preservation conditions.

Depending on the nature of the operation, it can be necessary to determine preservation methods for any part or component that will be incorporated in the final product (e.g., raw materials that will be manufactured or components that will be assembled) or for equipment or information critical to the provision of a service (e.g., data needed for technical support following delivery to the customer of a home computer).

Preservation of product includes controls such as identification, handling, packaging, storage, and protection. The following list provides examples of activities/product to be considered:

- Protection of the product during moves or handling
- Assessing stock during inventories
- Physical security
- Environmental controls (temperature and humidity)
- Electrosensitive devices (ESD)
- Legible, durable marking
- Expiration dates and stock rotation for materials with shelf life
- Hazardous materials

Preservation applies not only to the product being built but also to any parts of the product. An example would be a battery that is placed into a product or a raw material with shelf life.

Transition

Subclause 8.5.4 was addressed in ISO 9001:2008, subclause 7.5.5. The intent of the requirement remains unchanged in ISO 9001:2015. The word "output" is used in the requirement where in the past internal processing and delivery to the intended requirements was used. In addition, the requirements for handling, packaging, storage, and protection were previously included in the text of the requirement. It's now a note. Both of these changes were made to make the requirements easier to apply for service organizations.

Most organizations won't need to make any changes, but should consider how they have implemented the requirements based on the revised terminology to determine if changes are needed.

8.5.5 Post-delivery activities

- Meet requirements for post-delivery activities.
- The organization shall consider:
  - ✓ Statutory and regulatory requirements
  - ✓ Potential undesired consequences
  - ✓ Nature, use, and lifetime
  - ✓ Customer requirements
  - ✓ Customer feedback

- Note: Examples of post-delivery activities include warranty provisions and contractual requirements (e.g., maintenance, recycling, final disposal).

Keys to understanding

Planning activities—at all levels (system, design and development, operations)—should consider any need for a post-delivery activity. It's possible that an organization would determine that there are no applicable post-delivery activities based on the product being provided or service being delivered. When post-delivery activities do exist, the organization must apply the requirements.

The post-delivery requirements can be established by customers or other relevant interested parties. They may also be based on statutory and regulatory requirements that require organizations to take specific post-delivery actions.

When determining the extent to which post-delivery activities are needed, the organization needs to determine any potential consequences that need to be avoided. For example, if your organization provides a product such as a battery, consideration would be required to the activities needed for its disposal.

Organizations also need to consider what the product will be used for, how it will be used, and the lifetime of the product. For this reason, most organizations put a time frame on the product in which post-delivery activities will be considered. There are also considerations of any alterations the customer might potentially perform on a product that would nullify the warranty.

Post-delivery activities are typically the final stage of the product or service provision (e.g., shipping of the product to the customer facilities or on-site installation of a product). In certain cases, these activities are needed when the customer has a problem or a technical need after the product or service was provided (e.g., a patient calls his or her doctor for a clarification of a certain prescription or a warranty claim or a need of maintenance of a product).

For a home appliance distributor, for example, the post-delivery activities can be stated in the purchase orders or invoices submitted to the customers. An organization might also state these activities on its website, which includes contact information and a feature that the customer can use to provide feedback or request support.

Post-delivery activities are most frequently associated with processes such as sales, technical support, shipping and installation, and customer care.

There is no requirement for documented information in this subclause. However, as part of the subclause for determining the requirements related to products and services in subclause 8.2, it's reasonable to include this in the documented information that will be retained.

Transition

Subclause 8.5.5 was addressed in ISO 9001:2008, subclauses 7.2.3 and 7.5.1. Requirements for post-delivery activities are not new for ISO 9001:2015. However, these requirements in a stand-alone subclause is new. The subclause provides more specific requirements for post-delivery activities.

Organizations should analyze when these activities are taking place in their normal operations. An analysis of its implementation should identify opportunities for improvement and ensure that all the specific requirements will be addressed by the relevant processes.

8.5.6 Control of changes

- Review and control changes.
    - ✓ To extent necessary
    - ✓ Ensure conformity with requirements.

- Retain documented information.
    - ✓ Results of the review of changes
    - ✓ Persons authorizing the change
    - ✓ Necessary actions

Keys to understanding

These requirements address changes that occur during the production and service provision activities that can affect conformity with requirements. Requirements for changes to the QMS are included in clause 6. Requirements for design and development are addressed in subclause 8.3, which was discussed earlier in this chapter.

A need for change can be initiated by an internal issue (e.g., recurring nonconforming outputs or a sudden failure of a key equipment in the operations), an external provider (e.g., quality issues with the provided product, service or process, or delays in the schedules of provision), or another external issue (e.g., new or modified customer or regulatory requirements).

Change is a natural condition in any operation and the integrity of production and service provision should be maintained through the implementation of adequate activities for addressing it. These activities should be implemented using a cross-functional approach considering the different disciplines of the organization.

The organization can also use the requirements for considering risks and opportunities and actions to address them when establishing the methods for how changes will be controlled.

Typical activities of such a process include:
- Review
- Verification and validation before implementation
- Approval, including customer or regulatory authorization, where needed
- Implementation measures to ensure an effective implementation of the change

The organization can decide the extent of the documented information needed for the implementation of the control of changes activities. Customer or regulatory requirements may mandate the need for documented information.

Examples of documented information to be retained include:
- Minutes of the review activities
- Verification and validation results
- Database used for tracking changes
- Form that captures the documented information
- Description of the actions taken for addressing the change

The documented information to be retained needs to include the person(s) who authorized the change. This could be specific persons who are responsible for implementing the change in a specific discipline (e.g., purchasing to make a change to raw materials or production to incorporate a change in how nonconforming product is identified).

A best practice is that the change is not official until all of the required actions are completed.

Transition

Subclause 8.5.6 is a new requirement in ISO 9001:2015. Change is addressed in a generic way in ISO 9001:2008, subclause 5.4.2, which included requirements for the entire QMS. Subclause 8.5.6 is focused on the requirements for changing the way product is provided or the service is delivered.

Most organizations implementing ISO 9001:2015 already have methods in place to control change during production or service provision operations. These activities should be considered in the scope of the QMS.

Some organizations may find the need to make some level of change to incorporate specific requirements such as the authorization of the change and ensuring that documented information is being retained.

8.6 RELEASE OF PRODUCTS AND SERVICES

- Implement planned arrangements.
  - ✓ At appropriate stages
  - ✓ Verify requirements have been met.

- Release shall not proceed until plans have been completed, unless approved by a relevant authority and, as applicable, the customer.
- Retain documented information.
  - ✓ Evidence of conformity with acceptance criteria
  - ✓ Traceable to the person authorizing the release.

Keys to understanding

Subclause 8.6 deals with release activities that occur at appropriate stages during operations. Its intent is to ensure products and services are verified for conformity before release to other operations or the customer in accordance with the planned acceptance criteria.

Although not a specific requirement of the standard, the organization can choose to map its operations (e.g., a quality plan or flow diagram) and identify where the release is occurring. This should be done in accordance with the determined activities when the organization was planning the operations (see subclause 8.1).

For example, when materials are received, a release activity is implemented. During production there are different verification activities aimed for identifying conforming or nonconforming outputs. From there, a final verification or inspection is realized to ensure only conforming product or service will be provided.

For a service, the nature of release activities is unique and is based on the service that is provided. For example, a catering service may have a release activity for all the ingredients that will be used during the cooking operations. Another release activity will be for ensuring the cutlery, linen, glasses, and furniture are ready in accordance with customer requirements. The organization might also need to consider the temperature of the food or appearance when serving (i.e., releasing) food to the guests.

As part of the operational planning (see subclause 8.1), a clear definition of the acceptance criteria at every stage is critical. These acceptance criteria can result from design and development activities (e.g., specifications), customer or regulatory requirements (e.g., special characteristics or technical information), or internal requirements (e.g., production levels).

This subclause gives special attention to those release activities of the products or services to the customer because if something isn't done correctly, it can result in a nonconforming product or service and potentially a complaint.

For some services, this final release activity is very complex because the customer can be present when the service is released (e.g., reception in a hotel, online transactions like renting a car, or transferring money). In these cases, the activities could be considered as a process where the subsequent output cannot be verified prior to release (see subclause 8.5.1) and some specific controls should be implemented before the service is provided.

This subclause also requires that the documented information—in any format—clearly indicate the acceptance criteria and who authorizes the release. In a production environment, this will frequently be an operator, supervisor, or inspector. In the service environment, it can be a specific employee, a manager, or even the customer.

It's possible that the activities determined to establish release might not be completed in certain situations. This could be due to a rush job, such as when customers determine they cannot wait for final testing. For a service industry, it could be a tired customer who wants to go to his or her hotel room immediately. The customer might indicate that the review of hotel room typically performed by the supervisor prior to occupancy is not required.

Subclause 8.6 is a critical part of ISO 9001:2015 because it deals with one of the intents of the standard as expressed in clause 1, which is "...*to consistently provide products and services that meet customer and applicable statutory and regulatory requirements...*" Organizations should consider that if a nonconforming output is detected, the requirements of subclause 8.7 will be applied, followed by the requirements of subclause 10.2 for taking corrective action as necessary.

Transition

Subclause 8.6 was addressed in ISO 9001:2008, subclause 8.2.4. The intent of the requirement remains the same. Organizations that meet the intent of the current standard should find the transition simple. Organizations should analyze when release of product and service is taking place in their normal operations. An analysis of the implementation needs to be carried out to identify opportunities for improvement and to ensure that all the new requirements will be addressed by the relevant processes.

8.7 CONTROL OF NONCONFORMING OUTPUTS

Subclause 8.7.1

- Outputs that do not conform are identified and controlled.
  - ✓ Prevent unintended use or delivery.

- Take appropriate action.
  - ✓ Dependent on type of nonconformity and its effect

- Requirements apply to nonconforming products and services prior to or after production/delivery.
- Deal with nonconforming outputs in one or more of the following:
  - ✓ Correction
  - ✓ Segregation, containment, return, ceasing production or service delivery
  - ✓ Informing the customer
  - ✓ Obtaining authorization by concession

- Nonconforming outputs need to be verified when correction is made.

Keys to understanding

The main intent of the requirements in this subclause is to ensure that any nonconforming output will not be released to the next operations or to the final customer. Nonconforming output is something that we usually associate with manufacturing organizations. However, while more difficult, it can also be applied to service organizations. The purpose of the control of nonconforming product subclause is preventing the unintentional release of product or delivery of service that does not meet requirements.

The organization must take appropriate action when a nonconforming output is identified. The actions that are taken may differ based on the potential effect of the nonconforming output. For example, if an organization determines that there is a product defect that is a safety issue, there will be a more immediate notification to the customer than if the defect is less severe.

Once the nonconforming product is detected, the organization can take action in more than one way to deal with it. Because of the nature of the nonconforming output, some methods for dealing with the nonconforming product may be more practical than others. When determining if a service has a nonconforming output, it's difficult to detect prior to delivery to the customer. For that reason, the organization may focus more on the requirements for informing the customer. In some cases, the organization may find that more than one of the methods shall be used.

The first action is to identify and segregate the nonconforming output. In a production environment, specific labeling and placing the nonconforming output in specific areas or containers is a common practice. The organization could also stop production until any necessary corrections to the process are made. In a service environment, different ways are used for identifying that something is wrong with the service provision (e.g., a sign in front of the counter or stopping delivery of the service until it is resolved).

The organization can also correct the nonconforming output. Correction can include rework in a production environment or providing additional training to a person providing the service to meet service requirements for the organization.

The organization can also deal with a nonconforming output by informing the customer. This could be due to the fact that the nonconforming product is detected after delivery or the product is en route to the customer premises. In a service situation, a supervisor might observe that a person providing the service is not meeting the service goals for the organization. The supervisor might step in and make any necessary apologies and make adjustments as necessary. Each situation will probably require a different set of actions aimed to reduce customer dissatisfaction (e.g., a replacement or compensation). The nonconforming output process is directly related to customer return policies.

Another action that can be taken to deal with nonconforming output is to obtain acceptance through concession. Organizations should exercise extreme caution when accepting nonconforming outputs not meeting requirements. The organization needs to specify who has the ability to accept through concession. This could be an engineer or supervisor.

In some situations, there are specific customer or statutory requirements that would require the approval of the customer or a regulatory agency. In this scenario, the organization contacts the customer and informs them of an issue. The customer might determine that even though a specific requirement has not been met, they will accept the product under this condition. For service industries, it could be as simple as a "privacy please" sign on a hotel room, which means that the customer is granting a concession that the room will not be serviced.

When the action taken for nonconforming output is correction, the nonconforming output is to be verified. This could be completed by conducting the same inspection process or by a supervisor monitoring the performance of a person delivering the service.

Subclause 8.7.2

- Retain documented information.
  - ✓ Description of nonconformity
  - ✓ Description of actions taken
  - ✓ Description of the concessions obtained
  - ✓ Identity of authority who decided action for nonconformity

In manufacturing and service industries, the organization must retain documented information of what actions it took regarding the nonconforming output. The documented information needs to indicate a description of the nonconformity. This includes any concessions, including internal and customer. Documented information might reside on a form or in a database. The information also needs to include the person who authorized the actions that were taken.

Transitions

Subclause 8.7.2 was addressed in ISO 9001:2008, subclause 8.3. There is no longer a requirement for a documented procedure. Organizations have the option of determining if a documented procedure is needed. However, most organizations will find that this type of information is needed to ensure control.

In addition, some of the methods for dealing with nonconforming outputs use different language. Although ISO 9001:2015 includes methods to consider for dealing with nonconforming outputs, an organization can go beyond these minimum requirements if it so chooses.

With the transition to the language of nonconforming outputs from nonconforming product, organizations, specifically those that deliver a service, should consider the new language to determine if change is needed.

CHAPTER 12

Clause 9—Performance Evaluation

ISO 9001:2015 focuses on quality performance and achieving intended results. Simply put, output matters. This focus is reflected in clause 9 by requiring the collection of data related to the performance of the organization and the subsequent analysis and evaluation of the data. It's directly related to quality management principle (QMP) No. 6: Evidence-based decision making, which requires that decisions be based on the analysis and evaluation of data. This concept combined with the requirements in this clause provide the foundation for evaluating data and making necessary changes to the organization.

Many organizations collect a lot of data but do little or nothing with the information they collect. This is best illustrated by the fact that some organizations collect data related to their quality objectives but don't necessarily take action when they're not being met.

Because ISO 9001:2015 requires organizations to be results and performance based, they need to ensure that data is being collected, analyzed, and evaluated to ensure their quality management system (QMS) is achieving its intended results.

Each specific subclause in this section includes the requirements to drive these behaviors.

9.1 MONITORING, MEASUREMENT, ANALYSIS, AND EVALUATION

9.1.1 General

- Determine:
    - ✓ What methods will be used to ensure valid results?
    - ✓ When will monitoring and measuring be performed?
    - ✓ When will analysis and evaluation be performed?

- Monitoring and measurement activities shall be implemented in accordance with requirements determined by the organization.
- Determine the documented information to be retained.
- Evaluate the effectiveness and the performance of the QMS.

Keys to understanding

General subclauses outline the requirements of the clause. Although the specifics for how the requirements in this subclause can be met are included in subsequent subclauses in clause 9, it's important to note that the requirements outline a systematic way of looking at the organization's performance and analyzing and evaluating the results.

For example, subclause 9.3.2, Management review inputs, requires organizations to retain documented information of the results of the review. This can be directly related to the requirement in the general subclause related to retaining documented information. They don't need to be treated as different requirements.

It's also important to note that while some of the subclauses specifically identify documented information to be retained, organizations can also determine what additional documented information they need based on this requirement.

Transition

Subclause 9.1 was addressed in ISO 9001:2008, subclause 8.1, General. General subclauses are typically setting the stage for follow-up subclauses. Organizations that are currently certified or compliant to ISO 9001:2008 may need to make some adjustments to their QMS to ensure that correct data is being collected, analyzed, and evaluated, and that the data is being used to make decisions about the organization to ensure that performance results are achieved.

9.1.2 Customer satisfaction

- Monitor customers' perceptions on whether needs and expectations have been met.

- Determine the methods for obtaining this information and how the organization will monitor and measure it.
- Note: Examples of monitoring include customer surveys, customer feedback, meetings with customers, market-share analysis, complaints, warranty claims, and dealer reports.

Keys to understanding

With the focus on achieving intended results, it's important to understand that determining whether you are meeting the needs and expectations of customers is a key indicator. Organizations should understand that the focus on this requirement is the perception of the customers. So while an organization may believe it's satisfying its customers, in reality the customer may not actually be satisfied.

Organizations should determine from which customers they need to obtain feedback. In some cases, the organization may choose to sample only a portion of the customers or only those customers with which they do a certain volume of work. Some service organizations choose to obtain the data after the completion of the customer service activity (e.g., completion of a call, after a car is purchased from a dealer). Regardless of the method, the organization is reliant on receiving the information from the customer.

This is why surveys may not always be the best method for obtaining this data. Many customers find completing a survey a burden or time consuming. If an organization uses surveys to obtain customer feedback, it should ensure the survey is simple and easy to complete. Ultimately, the biggest question organizations need answered is whether the customer would choose to do business with them again.

Because surveys are often not completed, organizations should consider other methods for obtaining this information. This can include feedback received during meetings, analyzing market share, warranty claims or returns, and complaints. Organizations should also consider including compliments that are received to obtain data based on this feedback. This provides a balanced viewpoint on suggested improvements, as well as areas where the organization is performing well.

Customer feedback that is received from this subclause is analyzed and evaluated in subclause 9.1.3, Analysis and evaluation. The results of this evaluation are used in subclause 9.3, Management review, as an input where an organization should make decisions and take any necessary actions.

Transition

The requirements in subclause 9.1.2 are similar to the requirements in ISO 9001:2008, subclause 8.2.1. There are no new requirements in this subclause. Organizations with a mature QMS will not need to make any changes to accommodate the requirements in this subclause. However, organizations can use the transition as an opportunity to update the methods they use to obtain customer feedback.

9.1.3 Analysis and evaluation

- Analyze and evaluate data from monitoring and measurement.
  - ✓ Conformity of products and services
  - ✓ Customer satisfaction
  - ✓ Performance and effectiveness of the QMS
  - ✓ Effectiveness of planning
  - ✓ Actions to address risks and opportunities
  - ✓ External providers
  - ✓ The need for improvement to the QMS

Keys to understanding

One of the critical steps in having a QMS that meets requirements is evidence-based decision making. Successful decision making has its foundation in the analysis and evaluation of data. This subclause identifies the minimum amount of data to analyze to make those decisions. The type of data from each of the data points may vary based on whether your organization is a manufacturing or service organization.

Organizations should also ensure that the data they choose to collect provides the ability to make decisions about the performance and effectiveness of their QMS. This is why organizations may choose to benchmark another organization to determine its methods for analysis and evaluation. If benchmarking is used, the organization should ensure that the data sources are appropriate for the organization based on its product or service.

The results from analysis and evaluation are an input to subclause 9.3, Management review. Therefore, the determined actions identified in subclause 9.1.3 would also relate to any actions or changes needed from the QMS that are outputs to management review.

Organizations should ensure that the data they are analyzing is valid and that no manual manipulations are done on the data to achieve the desired numbers. For example, at times organizations will adjust the on-time delivery numbers because the customer changed its mind. However, this should only be allowed if the proper changes were made to the order entry system prior to delivery to the customer.

Figure 12.1 — Data Sources and Results/Indicators

Data	Sources	Results/Indicators
Conformity of products and services	• On-time delivery • First-pass yield • PPM • Wait times (customer service lines, telephone calls) • Rejects • Customer complaints (service)	Indicates whether the products and services of the organization are meeting requirements.
Customer satisfaction	• Complaints • Compliments • Warranty/returns • Market share • Customer meetings • Surveys	Indicates the degree of customer satisfaction.
Performance and effectiveness of the quality management system	Overall results from analysis and evaluation.	Determines if the quality management system may be meeting the intent of requirements but improvements could be made to be more effective (e.g., cost-effective).
Effectiveness of planning	• On-time delivery • Completion of projects • Organization is meeting requirements (e.g., drawings, specifications, procedures).	Actions are needed to improve meeting the requirements. Consideration could be given to understanding the organization's capabilities and capacity.
Effectiveness of actions taken for risks and opportunities	• Review of status of action items or plans • Meeting minutes • Status of improvement projects • Growth (sales)	Changes are needed to methods being used to avoid risks or obtain opportunities.
External providers	• On-time delivery • Rejects • On-site audits	Corrective actions issued to providers.
Need for improvements	Review of data sources from analysis and evaluation indicating any trends.	Corrective actions Improvement initiatives such as Six Sigma or *kaizen*

Transition

Subclause 9.1.3 was addressed in ISO 9001:2008, subclause 8.4, Analysis of data. There are some additional requirements in subclause 9.1.3 related to determining the effectiveness of planning, as well as the effectiveness of risks and opportunities. Subclause 9.1.3 is also more specific in its requirement for identifying any need for improvement.

Organizations will need to ensure that all types of data are being analyzed and evaluated. They will also need to ensure that the linkage is made to management review.

9.2 INTERNAL AUDIT

Subclause 9.2.1

- Conduct audits at planned intervals to ensure the QMS:
  - ✓ Meets requirements of the organization
  - ✓ Meets requirements of ISO 9001:2015
  - ✓ Is effectively implemented and maintained

Keys to understanding

Internal audits are the source for ensuring that the organization has implemented requirements and that the implementation is effective. This includes when an organization makes a change to its QMS. This is why it's important that organizations allow some time to pass prior to conducting an audit when making a change. For example, if an organization implements a new requirement one day and then audits for compliance to the requirement the next day, there may be little or minimal evidence that the requirement is effective. It simply demonstrates that the initial implementation was effective.

Subclause 9.2 includes a note to see ISO 19011, Guidelines for auditing management systems, for further guidance. This guidance document provides information on the methods an organization may use to implement its internal audit program. It's a valuable resource for the person responsible for the management of internal audits for the organization. However, as this is a note for clarification, it's not auditable and not mandatory for an organization to comply.

Auditing to established requirements provides better feedback for organizations. This is why an organization should allow a period of time to pass before scheduling audits in these areas. Some organizations use 30 days as a general guideline. At the same time, if an organization knows that a process is going to change, the audit should be delayed until after the change is made to eliminate nonvalue-added auditing. The only time where an audit might be needed without this preferred waiting time frame is during an initial audit where the audit must be demonstrated prior to certification.

The organization must also determine the frequency for conducting audits. Many organizations have implemented a practice of auditing all of ISO 9001's requirements annually. However, there is no requirement to do so. The organization has the flexibility to determine the frequency. Typically, the audit frequency is demonstrated in an audit plan or schedule. Based on the established frequency, the organization would need to be able to demonstrate that all of the requirements of this clause have been audited. These methods are part of the audit program that is discussed in subclause 9.2.2 as well as criteria to be considered when determining the frequency.

Transition

Subclause 9.2.1 was addressed in ISO 9001:2008, subclause 8.2.2. There are no new requirements in this subclause. However, organizations may want to review and determine if they can improve the methods in which they plan internal audits.

Subclause 9.2.2

- Establish, implement, and maintain an audit program.
  - ✓ Frequency, methods, responsibilities, planning requirements, and reporting
  - ✓ Consider processes, changes affecting the organization, and the results of previous audits.

- Define audit criteria and scope.
- Ensure that auditors shall be objective and impartial.
- Report audit results to relevant management.
- Take correction and corrective actions without undue delay.
- Retain documented information of the audit program and results.

Keys to understanding

A key aspect for ensuring the effectiveness of the internal audit process is the involvement of top management in the process during the establishment of the audit program, the establishment of objectives for the program and each individual audit, and the closure of any identified nonconformity. Active participation of top management in this process should be perceived by the people in the organization.

Without their support, the internal audit process could be more difficult, thereby minimizing its effectiveness.

In addition to the needed top management support, when an organization establishes an internal audit program, specific actions are required in several areas to help ensure an effective program.

Frequency

The organization needs to consider how frequently it will conduct audits. Many organizations prepare the audit program annually but review it on an ongoing basis. Planning audits on a more frequent basis such as monthly or quarterly allows for adjustments that are needed to the schedule based on other activities in the organization (e.g., new work or increased workload). Larger organizations should consider conducting audits more frequently because they may need to audit multiple areas for the same requirements. Smaller organizations may find that annual audits are sufficient, but should keep in mind that the QMS must be sustained throughout the rest of the year.

If an activity is only performed one or two times a year, audits should be scheduled around this time for observation and review.

Methods

There are many methods to conduct audits. These include interviews; review of documented information such as procedures, drawings, forms, and specifications; and observation of employees performing the work. Auditors should consider multiple methods when conducting audits to broaden the sample size. The internal audit program should also establish general guidelines for conducting audits. For example, auditors should review a sample size larger than one, but also consider that sampling should not be continued just for the point of identifying a nonconformance. The sample size is typically proportionate to the size of the organization.

For organizations with more than one site, it's possible to conduct the audit remotely through telephone interviews and online meetings. However, this technique doesn't work when the actual process needs to be observed (e.g., an audit of the product being manufactured or the service being delivered).

Many organizations use checklists to complete internal audits. If this method is used, organizations should strive to indicate what evidence was observed (e.g., drawings reviewed, date service was provided and by whom, part numbers reviewed) to provide confidence that actual processes were reviewed.

Clause 9—Performance Evaluation

Responsibilities

The audit program should establish responsibilities. This could include the responsibilities for planning the audits and approving audit reports. Although ISO 9001:2015 doesn't require documented procedures, these responsibilities could be included in a procedure. If an organization chooses not to have documented procedures, these responsibilities can be communicated to the responsible persons. This can be confirmed through the audit by conducting interviews and establishing that the necessary persons understand the responsibilities.

Planning requirements

The audit program should establish what planning should be conducted in preparation for an audit. This can include reviewing documented information such as procedures, forms, and drawings as well as reviewing the results (e.g., documented information) from previous audits.

When planning the internal audit program, there are several areas that should be considered. These areas help determine the frequency and the overall audit plan. The organization should review the importance of processes. The more critical the process, the more frequently it should be audited. This could include processes where the organization isn't meeting requirements, where there are customer concerns, or the consequences of a process not being followed could have severe effects on the organization.

Changes affecting the organization

During the annual audit program, the organization should consider any known changes that could affect the QMS. This could include a new enterprise management system, a new design, a new customer service tool, or training on a new technique for providing service. The area where the change is being made should be scheduled for an audit to allow for review and determine if the implementation has been effective.

Results from previous audits

If audits are conducted impartially and are a true indication of the performance of the QMS, then the results from previous audits are an excellent source for helping determine where audits should be planned. It should be common sense that areas that struggle to meet requirements should be scheduled for internal audits more frequently than those departments or areas of the organization that are performing well.

Although not a requirement of ISO 9001:2015, a best practice is to make an inquiry from the leadership team if there are any areas of concern in their specific departments. This information can be used alongside the other considerations to prioritize the audit schedule.

Reporting

The audit program also needs to establish the reporting requirements for conducting internal audits. This can include a standard format for providing the results as well as categories for nonconformities. Many organizations establish criteria for different types of nonconformities. These criteria help to ensure consistency when audits are conducted by multiple internal audits. Annex B.8 in ISO 19011 provides guidance for writing findings.

There may be different categories for classifying audit findings used by organizations in their internal audits and by certification bodies in their certification audits. To achieve consistency, ISO/IEC 17021-1:2015 includes definitions for major and minor nonconformities.

Subclause 3.12 of ISO/IEC 17021-1:2015 defines a *major nonconformity* as a "Nonconformity that affects the capability of the management system to achieve the intended results."

For clarification, this subclause continues, "Nonconformities could be classified as major in the following circumstances:
- If there is a significant doubt that effective process control is in place, or that products or services will meet specified requirements
- A number of minor nonconformities associated with the same requirement or issue could demonstrate a systemic failure and thus constitute a major nonconformity."

A *minor nonconformity*, according to subclause 3.13 of ISO/IEC 17021-1:2015, is a "Nonconformity that does not affect the capability of the management system to achieve the intended results."

Sectors such as automotive and aerospace have specific definitions for major and minor nonconformities that are consistent with the definitions included in ISO/IEC 17021-1:2015.

Some organizations have decided to consider other types of classifications.

Observation

Observations are categorized differently for various organizations. Some organizations treat them as one-time occurrences. For example, one document is found to be uncontrolled. Other organizations treat them as something that isn't a current nonconformance, but a potential one.

Audit findings that identify conformity with requirements are often classified as an opportunity for improvement (OFI) or noteworthy effort (NE).

- *Opportunity for Improvement.* An OFI is a finding for which the audit evidence demonstrates conformity with requirements, but where there is the possibility for the organization to perform better using a different approach. ISO/IEC 17021-1:2015, subclause 9.4.5.2, states that a nonconformity shall not be recorded as an OFI. This requirement is only applicable to certification bodies, but an organization implementing ISO 9001:2015 may consider the requirements of ISO/IEC 17021-1 as a reference.
- *Noteworthy effort.* Many organizations identify positive things that the organization is doing during an internal audit and classify these findings as an NE. An NE does not require any action by the organization, but can provide balance to areas where improvement needs are identified.

It's highly recommended that organizations use a common approach for recording audit findings. Because internal auditors are familiar with the organization's processes, they know where potential issues are. This is why internal audit reports that show no nonconformities or observations should be treated as suspect.

Audit criteria and audit scope

When planning an internal audit, it's important to establish the audit criteria and the audit scope as one of the initial planning activities. The audit criteria might be specific statutory and regulatory requirements that are applicable to the products or services of the organization, the ISO 9001 requirements, or any other requirements that a specific process should be following such as standardized work, corporate policies, or specifications. The audit scope constitutes the boundaries of the audit. It typically includes factors such as physical locations, organizational units, activities, and processes to be audited. Organizations should realize that even though an audit scope has been identified, when conducting process audits, the audit trail might take you to another process. For that reason, this should be made clear in any opening meetings or communication related to the audit.

It's essential to select impartial auditors to ensure objectivity. To have the most impartial view of the QMS, organizations should strive to assign auditors based on their ability to be independent of the process. When auditing your own work, it's difficult to always see areas of nonconformity due to the familiarity you have with it. In short, if you developed it, you already believe that the process is working well.

However, small organizations and even medium-sized enterprises often find that maintaining this level of impartiality and objectivity isn't possible simply due to the number of employees available and the fact that they often perform multiple jobs. In this situation, an organization can establish a method to maintain the impartiality while still meeting ISO 9001:2015's requirements. For example, a two-person team can be established. Another option is to have the internal auditor conduct the audit but have the audit reviewed for impartiality by someone who is unbiased, such as a peer or manager.

Another method is to trade resources with another organization. Some smaller organizations will trade internal audit services with another small business so that auditors can maintain objectivity and impartiality.

Competence requirements for internal auditors should be established according to subclause 7.2, Competence. Those assigned to conduct audits must meet the established criteria. Organizations might choose to have internal audits conducted by an external provider. In this scenario, the external provider must also meet the criteria established for competence.

Report to relevant management

The internal auditor identifies nonconformities or other observations and reports them to the relevant management. This can be done with a documented internal auditor report or through a closing meeting. Although not a requirement of the standard, it's important that any nonconformities are discussed and agreed upon prior to proceeding in order to maintain management support of the audit process.

Take appropriate correction and corrective action without undue delay

There are two possibilities when taking actions related to nonconformities identified during internal audits. The nonconformity can be corrected at the time of the audit, which means immediate action is taken. This is sometimes called "containment." For example, an outdated documented procedure might be posted in the area. The documented procedure is removed, thereby correcting the nonconformity. Based on the severity of the issue, the organization might determine a corrective action isn't required.

In other cases, corrective action might be required. When this determination is made, the requirements in subclause 10.2, Nonconformity and corrective action, should be followed.

Correction and corrective action should be taken without undue delay. Because undue delay isn't defined, the organization needs to identify what this means for its environment. Some organizations allow as many as 60 days for responses, while others only allow 30 days. The organization needs to evaluate potential effects to the business as well as any other requirements, including customer requirements, that need to be met when establishing this time limit.

Retain documented information as evidence

The organization must determine what evidence is necessary to show effective implementation of the internal audit program and the audit results. This can include audit plans or schedules, audit reports, auditor working notes, or the results of correction or corrective action (see subclause 10.2).

Transition

Subclause 9.2.2 was addressed ISO 9001:2008, subclause 8.2.2. The requirements are fairly similar. ISO 9001:2015 provides for more flexibility in allowing auditors to audit their own work as long as impartiality is maintained. ISO 9001:2015 also requires that an organization consider changes. This means that organizations will need to consider how internal audits are planned when changes are incorporated into the QMS.

9.3 MANAGEMENT REVIEW

9.3.1 General

- Conduct management review at planned intervals.
- Ensure the suitability, adequacy, and effectiveness of the QMS.
- Ensure alignment with the strategic direction of the organization.

Keys to understanding

ISO 9001:2015 requires top management to conduct management reviews. The purpose of management review is to determine if the QMS is suitable, adequate, and effective. The management review also must ensure that the QMS is in alignment with the strategic direction of the organization. This requirement is to help ensure that the management review is not a stand-alone activity but integrated into actions where the performance and effectiveness of the QMS are analyzed.

Top management must provide objective evidence that they have reviewed inputs identified by the standard, assessed the QMS, and developed identified outputs. In large organizations where there could be remote senior leaders, the organization should specifically identify who top management is.

The organization must plan at what intervals or frequency it will conduct management review. The organization has the flexibility to determine the frequency and format that works best for it. It's important to remember that changes can be made to the management review interval if the organization finds that the format and frequency aren't working.

When establishing the format, the organization needs to consider if it has existing meetings that can be modified to include management review inputs or what it wants to accomplish from management reviews. Many organizations already have a meeting (e.g., weekly, monthly, or quarterly) to review the performance of the business. The organization may also want to consider whether it can review multiple systems at the same time (e.g., environmental and quality). These meetings can be modified to include management review inputs. This allows the organization to leverage an existing process and eliminates the need for top management to participate in an additional meeting.

If the organization doesn't have an existing meeting in place or believes that management review warrants a stand-alone meeting, it will need to determine the frequency of this meeting. Many organizations find a frequency of twice a year provides a format that allows a review of the QMS without adding too many meetings.

Smaller organizations may find that management review can be scheduled less frequently because most persons of the organization are involved in day-to-day business operations.

It is also possible for some organizations to conduct management review through a documented report that addresses the required inputs and outputs. This can be a good method when the organization is small or when the topics are addressed in other meetings.

In addition to planning the frequency, the organization will need to consider whether it will cover all inputs at one meeting or cover the inputs over several meetings. If an organization chooses to cover inputs over multiple meetings, it will need to provide evidence that all required inputs have been covered. An easy way to provide this objective evidence is to create a cross-reference of topics to meetings.

Figure 12.2   Management Review Cross-Reference

Input	Date of Review
Results of audit	12/2 Staff meeting
Status of preventive and corrective actions	12/2 Staff meeting
Customer feedback	1/3 Staff meeting

Transition

Subclause 9.3.1 was addressed in ISO 9001:2008, subclause 5.6. It's generally the same in ISO 9001:2015 with the addition of determining if the QMS and the management review align with the strategic direction of the organization.

9.3.2 Management review inputs

- Consider the following inputs when carrying out management review:
  - ✓ Actions from previous management review
  - ✓ Changes in external and internal issues
  - ✓ Information and trends that provide an indication of the performance and effectiveness of the QMS
    - ◆ Customer satisfaction and feedback from relevant interested parties
    - ◆ Quality objectives
    - ◆ Process performance/conformity of products and services
    - ◆ Status of nonconformities and corrective actions
    - ◆ Monitoring and measuring results
    - ◆ Audit results
    - ◆ External providers
  - ✓ Resources
  - ✓ Actions to address risks and opportunities
  - ✓ Opportunities for improvement

Keys to understanding

Although the organization can include any topic it wishes to discuss during management review—and many do to eliminate the need for an additional meeting—ISO 9001:2015 requires that certain minimum topics be reviewed.

Organizations should consider meetings and data they currently use to determine if existing data can be used to meet the requirement. The output from subclause 9.1.3, Analysis and evaluation, should be used as an input to management review. If the organization doesn't currently review a specific topic, it will need to establish what data it will review.

Figure 12.3 shows a list of inputs and examples of data that could be used to meet the intent of the requirement.

Figure 12.3 Management Review Inputs and Data Examples

Management review input	Examples of data
Follow-up actions from previous management reviews	List of action items from previous management review including an update on the status. Note: Organizations may want to consider how to monitor this list on an ongoing basis if management review isn't held frequently.
Customer feedback/feedback from relevant interested parties	• Survey results • Customer rejects • Results from regulatory reviews • Output from subclause 9.1.2, Customer satisfaction
Quality objectives	• Output from subclause 6.2, Quality objectives and planning to achieve them • Review of metrics associated with quality objectives
Process performance and product conformity	• Number of defects • On-time delivery • Customer wait time
Status of preventive and corrective actions	• Number of corrective actions closed • On-time closure • Number of corrective actions open for an extended period of time with no action
Monitoring and measurement results	• First-pass yield • PPM • Cost of nonconformance
Results of audits	• Number of audits conducted • Areas/departments audited • Trends in audit findings
External providers	• On-time delivery • Quality issues (e.g., rejects) • Additional data related to criteria established in subclause 8.4, Control of externally provided processes, products, and services

Adequacy of resources	• Review of any concerns related to whether the organization has adequate resources:
	  ✓ People (7.1.2)
	  ✓ Infrastructure (7.1.3)
	  ✓ Environment (7.1.4)
	  ✓ Competence of people (7.2)
	  ✓ Training or mentoring to gain competence

Actions to address risks and opportunities	• Status of actions related to risks and opportunities identified in subclause 6.1. • Action items and current status • Status of opportunity projects such as *kaizen* events or other improvement initiatives.
Opportunities for improvement	Improvement opportunities that have been identified via audits or data from this management review that have not been implemented.

Transition

Subclause 9.3.2 was addressed in ISO 9001:2008, subclause 5.6.2. Although many of the management review inputs are the same as in ISO 9001:2008, some of the inputs are new. These include external and internal issues, feedback from relevant interested parties, performance of external providers, and effectiveness of actions taken to address risks and opportunities. There is also an emphasis in ISO 9001:2015 to consider trends in evaluating the management review inputs.

Quality objectives are now used in ISO 9001:2015 as an input as opposed to ISO 9001:2008, which only required that consideration be given to whether changes were required. Adequacy of resources are now considered as an input in addition to the determination of whether any resources are needed. ISO 9001:2008 required that management review include changes that could affect the organization as an input. ISO 9001:2015 indicates that the organization should include decisions and actions related to whether changes are needed to the QMS as a result of looking at the information presented in management review.

Based on the new inputs, organizations will need to ensure these topics are covered. Many organizations will find that they have activities in place that will address the inputs but need to link them to management review.

9.3.3 Management review outputs

- Include actions and decisions related to:
  - ✓ Opportunities for improvement
  - ✓ Changes needed to the QMS
  - ✓ Resource needs

- Retain documented information as evidence of reviews.

Keys to understanding

At the conclusion of the management review, certain outputs should be developed that indicate that decisions and actions have been taken related to specific criteria. These outputs can include information that the organization believes is beneficial to maintaining the QMS, but at a minimum must include decisions and actions relating to:

- *Opportunities for improvement (OFIs)*. This should be a list of any actions needed that are based on trends in the information reviewed. OFIs could include corrective actions (subclause 10.2) or continual improvement (subclause 10.3).
- *Changes needed to the QMS*. Based on the trends and whether the performance of the QMS is effective, changes needed to the QMS should be identified. This could include a variety of things, but most would require some type of process change.
- *Resource needs*. As one of the inputs to management review, the organization considers whether resources are adequate. Decisions and actions related to resources are also ouputs. The organization must determine whether any resources are needed and actions necessary to achieve them. Resource needs could be related to both people and infrastructure.

To ensure these outputs are adequately addressed, some method of demonstrating that these outputs were considered is necessary. This can be achieved by either including an agenda topic in management review or including decision points in any meeting minutes.

The organization is required to retain documented information that demonstrates there is evidence that the management review was conducted. This documented information can be demonstrated in meeting minutes, slides or presentations, or information that is retained in a posted area (e.g., town hall meetings).

Transition

Subclause 9.3.3 was addressed in ISO 9001:2008, subclause 5.6.3. The determination of whether the QMS is suitable and adequate is now addressed in subclause 5.6.1. There is also some slight variation of what the output of the management review should be, but this requires minimal change to an organization's existing QMS.

CHAPTER 13

Clause 10—Improvement

The requirements in clause 10 are focused on improving the organization as well as taking actions to correct nonconformities. Improvement actions should be taken for products and services as well as the quality management system (QMS).

10.1 GENERAL

- Meet customer requirements and enhance customer satisfaction.
  - ✓ Improve products and services.
  - ✓ Correct, prevent, or reduce undesired effects.
  - ✓ Performance and effectiveness of QMS

- Examples include:
  - ✓ Correction
  - ✓ Corrective action
  - ✓ Continual improvement
  - ✓ Breakthrough change
  - ✓ Innovation
  - ✓ Reorganization

Keys to understanding

Subclause 10.1 is a high-level requirement that outlines the requirements for the remaining requirements in clause 10. It includes requirements for improvement where an organization takes an existing process and makes a change to make it better. Other requirements focus on taking action to meet requirements or ensure the satisfaction of customers. Because nonconformities and corrective action are frequently related to a performance issue, many organizations don't consider them as improvements, but corrections.

Subclause 10.1 includes a note with examples of different types of improvement. Because this note is provided for clarification, organizations aren't required to demonstrate conformance if the requirement isn't included elsewhere in the standard. Innovation, breakthrough change, and reorganization are examples of these types of improvement.

The organization needs to specifically consider improvements to products and services. These improvements may be a result of analysis and evaluation of data or management review. They may also be necessary to accommodate a future customer need. For example, if a customer needs a certain functionality that isn't available, the organization would need to consider what improvements are needed as well as potential design and development activities to achieve the improvement.

Other actions might result in actually correcting a nonconformity. These requirements are addressed in subclause 10.2. Preventing or reducing undesired effects can be directly related to subclause 6.1, in which an organization determines the actions that it will take to address risks and opportunities.

The organization also needs to determine and select opportunities for improving the performance and effectiveness of the QMS. Subclause 10.3 describes the requirements for continually improving the QMS.

Most organizations have some type of improvement program. These may include *kaizen* events to make improvements to processes or lean activities to improve the efficiency in how a product is provided or a service is delivered. Organizations should leverage these existing activities in demonstrating conformance to improvement activities.

Transition

The requirements in subclause 10.1 were previously addressed in ISO 9001:2008, subclause 8.1, General. Subclause 10.1 also includes requirements for correcting and preventing undesired effects, which weren't previously addressed in ISO 9001:2008, subclause 8.1. Because these actions were previously required in other clauses, most organizations won't need to make any changes to their QMS.

10.2 NONCONFORMITY AND CORRECTIVE ACTION

Subclause 10.2.1

- React to nonconformities, including complaints.
  - ✓ Take action to control/correct it.
  - ✓ Deal with the consequences.

- Evaluate need for action.
  - ✓ Eliminate cause so it doesn't happen again.
  - ✓ Review and analyze.
  - ✓ Determine cause.
  - ✓ Determine if similar nonconformities exist or could occur.

- Take action.
- Review effectiveness of actions.
- Update risks and opportunities (if necessary).
- Make changes to the QMS (if necessary).
- Actions shall be based on the nonconformity.

Keys to understanding

There are many references in ISO 9001:2015 to the organization taking correction or corrective actions. Each time this reference is made, the organization needs to apply the requirements of this clause. Application needs to be appropriate to the potential effects of the nonconformity. What does this mean in simple terms? "Don't implement a $1 million solution for a $5 problem." For some nonconformities, the organization may determine that correction only is needed based on the severity of the issue and whether a cause can be determined. For example, an organization may receive a nonconformity from a customer related to a shipping error where the organization shipped the wrong number of parts. In this scenario, it's not always possible to determine the cause. Therefore, the organization may simply choose to send the missing parts.

For each potential source of corrective action, the organization should establish a threshold for when corrective action is required. The threshold may be based on a dollar amount, the amount of rework required, or the severity of a finding. Based on the threshold or criteria, the organization may determine that the level of needed correction will vary. Thresholds should also be established for customer complaints. It's important to review and receive approval from customers, where required.

The following list includes examples of nonconformities that might require corrective action:
- Internal audit reports
- Nonconforming outputs, including nonconforming products and services
- Customer audits
- Customer complaints
- Third-party audits
- Engineering change requests
- Focus groups
- Employee feedback
- Returns
- Scrap reports
- Late-ship reports
- Performance data
- Issues identified by top management during any review activity, including management review

When the organization identifies a nonconformity, it must first take action to control or contain it. This might include stopping production or delivery of service. For customer complaints, it might include communicating with the customer on the actions it plans to take. In some situations, where there have been adverse effects, the organization might need to mitigate any potential effect.

The organization will need to determine if actions are required to eliminate the cause(s) of the nonconformities. In making this decision, the organization should review and analyze the nonconformity. Many organizations tend to think that they know what corrective action should be taken without doing this analysis. In these situations, organizations will sometimes miss correcting the nonconformity.

There can be one or many causes of a nonconformity. Although not a requirement of ISO 9001:2015, some organizations use a specific methodology for determining the cause of nonconformities. These could include but are not limited to the 5 Whys, fishbone diagrams, 8D approach, fault tree analysis (FTA), or failure mode and effects analysis (FMEA). The determination of this cause should be considered in what actions are needed.

The organization should review to see if there have been similar nonconformities. This can be done by reviewing past nonconformities or reviewing existing work to check for nonconformities. For example, if an organization determines that product isn't being identified properly, it might review other production departments to see if the nonconformity exists.

Once the organization determines that actions are needed, it must implement them. Implementation should be completed according to established timelines. This may include revising a process, such as a method for identifying product or a technique used in delivering the service. Training or revising documented information is frequently used to demonstrate implementation of a corrective action. However, organizations should consider whether these actions alone will result in correcting the nonconformity.

Organizations need to also review the effectiveness of corrective actions. To determine if the verification is effective in the long term, the organization should consider waiting prior to conducting the review. For example, if the corrective action was to train employees, the person conducting the verification review could confirm that the training has been completed. However, the reviewer might wish to wait 30 days to see if the activities provided in the training are still being followed.

The actions taken have a direct correlation to the organization's risks and opportunities and the actions taken to address them. The organization should review the risks and opportunities identified in subclause 6.1 and determine if the actions taken as part of the corrective action should be incorporated into this information.

The organization is responsible for making any changes needed to the QMS as a result of the nonconformity. This could be a change in a specific process such as how products from external providers are verified or the method in which a service is delivered. It could also be the revision of documented information that describes the processes to be followed.

Subclause 10.2.2

- Retain documented information.
  - ✓ The nonconformity and any actions taken
  - ✓ Results of any corrective action

Keys to understanding

The organization is required to retain documented information. This is frequently a corrective action form or a database that is used to manage corrective actions, including customer complaints. The method used needs to include the required evidence of the review, determination of cause, verification of effectiveness, and necessary changes to the QMS. The level of documented information can also be related to the effects of the nonconformities. An organization can establish that not all of the required elements of a documented information method are required for certain types of nonconformities. However, this needs to be clearly defined.

Transition

The requirements in subclause 10.2.2 were addressed in ISO 9001:2008, subclause 8.5.2, Corrective action. ISO 9001:2015 includes additional requirements, including updating the risks and opportunities that are determined during the planning process as well as being specific that the organization needs to make necessary changes to the QMS when determining corrective action to be taken.

However, the changes to the QMS would have been implied in previous versions. Organizations will need to make adjustments to ensure a closed loop for considering updates to risks and opportunities. This could be incorporated on a case-by-case basis where the nonconformity is significant or through some type of analysis of data that would show trends in the nonconformities. Management review includes both nonconformities and corrective actions as well as reviewing the actions to address risks and opportunities. This analysis and consideration of needed updates could be done at that time.

10.3 CONTINUAL IMPROVEMENT

- Continually improve the QMS.
  - ✓ Suitability
  - ✓ Adequacy
  - ✓ Effectiveness

- The organization should:
  - ✓ Consider results of analysis and evaluation and management review.
  - ✓ Determine if there are needs or opportunities for continual improvement.

Keys to understanding

According to ISO 9000:2015, improvement is an activity to enhance performance and continual improvement is a recurring activity to enhance performance.

Performance is a measurable result. Therefore, improvement of the processes and the QMS should be tangible by providing data.

Although many organizations have continual improvement efforts in place, a formal and regular approach may be missing. The requirements in subclause 10.3 can help organizations implement an effective approach to continual improvement.

Organizations should consider existing methods in establishing an approach. These could include Six Sigma tools, employee suggestion programs, or other initiatives that the organization has developed to encourage continual improvement. This subclause requires that those continual improvement efforts include actions related to the suitability, adequacy, and effectiveness of the QMS and its processes.

Organizations can consider many different inputs when determining continual improvement opportunities. At a minimum, the organization needs to consider the results of analysis and evaluation as well as management review. Both of these requirements focus on many different requirements of the standard.

Although management review considers an analysis of the overall continual improvement needs of the QMS and decisions that need to be taken to achieve improvement, organizations should also consider improvement at the process level. This can be done by considering any established performance indicators for the processes and determining needed actions as required by subclause 4.4.

Transition

The requirements in subclause 10.3 were addressed in subclause 8.5.1 of ISO 9001:2008. The requirements now include the continual improvement of the suitability, adequacy, and effectiveness of the QMS. Because these two subclauses include many of the prescriptive items to be considered in the consideration of continual improvement, there is little change.

There are some new inputs in management review that might drive different actions in continual improvement. The trends in evaluating the performance of the QMS will help identify continual improvement actions.

Most organizations will meet the intent of the requirements but may find that they need to ensure that continual improvement actions are completed. Some organizations with unstructured programs may find that the follow-through on these actions are limited, making it difficult to demonstrate compliance.

SECTION III

Implementation and Integration

This section provides practical guidance on how an organization implementing ISO 9001 for the first time or integrating multiple management systems should conduct the implementation and integration activities.

Chapter 14

Engaging Leadership

Leadership in an organization isn't just about where people fall on the organization chart or their titles. Leadership extends to all those who have a significant influence on those performing work within the quality management system (QMS). One classification that has specific requirements identified within ISO 9001:2015 is "top management."

ISO 9000:2015 defines top management as a "person or group of people who directs and controls an organization at the highest level." For any QMS to be successful, it's important for all leadership—especially top management—to be engaged.

In this chapter, we'll specifically address the requirements for top management and leadership in the broader sense for successful adoption and improvement of the QMS.

For any organization seeking to deploy ISO 9001:2015 as the framework for its QMS, adoption by leadership is key to the overall success of the effort. There are many methods and practices to identify good organizational change management to achieve successful adoption. However, a simplification is that the organization must have the right business case to justify the need for a comprehensive QMS. Once leadership accepts the business case, it's necessary to identify and engage all key stakeholders in planning the components of the QMS. Adoption is then possible with constant transparency, accountability, and communication throughout the deployment, execution, and improvement of the QMS.

It's important when engaging leadership to not confuse compliance with buy-in. Just because leadership understands the requirements, it doesn't indicate that there is buy-in. There are many times in one's career when you get visible agreement through a head nod. If the QMS is intended to be effective and drive the typical "better, faster, cheaper" mentality that is demanded by most customer groups, it's important to gain adoption and support rather than the blind obedience of compliance.

Some of the elements an organization can consider in gaining this buy-in among leadership are:
- *Protecting the brand or reputation.* An effective QMS is a key mechanism to protect a company's brand image or reputation. It mitigates the risk to customers of receiving products or services that do not meet their needs. Full adoption of this notion extends beyond the traditional quality department into all areas that affect customers.
- *Zero defects is the ultimate lean program.* Adoption of the QMS throughout the organization is vital in helping the organization achieve efficient use of resources. There is no more lean way to run an organization than when there are zero defects coming out of key processes. An organization simply needs to take stock of how many activities are needed to minimize the effect of defects throughout the processes, whether manufacturing, service, or front office processes.
- *Lock in the gains.* Almost all organizations now talk about knowledge management and buzz words like "learning organizations." The QMS enables the lessons that are learned through planning, improvement, or corrective actions.
- *Providing health checks.* A QMS based on ISO 9001:2015 provides for management reviews and audit checks that can be done to gauge the status and health of the organization's key processes.

So, what exactly is the business case for adoption of a comprehensive QMS based on ISO 9001:2015? What value should leadership see in a QMS? One of the primary drivers of any organization revolves around the economics of quality. Having an effective and efficient QMS can affect both the cost and revenue side of the equation for an organization. Simply put, it can drive value in the mind of the customer, address prevention and cost avoidance, and produce the organization's products or services.

The effect of poor quality is clear. A lack of a clearly defined QMS can create many inefficiencies in the organization. These inefficiencies can lead to unnecessary wastes in precious resources, including:
- *Duplicating efforts (whether internal or external).* Lack of visibility to defined processes.
- *Wrong or even misleading measures.* Not having a clear understanding of the expected or desired output of processes.
- *Lack of clarity.* No clear expectations or requirements.
- *Operational inefficiencies.* No defined control methods to prevent excessive variation and defects.

In the early stages of the adoption of a QMS, there are some concrete steps the organization may take to engage leadership. Start by identifying the process owners to leverage their knowledge of the business. Understand the early supporters for collaboration and the detractors to recognize roadblocks. Establish a trusted facilitator to provide a sense that all decisions are being made while respecting the best interests of the business rather than any functional bias. Continually confirm the value of identifying gaps or possible inefficiencies. Find every opportunity to take advantage of a stakeholder "pull" rather than appear to push a particular system on the organization. Finally, constant communication and transparency with leadership will promote collaboration, support, and visible leadership.

There are some drivers that an organization can use to further the adoption of the QMS and engagement with leadership. It's important to build management accountability into the QMS. Clear expectations and accountability are routinely identified as key elements of engagement. Visible and active cross-functional ownership of the key processes sends an obvious signal to the organization that it's not just the responsibility of the quality department. Finally, the ease and understanding of the QMS for the users is a key acceptance factor. If the system is difficult or even if it's just perceived to be difficult, it can create barriers that are quite difficult to overcome. An organization should consistently evaluate and challenge itself on these drivers.

Although it has been mentioned that the QMS should involve the entire organization and not just quality personnel, quality does provide a significant and obvious role in most organizations. These roles typically include:

- Product and process compliance
- Safeguarding the reputation of the organization
- Consultation on requirements and best practices
- Custodian of documentation and records

While planning the implementation of a QMS, there are important decisions that increase collaboration and adoption when made as a team. Collaboration on the scope of the QMS will help to assure that all aspects within the business case are met. There may be electronic management tools needed to control documents, records, and data. The team may determine to what extent they will modify current systems and processes vs. a more significant redesign. There may even be consideration as to the extent of centralization vs. decentralization in larger or more complex organizations. The more that the full leadership team is engaged in the critical decision making, the greater the support and acceptance will be.

To ensure ongoing success in engaging leadership, there must be constant attention to driving accountability for the QMS. To have accountability, all stakeholders need to understand that change is inevitable and their role is clear in managing change. Providing ongoing opportunities to teach and educate the leadership in the requirements of the QMS allows for informed collaboration and can minimize fears or misconceptions. Finally, providing small, regular, and specific targets can provide an opportunity to demonstrate the commitment and accomplishment needed for trust to build.

The moral of the story is achieving all of the goals of a business case for implementing a QMS based on ISO 9001:2015 is critically tied to the level of engagement of leadership. Remember two key points: Compliance does not necessarily equal adoption and there is much more to leadership than where someone falls on the organization chart.

Chapter 15

Certification vs. Declaration of Conformity

Organizations have two options when implementing ISO 9001:2015. They can choose to demonstrate their conformity with the standard through self-declaration or they can choose to achieve third-party certification through a certification audit carried out by an accredited certification body. There are considerations the organization must make to determine if certification or declaration of conformity is the right decision.

Organizations that want to demonstrate to customers that they meet ISO 9001:2015's requirements would benefit from certification. Organizations that have strong competition in the marketplace may also benefit. In fact, many business sectors or industries require organizations to achieve certification as a condition of doing business. Other benefits include providing consumers and interested parties confidence in the organization as well as meeting regulatory body requirements.

Organizations that choose to make a declaration of conformity instead of obtaining certification are usually on a limited budget and may not have the funds for certification. ISO 9001:2015 certification might not be a customer requirement or there is no marketing advantage to the organization. The organization may choose to implement ISO 9001:2015 purely for internal reasons. In those cases, the organization can still implement the standard, make a claim of conformity if needed for a proposal, and quickly close the gap with a certification audit if needed.

ACCREDITATION AND CERTIFICATION

Two key aspects with conformity assessment are accreditation and certification. These are key for any organization seeking ISO 9001:2015 certification.

Certification is written assurance (a certificate) by an independent body that an organization's quality management system (QMS) meets specific requirements. Certification is also known as third-party conformity assessment. Certification can be useful in adding credibility to an organization by demonstrating that its QMS meets customer expectations. For some industries, it's a legal or contractual requirement. The independent bodies that provide conformity assessment of a management system standard such as ISO 9001:2015 are known as certification bodies or registrars.

Accreditation is the independent evaluation of certification bodies (CBs) against recognized standards to ensure their impartiality and competence. Through the application of national and international standards, governments, procurers, and consumers can have confidence in the certifications provided.

Accreditation bodies are established in many countries with the primary purpose of ensuring that CBs are subject to oversight by an authoritative body. Accreditation bodies that have been evaluated by peers are competent and sign arrangements that enhance the acceptance of products and services across national borders. This creates a framework to support international trade through the removal of technical barriers.

For ISO 9001:2015, these arrangements are managed by the International Accreditation Forum (IAF). The IAF established the Multilateral Recognition Arrangement (MLA) to ensure mutual recognition of accredited certification between signatories to the MLA and subsequent acceptance of accredited certification in many markets based on one accreditation.

Accreditation body members of IAF are admitted to the IAF MLA only after a stringent evaluation of their operations by a peer evaluation team charged with ensuring that the applicant member complies fully with both the international standards and IAF requirements. Once an accreditation body is a signatory of the IAF MLA, it's required to recognize the certificates issued by CBs accredited by all other signatories of the IAF MLA with the appropriate scope.

There are many CBs to select from, but it's important to select a CB that is accredited by an IAF signatory member and has a good reputation in the industry.

When choosing a CB, an organization should evaluate several CBs to verify that they use the relevant ISO/CASCO standard and determine if they are accredited. Accreditation is not compulsory and non-accreditation does not necessarily mean a CB isn't reputable, but it does provide independent confirmation of competence. To find an accredited CB, contact the national accreditation body in your country or visit the IAF at *www.iaf.nu*.

In addition to establishing the guidelines that accreditation bodies and CBs must follow, the IAF also establishes specific requirements such as the number of audit days based on criteria such as complexity of processes, number of employees, and number of sites. This allows for consistency between organizations and prevents audit days from being a reason for selecting a specific CB.

Achieving and maintaining certification includes multiple steps. During each of the steps, the goal is to provide feedback that allows the organization to progress to the next stage.

Sometimes, as part of pre-certification activities, a pre-audit or pre-assessment can be scheduled. This activity is not referred to in ISO/IEC 17021-1 and is optional. An auditor assigned by the certification body will audit conformity to the requirements of ISO 9001:2015 and provide feedback. The organization can consider this feedback during preparation for the initial audit.

If the organization and the certification body agree to a pre-audit, independence and impartiality must be given special consideration. The pre-audit is not part of the initial certification audit.

PRE-CERTIFICATION ACTIVITIES

Pre-certification activities are those actions carried out by the organization and the CB to establish an audit program for the full certification cycle and determine the audit time, including the application activities.

The audit program for the initial certification includes a mandatory two-stage initial audit, surveillance audits in the first and second years following the certification decision, and a recertification in the third year prior to expiration of certification.

In determining the audit time, the CB will consider, among other things, the requirements of the relevant management system standard, the complexity of the client and its management system, the technological and regulatory context, outsourcing of any activities included in the scope of the management system, the results of any prior audits, size and number of sites, geographical locations and multi-site considerations, and the risks associated with the products, processes, or activities of the organization.

PLANNING AUDITS

Planning should be performed for each audit included in the audit program. The planning activities should consider the determination of the audit objectives, scope and criteria, and the audit team selection and assignments.

An audit plan should be established that includes or refers to the audit objectives, the audit criteria, the audit scope (including identification of the organizational and functional units or processes to be audited), the dates and sites where the on-site audit activities will be conducted, the expected duration of on-site audit activities, and the roles and responsibilities of the audit team members and accompanying persons, such as observers or interpreters.

The organization will receive the audit plan from the CB before the start of the initial audit.

INITIAL CERTIFICATION AUDIT

Stage 1

During stage 1, the auditor from the CB conducts a review of the organization, including its documented information. This could include the documented information related to the context of the organization and any other documents the organization is using to demonstrate implementation. Stage 1 allows the auditor to become familiar with the organization's processes, obtain necessary information regarding the scope of the QMS, and to complete an effective audit plan for stage 2. The auditor is looking for conformity in key areas such as planning, support and operation processes, management review, internal audits, documented information, and nonconformity and corrective action. Stage 1 also provides the opportunity to ensure that ISO 9001:2015 requirements have been correctly applied and that the organization has an understanding of the requirements.

At the end of the stage 1, documented conclusions will be communicated to the organization, including identification of any areas of concern that could be classified as a nonconformity during stage 2.

Tip: Organizations should own a copy of ISO 9001:2015 and be familiar with it. They should understand the core requirements and be able to describe and/or show objective evidence of how they meet these requirements.

Stage 2

During stage 2, the CB determines if an organization conforms to ISO 9001:2015. The purpose of stage 2 is to evaluate the implementation, including effectiveness of the QMS. Stage 2 takes place at the organization's site(s).

Once stage 2 activities are completed, an audit report is provided to the organization. This report will include the audit conclusions, the audit findings, and recommendations from the audit team.

The organization can be recommended for certification as long as there are no major or systemic nonconformities in its implemented QMS.

A *major nonconformity* is a nonconformity that affects the capability of the QMS to achieve the intended results, such as nonconforming product or services provided to the customer without any action implemented for improvement or a series of minor nonconformities in one area that indicate systemic issues exist. A *minor nonconformity* is a nonconformity that does not affect the capability of the QMS to achieve the intended results.

If a nonconformity is identified, the CB will require the organization to implement a correction and corrective action within a defined time. The CB will review and verify the effectiveness of any correction and corrective action taken. Normally, major nonconformities are verified on-site and minor nonconformities are verified off-site, either through documents or pictures.

After verification, the organization is then recommended for certification.

CERTIFICATION DECISION

Prior to making a certification decision, the CB will review the information provided by the audit team to determine if it meets the certification requirements and the scope of certification; if correction and corrective actions for any major nonconformities have been reviewed, accepted, and verified; and if the organization's plan for correction and corrective action for any minor nonconformities has been reviewed and accepted.

For granting the initial certification, the CB will consider the audit report and comments on the identified nonconformities after their verification, including confirmation that the audit objectives were achieved, among other relevant elements.

Normally, the certification is granted for three years and the corresponding certificate will include the expiration date.

SURVEILLANCE AUDIT

Once the organization is certified, the CB provides an audit plan for the length of the certification (three years). The CB conducts periodic or surveillance audits. These audits will be conducted either every six months or once a year. In considering the frequency of surveillance audits, the organization should consider the size or complexity of the system, overall maturity of the system, and results of the initial audit. Many major nonconformities during the initial audit could be an indication that, at least for one cycle of audits, it would be beneficial to have the surveillance audit conducted every six months. Smaller organizations usually find that annual surveillance audits are adequate.

During the surveillance audit, the CB reviews the predetermined requirements of the audit plan. Each of the core requirements, including documented information, management review, internal audits, and nonconformities and corrective action are also audited at each surveillance audit. A major nonconformity might be issued when an organization fails to effectively implement the corrective action from a previous audit or if there is a breakdown in the QMS. For example, an organization might make a change to its QMS that no longer meets the requirements of ISO 9001:2015 or it might have a series of nonconformities in a specific area such as monitoring and measuring resources (calibration) that together indicate a systemic failure.

Organizations might find that they become more disciplined around audit time and less disciplined during the other times in the year. These organizations may find that they frequently have nonconformities, including major nonconformities. For major nonconformities, follow-up audits are required by the CB, which results in additional costs. Organizations should remember that they are on a journey and maintain their QMS accordingly.

RECERTIFICATION

The purpose of the recertification audit is to confirm the continued conformity and effectiveness of the QMS of a certified organization. A recertification audit should be planned and conducted to evaluate the continued fulfillment of all of the requirements of ISO 9001:2015. This audit should be planned and conducted in due time to enable timely renewal before the certificate expiration date.

APPEALS PROCESS

Each CB has an appeals process that it should explain during the opening and closing audit meeting. The appeals process should highlight the steps organizations should use if they don't agree with a nonconformance.

Many organizations are reluctant to challenge a nonconformance because they believe the auditor holds the fate of their certification in their hands. Although it's true that the auditor makes a recommendation for certification, this doesn't eliminate the potential for honest disagreement.

Steps an organization should take in determining if an appeal is necessary

Organizations shouldn't accept a nonconformance just because the auditor states it. It is, however, the organization's responsibility to provide information as to why it disagrees with the nonconformance and ask for clarification from the auditor. The auditor needs to specifically provide the organization with the ISO 9001:2015 requirement, the organization's own requirement, or a regulatory requirement that the organization does not comply with.

If after this discussion the auditor and the organization still don't agree, the organization should request an official technical interpretation from the auditor's CB. If there is still a disagreement, the organization can file an appeal with its accreditation body.

Although the appeals process is available to the organization, it should first focus on resolution with its auditor before proceeding.

DECLARATION OF CONFORMITY

In lieu of seeking certification, some organizations implement ISO 9001 but don't go through an independent third-party audit with an accredited CB. This is known as a declaration or self-declaration of conformity by the organization. When an organization claims conformity, it will routinely find there are gaps in its system. This may arise from the fact that an organization doesn't have a CB (e.g., a third-party independent auditor) reviewing its system on a regular basis. These organizations may also have less disciplined systems that are prone to findings.

ISO/CASCO has published standards that organizations can use as a reference. These standards are ISO/IEC 17050-1, Conformity assessment—Supplier's declaration of conformity—Part 1: General requirements, and ISO/IEC 17050-2, Conformity assessment—Supplier's declaration of conformity—Part 2: Supporting documentation.

ISO/IEC 17050-1 specifies general requirements for a supplier's declaration of conformity in cases where it is desirable—or necessary—that conformity of an object to the specified requirements be attested, irrespective of the sector involved.

For the purpose of ISO/IEC 17050-1, the object of a declaration of conformity can be a product, process, management system, person, or body.

CHAPTER 16

Implementation

A common mistake made when implementing ISO 9001 is attempting to do so without a plan. This chapter outlines the steps an organization should take to help manage a successful ISO 9001:2015 implementation. Although not all of these steps may be necessary or possible due to the size of the organization, they do provide a general guideline.

ISO 9001:2015 was written as a generic standard so that it could be applied to all types of organizations regardless of the type, size, or product provided. It is equally applicable to service as well as manufacturing organizations. Because all organizations are different, quality management systems (QMS) will differ from one organization to the next. That's why it's important to tailor your organization's QMS around your specific processes, products, and services, and why a generic model might not provide you with the best outcome.

ISO 9001:2015 provides a structured model of quality management. Many organizations over-interpret the standard and develop systems that focus solely on meeting ISO 9001's requirements. Organizations with more effective implementations typically follow a model that reviews existing work activities to provide objective evidence of conformity to ISO 9001, identify gaps between the organization's QMS and ISO 9001, and develop an implementation plan to close any of the identified gaps.

Fortunately, there is a simple model organizations can use during their ISO 9001:2015 implementation. This is illustrated in figure 16.1.

Figure 16.1	Simple ISO 9001:2015 Implementation Model
Say it!	Document your processes.
Do it!	Follow your procedures.
Prove it!	Maintain documented information.
Improve it!	Improve processes.
Tip: Focus ISO 9001 implementation on requirements that establish the foundation for the quality management system.	

Although ISO 9001:2015's requirements cover a variety of topics that document the QMS, there are certain requirements in the standard that provide a broad verification of efficiency. This holds true for the organization as well as any second or third party that might assess your QMS for conformity.

LEADERSHIP

Organizations that have strong management commitment and conduct management reviews that align with their strategic direction are seen by third-party auditors as engaged in the process. When managers are actively involved in the management review process and recognize it not only as an ISO 9001 requirement but also as an avenue to drive business improvement, they will find that management review adds value to the organization.

RISKS AND OPPORTUNITIES

As part of its planning activities, the organization should determine the risks and opportunities that can affect the ability of the QMS to achieve its intended results and to enhance customer satisfaction.

These risks and opportunities become a key input for QMS processes, as appropriate. Specific actions or controls to address these risks and opportunities will be established and implemented at relevant QMS processes. Some processes will be more relevant in ensuring the effectiveness of the actions to address these risk and opportunities.

INTERNAL AUDITS

Internal audits provide information to the organization on whether the QMS conforms to requirements. These requirements can be internal, customer, statutory and regulatory, or ISO 9001 requirements. If these audits are being conducted as required and used to identify opportunities to provide more control, the overall management system will improve.

It's sometimes difficult for organizations to see internal audits as little more than a "check the box" activity. It's important to drive a culture that embraces internal audits as a valuable improvement tool. No matter how hard we try, we develop our systems in the way we think that they should function. Internal audits give us a view into what can—and will—go wrong when the system is under the regular stress of the business.

The most successful organizations initiate their internal audit programs early in the implementation process and continue to use them as a way of improving.

Although ISO 9001:2015 doesn't specifically require the implementation of ISO 19011, Guidelines for auditing management systems, this document provides comprehensive guidance for a successful implementation of an audit program and the performance of internal audits. It also provides valuable guidance on the competence of internal auditors.

CORRECTIVE ACTION SYSTEM

An organization should have a system for tracking corrective actions and ensuring that actions are robust and are completed in a timely manner. Taking corrective action on nonconformities to ensure that they don't recur—and following up to ensure the corrective action is effective—shows that the organization is learning from its mistakes and making changes as needed.

DOCUMENTED INFORMATION

Start on your documentation system early. The intent of ISO 9001:2015 is that each process—through its process owner—determine what documented information is needed for its effective operation and demonstrate that the realization of the process is as planned.

The organization must have controls in place for each document type (e.g., forms, documented procedures, work instructions, and drawings) that it determines is necessary. Even though there are no specific documented procedures required by

ISO 9001:2015, there are several instances where documented information must be maintained or retained. Organizations should establish these documented information requirements early in the implementation of the standard and ensure their ongoing suitability after initial certification is achieved.

These core requirements are critical to most standards and can provide benefits to the organization even if it doesn't seek certification. This is also why an organization that's using a graded approach to implementation and only selecting a portion of the standard to implement might want to focus on these areas.

APPROACHES TO IMPLEMENTATION

There are different methods for implementing ISO 9001:2015. Each organization is unique and made up of different systems, so there isn't a cookbook with a list of special ingredients that are required to be successful. When an organization begins its journey to ISO 9001:2015 declaration of conformity or certification, it must make some decisions as it defines its implementation plan. For example, the organization needs to decide if it's going to start from scratch or build on an existing system. It also need to determine if it needs outside assistance from a coach or consultant. Organizations will also need to consider if they have the capacity to handle an implementation plan with aggressive dates.

Adapting your current system

For organizations that have existing processes and documented procedures, a gap analysis of the existing system will need to be conducted to determine what changes are needed. Some organizations that adopt this philosophy take only the minimum steps needed to achieve conformity with the standard. These organizations may find that sustaining their certification may be more difficult in the long term. Other organizations will use their gap analysis as an opportunity to adapt and improve their current system. These organizations may find that adapting systems that people are already using requires more monitoring than other systems. However, they may also find a more sustainable system in the long run.

It's important to remember that ISO 9001 is compatible with other initiatives the organization may be involved in such as total quality management, lean Six Sigma, CMMI, or excellence models such as the Malcolm Baldrige National Quality Award or the Deming Prize. Therefore, if your organization has these initiatives in place, the implementation team should look for ways to align them with its ISO 9001:2015 implementation activities.

Figure 16.2	Using Existing Systems for Implementation
Benefits	**Challenges**
Organization has a starting point.	Organizations do not always identify gaps by assuming current system meets requirements.
Use existing work.	Organizations are reluctant to make change.
Implementation may be quicker.	Sustaining certification may be more difficult because the implementation may be based on a short-term fix and not a long-term solution.

Establishing a new management system

Some organizations won't have an existing system of processes and documented procedures. Other organizations may have a current management system that's not mature enough to use as a baseline for an ISO 9001:2015 implementation effort.

In this scenario, an organization may find that starting over from the beginning will provide a better opportunity for success. Organizations need to review existing business processes and compare them to ISO 9001:2015's requirements to determine what type of actions are needed to achieve conformance to the standard.

It might require a significant change to the organization's methods for conducting business. However, it could be that the organization determines that minimal change is needed. Every organization is unique. This chapter includes information on conducting a gap analysis. Organizations that use this approach typically find that their QMS will endure over time. They also have more opportunity for improvement during the implementation process.

Figure 16.3	Starting from Scratch
Benefits	**Challenges**
Sustaining certification may be easier over time.	Implementation may take longer.
Less oversight of quality management system needed.	Required changes could require investment in resources (e.g., software)
Implementation may be quicker.	Increased need for senior leadership involvement during initial implementation.

Consultants

Some organizations use outside resources such as a consultant to provide support during their ISO 9001:2015 implementation efforts. Other organizations may determine that they need ongoing support.

When selecting a consultant, organizations should consider an approach that best suits the needs of the organization. There are two different approaches.

Consultant

In this approach, a consultant takes primary responsibility for implementing ISO 9001:2015. The organization has minimal "hands-on" actions during the implementation process. Therefore, it has less understanding of the QMS on an ongoing basis and may find it has to rely on the consultant to sustain the QMS.

Consultants as coach

Another approach is to select a consultant who will serve as a coach. The key differences? A consultant typically directs requirements for the QMS and even does much of the development work such as creating documented information and setting any requirements. A coach typically provides some steps to implement the standard and may even provide some suggestions on how to implement it, but serves more as a person who the organization can utilize to validate that implementation steps are correct.

A coach will provide training on how to effectively implement the requirements of ISO 9001:2015. A coach will also provide feedback on whether a proposed technique the organization wishes to implement meets the intent of the standard. It's important that an infrastructure is developed for ongoing maintenance.

Organizations that use a coaching method for their implementation efforts should look for someone who will coach them on different approaches while letting the organization's implementation team make decisions and execute changes.

In short, the coach and the organization work together to find the best long-term solution, yet the organization owns the implementation process.

Developing an implementation plan

It's important to remember that an implementation plan is critical to the organization's success. Organizations that don't have an established implementation plan may find that they wander through the certification process without making forward progress.

Focus on some basic steps such as establishing management commitment, determining the needed resources, establishing the scope of certification, and identifying team members. Once this is completed, additional recommended steps can be conducted simultaneously or in any sequence the organization establishes.

Because each organization has varying goals, there is no standard implementation plan that can be used for all companies. Many organizations develop an implementation timeline of about twelve months. However, based on an organization's readiness, certification *can* be achieved in less time.

The amount of time required for a successful implementation depends on the results of the gap analysis. The gap analysis indicates what actions need to be taken to achieve conformity. An organization should also consider the resources it has available to commit to the implementation, management commitment, and any customer needs requiring ISO 9001:2015 compliance or certification *before* establishing its implementation plan.

MAKING THE DECISION TO IMPLEMENT ISO 9001:2015

When making the decision to implement ISO 9001:2015, the leadership team needs to review the reasons for certification and determine their benefits. In some cases, the organization may find that the level of effort and costs aren't in line with the current direction of the organization. After seeing the benefits of implementation, some may decide to use a graded approach and only implement some of the requirements of the standard. Others may choose to seek a declaration of conformity instead of independent third-party certification.

The following reasons are those frequently cited by organizations that choose to implement ISO 9001:

- *Mandated by customer.* Many customers use ISO 9001 as a way to ensure that their providers have implemented a management system that meets minimum requirements. In some cases, this certification can eliminate the need for the organization to conduct additional second-party audits.
- *Mandated by the corporation.* Corporations frequently require all of their organizations or subsidiaries to be certified. Implementing ISO 9001 across a corporation provides a framework for consistency in business operations.
- *Competitive advantage.* By obtaining ISO 9001 certification, organizations can differentiate themselves from their competitors and get leverage when seeking new contracts.
- *Internal decision.* ISO 9001 certification is most commonly seen as a way to meet requirements that someone else has put on the organization. However,

some organizations choose to implement ISO 9001 as a method for controlling *their* business management system and improving processes.

BENEFITS OF ISO 9001:2015 IMPLEMENTATION

It's important to remember that not all organizations will achieve the same benefits when implementing ISO 9001:2015. Because many people within the organization—including leadership and employees—will at times question the benefits of ISO 9001 implementation or certification, it's helpful that potential benefits be reviewed and established. It's important that once these potential benefits are established that they are communicated to the organization's interested parties. These parties can be both internal and external and could include leadership, employees, customers, and providers.

Although the benefits can vary, here are some frequent benefits that organizations might see. These can be evaluated as potential wins for the organization.

Benefits for employees

Organizations should strive to identify benefits that will communicate to employees "what's in it for me." Employees will be more likely to engage in the implementation process if there are potential personal benefits. Benefits for employees can include job security based on the organization's ability to increase the amount of work it has as an ISO 9001:2015-certified company or having defined requirements that make their jobs easier.

Benefits for customers

When an organization identifies benefits for customers, it's important that the benefits outweigh any perceived or real costs of implementation. Some customers believe these costs will be passed onto them in either higher costs for products or services or delayed delivery times.

A structured QMS provides a means for the customer to know that the organization has put controls in place that will help with providing quality products and services. In some cases, it may be as simple as improvements to existing controls. These controls include internal audits and corrective actions. The organization may wish to address a specific concern that customers have raised in the past and demonstrate how improvements are being made as a result of the ISO 9001 implementation.

Customers who see that an organization has a method for identifying nonconformities and taking action to correct them can have the confidence that problems are identified and corrected. It also provides a mechanism for improved communication between the organization and its customers.

Benefits to leadership

In most cases, the leadership team is involved in making the decision to seek ISO 9001 certification. However, organizational leadership might often be the most vocal about bureaucracy they believe ISO 9001 requirements adds as well as additional costs driven by controls. These organizations need to ensure that benefits are communicated to all levels of leadership. Benefits may also vary based on each level of leadership, but almost every management level can see an improvement in employees' understanding requirements and following them. Management will realize benefits from this by a decrease in nonconformities resulting from their processes. This means less rework and the ability to meet requirements with less cost.

Benefits to external providers

The benefits to external providers—or suppliers—are typically simpler. When an external provider is familiar with ISO 9001, it will know ahead of time what its customer's expectations are. Benefits might also include improvements in communication regarding the selection and approval of providers. This also might mean an improved relationship with the organization and more potential contracts.

Focus on the benefits not the challenges

In the beginning stages of implementation, organizations may have the tendency to focus on the negative aspects of their implementation efforts. Organizations need to challenge themselves to identify actions that are improving their organization. It's important to gather information and act on facts. It's also important to realize that if the organization is looking at benefits, they may not always be tied to dollars. In fact, many of the benefits are intangible.

A successful ISO 9001:2015 implementation will lead to processes that are understood, employees that are competent, and business operations that are consistent. In addition, customer requirements are addressed and there should be processes in place that meet established criteria, including any statutory and regulatory requirements.

The internal audit and corrective action systems will provide a focus on identifying opportunities for improvement and implementing them.

Establishing management commitment

Establishing management commitment is essential to a successful ISO 9001:2015 implementation and should be a priority for the organization.

Unless management makes ISO 9001 implementation a priority and demonstrates their commitment to it, employees won't see it as a strategic goal or important to the organization. It's also management's responsibility to listen to the implementation team if they're not involved in day-to-day activities associated with implementation.

For example, the implementation team may believe that there are challenges with the implementation. If leadership is seen as not actively involved in resolving these issues, the organization may not achieve certification.

ASSIGN IMPLEMENTATION TEAM

The size of an implementation team depends on the size of the organization and the level of effort needed to achieve certification. The more members of your organization who participate in the implementation, the better the buy-in.

There are many different roles and responsibilities for the ISO 9001:2015 implementation team. In small organizations, team members frequently serve in more than one role. However, it's important not to assign too much of the workload to one individual. The key is to identify the team members, understand their capacity, assign their responsibilities, and then communicate them to your organization. Clearly understanding who is working on the team and their individual responsibilities is a key success factor. A lack of clearly identified responsibilities could hinder implementation and result in employees not providing the necessary support to team members.

Some organizations may already have identified process owners. They can become members of the implementation team to help ensure that the implementation follows a multidisciplinary approach.

Leadership should participate in the implementation team's review activities. This way, the team leader will ensure the resource needs and implementation issues are shared with top management and appropriate decisions will be promptly taken.

CHARACTERISTICS OF AN ISO 9001:2015 IMPLEMENTATION TEAM MEMBER

Frequently, when an organization initiates an ISO 9001 implementation effort it selects team members it believes would help the effort. Other organizations simply

assign those who are available. Organizations need to make sure that the individuals they select meet some minimum criteria. These include:
- *Respect from others in the organization.* The team is going to work across all aspects of the organization, so members should have some level of respect at all levels, including leadership, peers, and other employees. In some situations, a good relationship with the customer may also be needed.
- *Ability to effect change.* Team members should have sufficient status that if they make a recommended change to the organization's QMS, it will be accepted with leadership's endorsement. The viewpoint of the team member needs to be valued by others in the organization.
- *Knowledge about the organization.* Team members should have enough knowledge about how the organization works and who to contact to get things done. This is particularly true in large organizations where there might be the need to direct employees to take specific actions.

Because it's possible that some team members don't come from a traditional quality background, they may feel uncomfortable with ISO 9001:2015's requirements during early phases of implementation. If a training class is held, it's possible that the concepts may not come naturally to them. They could be reluctant to ask questions because they feel everyone else in the class understands the material and their questions will appear simple. They still may be extremely effective, but the organization should be prepared to help them through these feelings and doubts.

Other team members may be uncomfortable with the ambiguity of ISO 9001:2015's requirements. These members are looking for very specific guidance on how to implement ISO 9001:2015 within the organization. This ambiguity makes them uncomfortable in their implementation efforts because it's often an additional job responsibility that's been tacked on to their day-to-day job.

ISO 9001:2015 implementation team members should remember that they were selected based on their overall skill set. Although it might seem difficult at times, team members should realize the feeling of uneasiness is very common. They shouldn't be overwhelmed and while they would most likely feel more comfortable in a working relationship with a consultant, they will be successful if they have the support and commitment of their organization's management.

To ease the discomfort, it may make sense to find a mentor for the implementation team. Mentors can come from professional organizations, similar organizations, or from somewhere else in the corporation.

The following is a list of frequently assigned roles in an ISO 9001 implementation. However, it's important to note that these are common practices and not all roles may be needed by the organization or additional roles may be needed.

- *Management sponsor.* Previous versions of ISO 9001 included a requirement for a management representative to be responsible for the QMS. This role is no longer required by ISO 9001:2015. However, the responsibilities for leadership remain the same. Therefore, it may still be helpful to your organization if a specific person or team is assigned.

  The management sponsor typically serves as the project champion. They would be responsible for ongoing communication to the senior leadership team regarding the status of implementation. They might also take responsibility for coordinating the management review process. Although ISO 9001:2015 implementation is for the organization's QMS, the management sponsor doesn't necessarily need to be part of the quality team. However, this person should be a member of top management.

- *ISO 9001 coordinator.* This person typically oversees the day-to-day coordination activities that support the implementation project. He or she ensures that implementation activities are on track and may even be responsible for making general implementation decisions. The coordinator supports the management sponsor and facilitates communication between clause/subject matter experts or departments on issues that may need resolution or independent facilitation.

- *Clause/subject matter experts.* These individuals serve as the subject matter experts on the standard itself. They are responsible for ensuring that the ISO 9001:2015 requirements are effectively implemented. This can include the implementation of specific requirements, development of documented procedures (if needed), and ensuring that training is provided to employees. Using clause/subject matter experts helps to ensure that it's not just a couple of employees who are responsible for implementing the standard. This also helps provide employees understanding of what requirements are related to their area and how they meet them.

At times, the organization might find that employees don't have experience in QMS implementation. For that reason, different roles on the implementation team might be performed by external consultants or coaches.

CONDUCT TRAINING

One of the biggest mistakes organizations make is trying to implement ISO 9001:2015 without any training for the employees responsible for implementing it. This is equivalent to having employees implement the standard without reading it.

There are several types of training that are critical to getting an organization's ISO 9001:2015 implementation off the ground. Each organization must decide the level and detail of training required for its employees. Some team members may benefit in attending an off-site implementation course. If your organization is large, it may be more cost effective to bring the training in-house so many employees can attend.

Here are some basic guidelines for training needed for an organization seeking ISO 9001:2015 certification.

Management overview

The senior leadership team should be trained on their responsibilities for implementing ISO 9001:2015. The training should include a special emphasis on clause 5, Leadership. In most cases, it's not necessary for the senior leadership team to receive training on the entire standard. However, it can certainly be helpful in organizations where there is a lack of trust by senior leadership. At a minimum, leadership should read the standard.

Some organizations choose to provide internal training. The implementation team needs to evaluate—based on management commitment—if an external source should provide the training. It's sometimes beneficial to have someone from the outside provide the details of the requirements as an independent voice.

ISO 9001 coordinator/clause experts

Subject matter experts need to receive training on all of ISO 9001:2015's requirements and how to implement them. This training can be combined with internal audit training because both auditors and clause experts will need training on ISO 9001:2015's requirements.

Based on the organization's budget, some of this learning may be completed through self-training or online courses. However, it's important that at least one person receive some type of formal training to facilitate a more successful implementation. In addition to external organizations that provide training, additional sources of training could be local technical colleges. In some states, there are programs where a portion of the training could be subsidized or reimbursed. Contact your state's economic development department to see if there is such a program in your state.

Employee awareness

Every employee should receive ISO 9001:2015 awareness training. This training should focus on each employee's responsibilities within the ISO 9001:2015 implementation process. It's not necessary for every employee to have an in-depth understanding of ISO 9001:2015's requirements but rather what their role is in maintaining the certification.

Examples include understanding their role in the QMS, knowing how to find documented information, understanding the quality policy and what it means in their job, knowledge of quality objectives relevant to their area and how they might contribute to them, and a general knowledge of what ISO 9001:2015 means for the organization.

Internal auditor

Employees who will serve as internal auditors will require training not only on internal audit methods but also on ISO 9001:2015 requirements. Employees selected as internal auditors will often take the clause experts' training in addition to internal auditor training. Without this type of training, auditors will tend to audit based on opinion and not actual ISO 9001:2015 or organization requirements.

Because the organization establishes competence requirements for internal auditors, they can be as stringent as the organization requires. Typically, the lead auditor training required for third-party auditors working for certification bodies would be considered too stringent for an internal auditor. For that reason, training on how to audit in general is more appropriate. ISO 19011 can be used for guidance and to train auditors.

DEVELOP A COMMUNICATION PLAN

When an organization begins the ISO 9001 implementation process, there are often comments made by employees about what they think the process means. This might come from someone else they know whose organization has implemented ISO 9001. Frequent comments heard include:
- "ISO 9001 causes more bureaucracy."
- "We don't need this; we already have a strong quality system."
- "ISO 9001 is non-value-added."
- "It's just another quality assurance initiative."
- "It will add cost to the system."
- "What are the benefits?"

When developing its communication plan, the organization needs to consider how it will alleviate the concerns of interested parties, including leadership and employees. This might include addressing some of the myths frequently associated with implementing ISO 9001. Although the organization may never be able to address all the apprehension that can come with a change in culture, it may be able to eliminate some of the concerns by creating a well-crafted communications campaign.

Keep in mind that these myths can become reality if an organization doesn't have an effective implementation plan.

The implementation team will need to identify interested parties it needs to communicate with. The team will also need to create the necessary communication tools. The organization may need to develop different methods based on the audience and the message that the organization wants to convey, as leadership is interested in different information than an outside interested parties.

Leadership

In addition to senior leadership, many organizations have other levels of management. It's important to emphasize to all levels of management what their role is for the ISO 9001:2015 implementation effort. The message may also include the priority the organization places on the implementation effort and how to manage employees who support the ISO 9001 implementation team. Senior management's commitment must be clear to all managers.

To have one consistent voice, it can be useful to provide common messages to pass on to customers and other interested parties.

Employees

For most ISO 9001:2015 implementation efforts, the organization will need to communicate with employees multiple times to be effective. It's important to consider the right time to begin communicating with employees and to consider what employees need to understand regarding ISO 9001:2015. It's not as critical that each employee understand every requirement of the standard, but why the organization is implementing it. It's also helpful for employees to understand the benefits to them personally and to the organization.

Customers

When developing a communication plan for customers, the organization needs to address both benefits and potential questions. It may be necessary to create different messages for different customers, especially if the organization is aware of customer concerns. The organization will want to communicate its reasons for wanting to achieve ISO 9001:2015 certification. Because some customers may feel that there could be increased costs, bureaucracy, or issues with timeliness of delivery during the implementation process, it's important for the organization to address how these will be minimized.

Communication to customers should be ongoing during the ISO 9001:2015 implementation to continue to address any concerns that may arise.

Providers

The message to providers may not need to be as formal as with other parties. However, it's still necessary that they understand any potential effects. For example, an organization may wish to communicate that it's seeking certification and will require it of all or critical external providers by some future established date. Other organizations may communicate that they are seeking certification but will not require it of providers. However, providers won't be responsible for meeting better established criteria and will be evaluated on an ongoing basis to that criteria. The message should be specific.

DETERMINE SCOPE OF CERTIFICATION

When seeking third-party certification, an organization must determine the scope of the registration to its QMS. This is referred to as the scope of registration for the organization.

Organizations that limit their scope to either a specific physical location or product/service should take extreme care because it defines how a third-party auditor will review the site. In particular, this is crucial if the organization is seeking certification based on external requirements. Organizations should consider the requirements in clause 4, Context of the organization, when determining the scope. They should define the following:

- *Application of the standard.* By design, ISO 9001:2015 was written in a generic style so that it could be applied to all types of organizations regardless of type, size, and product or service provided. There are some requirements that cannot be applied due to the product or service the organization provides. In this case, the organization may determine that a particular requirement won't be applied. It's important for the organization to remember that a requirement cannot be determined not to apply if it affects the organization's ability to provide products and services that meet customer and applicable statutory and regulatory requirements.
- *Geographic locations.* The organization must determine what physical locations are included in the scope, including different physical addresses or different buildings for a large site.

- *Products and services.* The organization will need to identify all of the products and services that will be included in the scope. If the organization is choosing a limited scope, it would identify only those products or services that will be included. Organizations that have an ISO 9001:2015 certification that covers only a portion of the business must exercise caution when providing information related to their certification. The organization can only make claims that align with the limited scope.
- *Portions of the value stream (the starting and ending points of the certified QMS).* The organization may choose to certify a specific department relating to a certain product (e.g., the engineering department for a specific part).

If an organization is part of a larger corporation and has difficulty determining what its product or service is, it may need to review whether it should pursue ISO 9001:2015 certification as a separate entity or as part of the corporation.

In determining the scope of the certification, an organization can be very specific or more general, but it should consider what it wants to convey to potential customers when developing the scope. If an organization wants to demonstrate a specific type of manufacturing, then a specific scope should be developed. General scope statements should be considered when an organization does not want to limit its scope.

Scope (Example)

The design and manufacture of electrical, mechanical, electro-mechanical, electronic, metal, rubber, and plastic components, products, assemblies, and systems; design/engineering services; and technology transfer to education, business, and industry.

CONDUCT GAP ANALYSIS

One of the most critical steps in any ISO 9001:2015 implementation is to conduct a gap analysis. Many organizations begin the implementation process without an understanding of what actions are necessary to achieve conformity with the standard. The timing of this step is difficult to establish. For example, if your organization plans to conduct the gap analysis itself, it's important that training is provided on ISO 9001:2015 prior to the gap analysis to ensure that the activity is value added.

Even with training, the implementation team may still not have an in-depth understanding of ISO 9001 initially. However, conducting the gap analysis will provide valuable insight into the organization and what needs to be done.

This is also a critical step when hiring a consultant or coach. Many organizations that determine they are going to an external source for implementation assistance will inquire as to what it will take to achieve ISO 9001:2015 certification. If your organization uses this method, ensure that your consultant provides an initial gap analysis to determine the overall level of effort needed. Without this step, both from an internal or external viewpoint, any implementation plans are simply guessing.

Some organizations use a third-party's checklist. If this type of tool is used, the checklist should be modified to not only include whether the organization meets the requirements, but also how it meets the requirements. This tool can also be used to identify what actions will be taken to close specific gaps.

The implementation team should frequently review and update the gap analysis as part of the implementation process to ensure all actions are taken.

IDENTIFICATION OF PROCESSES AND DEVELOPMENT OF DOCUMENTED INFORMATION

Determine/map processes

ISO 9001:2015 requires that the organization determine the processes and their interactions used for its QMS. The standard does not require the organization to map the processes. However, many organizations choose process mapping to instill process ownership and to better understand the organization's processes. These organizations use natural teams to map the processes. Those who are actually completing the work would then validate the processes. Completing this activity will help meet the requirements in clause 4.4, Quality management system and its processes, while also meeting a critical need in the implementation plan.

Development of documented information

ISO 9001:2015 requires that the QMS include specific documented information. Some of the documented information is maintained, which is traditional to what are called "documents," and other documented information must be retained, which is typical to records.

Documented information to be maintained
- Scope of the QMS (subclause 4.3)
- Specific records to demonstrate fulfillment of a requirement (subclause 4.4.2)
- Quality policy (subclause 5.2.2)

- Quality objectives (subclause 6.2.1)
- Documented information to demonstrate fulfillment of production and service provision requirements (subclause 8.1)

Documented information to be retained

- Specific records to demonstrate fulfillment of a requirement (subclause 4.4.2)
- Evidence that monitoring and measuring resources are fit for purpose (subclause 7.1.5.1)
- Evidence of competence based on education, training, and experience (subclause 7.2)
- Documented information to demonstrate fulfillment of production and service provision requirements (subclause 8.1)
- Results of review of customer requirements (subclause 8.2.3.2)
- Design and development inputs (subclause 8.3.3)
- Design and development controls (subclause 8.3.4)
- Design and development outputs (subclause 8.3.5)
- Design and development changes (subclause 8.3.6)
- External provider evaluation and reevaluation (subclause 8.4.1)
- Identification and traceability of outputs where required (subclause 8.5.2)
- Control of changes (subclause 8.5.6)
- Release of products and services (subclause 8.6)
- Control of nonconforming output (subclause 8.7)
- Internal audit results (subclause 9.2.2)
- Management review output (subclause 9.3)
- Results of nonconformities and corrective action (subclause 10.2.2)

Additional documented information

In addition to the documented information required by ISO 9001:2015, the organization may determine that additional documented information is required for its processes. This could include documented information needed for the operation of the process, such as documented procedures; work instructions; drawings; visual aids; technical specifications; manuals; job descriptions; and data contained in information systems.

Documented information is needed to demonstrate that a process is performed as planned or to demonstrate the performance of processes such as records, performance indicators, minutes, reports, completed checklists, calibration or test results, and data contained in information systems.

Documented procedures

A gap analysis helps to identify areas of the business where quality could be adversely affected if documented information, including procedures, were not in place. Procedures should be developed for these areas.

Train employees

One of the biggest mistakes organizations make is not providing adequate training. This training may include the process activities and the documented information needed as references or developed as evidence of intended performance. This training should be consistent with the desired competence of the people in the organization.

Update processes and documented information

Once processes are established and documented information is created, they need to be updated throughout their useful life. The need for updating a process can be the result of a change in the QMS or a process not achieving its intended results. ISO 9001:2015 requires that documented information be monitored, reviewed, and updated as appropriate. Documented information that does not specifically relate to an ISO 9001:2015 requirement must also be monitored for review. Some organizations put a frequency interval requirement on documented information to ensure information accuracy over time. During the implementation of ISO 9001:2015, it's common for documented information to be modified. Reasons for an update could include feedback from employees that documents are incorrect, internal audits indicating that the documented information isn't being followed or is inadequate, or corrective action to address a nonconformance that requires documented information to be modified. It's important to include this review and update steps in the implementation plan to allow time to make necessary corrections prior to a certification audit. This activity should be part of each process owner's responsibility.

ANALYSIS AND EVALUATION OF THE QMS

There are many steps in the implementation process that relate to the organization analyzing its QMS either through scheduled reviews or internal audits. These requirements not only meet the intent of ISO 9001:2015 but also help to drive the implementation effort and identify opportunities for improvement prior to the initial certification audit.

Management review

Subclause 9.3 requires that each organization conduct a management review. The organization should schedule a minimum of one management review prior to an on-site visit by a certification body. Whenever possible, it's helpful to conduct more than one management review, as this activity can also be used to drive the implementation effort. The review needs to include the identified inputs and outputs and provide objective evidence of next steps for the next management review.

Initiate internal audits/audit all ISO 9001:2015 requirements

Once an organization has documented its QMS, internal audits must be conducted to validate compliance. Internal audits must be completed for each requirement prior to the initial audit by the certification body. It's best to conduct audits of an entire process, but it could be necessary to audit specific requirements to ensure compliance. The earlier in the process that internal audits can be initiated, the better off the organization will be as internal audits can identify flaws in the implementation of certain requirements. Therefore, they could be corrected prior to organizationwide implementation. To ensure the audit adds value to the organization and is timely, these audits should be conducted when documentation or a process is considered complete.

Initiate corrective action

When an organization completes its internal audits, the findings should be entered into the corrective action system. It's important to ensure that the corrective actions were completed by conducting follow-up reviews in the areas where the findings were identified to verify that actions have been taken. Lack of effective corrective action is a common issue with initial audits and achieving certification.

THIRD-PARTY CERTIFICATION

Select certification body

Although this step comes fairly late in this implementation, it can be initiated at any time during the process and should be completed as early as possible. An organization should choose the certification body that best suits its industry. For example, there may be some certification bodies that have a small business focus. Larger organizations may want to consider the number of standards that the certification body is accredited to if they're looking to certify to more than one standard.

It's recommended that multiple certification bodies be considered prior to selection. Benchmarking with similar industries can provide valuable feedback to determine if the certification body is a good fit for your organization.

The organization has the right to review resumes of potential auditors and even interview them. This step is frequently overlooked, but can provide the organization a level of confidence with not only the auditor's knowledge but also how the auditor might approach an audit. Different organizations may need different types of auditors. Some organizations prefer a direct approach; others want to ensure that employees will be made to feel comfortable and not overwhelmed with the audit process.

Schedule audits

An organization should choose the dates for audits by the certification body early in the process. This is to ensure that the auditor of choice is available when needed. This includes the document review and initial visit, pre-assessment (if selected), and the initial audit. This will give the organization a date to plan for as well as ensure that the auditor is available. Early planning is also beneficial for the organization to ensure that key personnel are available for the audit.

Some organizations choose to bypass the pre-assessment and go straight to the certification audit. An organization should carefully weigh the benefits vs. the cost of this decision. Organizations that have made a significant amount of change usually find a pre-assessment helpful.

Complete corrective action

The certification body will identify nonconformities during each audit. It's critical that this feedback is considered to its fullest since it could lead to certification denial during the initial audit. Although the organization isn't required to provide corrective action responses to the auditor during the initial stages, the organization must demonstrate that correction or corrective actions have been taken.

Initial audit

During this audit, the certification body reviews the organization's QMS. During this audit, nonconformances will be categorized into two types of findings: major and minor. Major nonconformances require a follow-up audit prior to an organization being recommended for certification. Responses are required for minor nonconformances prior to a certificate being issued to the organization.

How does an organization know it's ready for the initial audit?

Many of the steps throughout the process, such as the document review, initial visit, and pre-assessment, are designed to help an organization know whether it's ready for an initial audit.

There are certain checks and balances that an organization can ensure are in place as well:
- Completion of at least one management review.
- Completion of a minimum of one round of internal audits with corrective actions issued and verified.
- Documented information to be maintained and retained in place.
- Data and records sufficient to indicate full implementation of key processes.
- Quality objectives established and being monitored.
- Quality policy in place with employee awareness.

Certification decision

After the organization completes its responses to corrective actions for any nonconformances identified during the initial audit, the certification body will make a recommendation that the organization be certified. The certification body will provide the organization a certificate and information on how to use the certification mark.

Celebrate!

ISO 9001:2015 certification is an accomplishment to be celebrated. Each organization should have a celebration that is appropriate to the level of effort that was put forth by employees and the overall benefit of the certification to the organization. Celebrations can include T-shirts with the company logo, cake, tacos, or pizza parties. If the organization celebrates frequently, the level of celebration should also reflect the importance of achievement to employees. If you have many pizza parties, try to celebrate in a different manner to differentiate this achievement from others.

MAINTENANCE

ISO 9001:2015 implementation is a journey

Many organizations are so eager to get certified that when it's over, it's a relief and the organization relaxes to a level that may compromise its ability to sustain its certification. As part of the implementation plan, organizations should include a corresponding plan that will ensure that the organization will continue on its journey. This includes ensuring that there is adequate oversight of the QMS on an ongoing basis.

Frequently, the ISO 9001 implementation team has the support of their organization to go to ISO 9001 training. However, when implementation begins they struggle with having ongoing management commitment to make changes that will move the organization toward a goal of ongoing compliance or certification. There can be challenges with training new employees or persons who will have responsibility for the QMS.

Some organizations will find that resources are available during the initial implementation, but after the euphoria is gone, there isn't the same level of support from management. It's important to remember that ISO 9001:2015 requires an ongoing commitment by management and employees to ensure that the QMS is still capable of achieving its intended results and is able to sustain the certification.

Keys to sustaining a QMS

- *Commitment of leadership.* Timely management reviews, support of internal audits, continual improvement
- *Resources.* Internal auditors, document coordinators
- *Engagement.* Regular engagement with process owners to ensure ongoing maintenance and improvement

Each organization needs to evaluate whether it is ready to make the commitment and provide the infrastructure needed to support the implementation after certification is achieved.

Chapter 17

Procedure Writing

The consideration of documented procedures has been an integral part of ISO 9001 since its first publication in 1987. ISO 9001:2015 introduces the concept of documented information including many different types of documents that are part of any quality management system (QMS). This includes documented procedures. ISO 9000:2015 defines "procedure" as a "specified way to carry out an activity or a process." It also states that "procedures can be documented or not."

In certain cases, it's critical for the operations of an organization to document one or more activities of a process. At other times, an organization may determine the entire process needs to be documented. In subclause 4.4.2 of ISO 9001:2015, the extent of documented information is up to the process itself. This means that whoever is responsible or owns a process should determine which documented information is critical for its operations. This includes documented procedures. The organization might also need to consider whether there are customer or statutory and regulatory requirements for specific documented procedures. Regardless of the reason, when documented procedures are created, the organization should ensure that the documented information adds value.

For example, the owner of a small restaurant can have a specific way to prepare "eggs topped with a spicy tomato sauce." He is the only person doing the cooking so in this case a documented procedure would most likely not be required.

If this restaurant was franchised in several states with a chef responsible for the creation of all the dishes on the menu, it might determine that a documented procedure or work instruction and a recipe must be used for preparing this food dish by the cooks at each restaurant.

In today's business world, there are information systems and enterprise resource planning (ERP) systems that have embedded the way to perform an activity. For example, an inventory module has a menu of different actions. Persons in the receiving area can access the menu, which includes an inventory update screen. The person can upload the part number, quantity, and other relevant information to the system. Actions that the employee can perform may be based on security protocols. In this case, the embedded logic in the ERP system most likely wouldn't require documented procedures.

Developing documented information is something that not every organization implementing ISO 9001:2015 will address in the same way. This section will assist organizations that rely on documented procedures or equivalent documents such as visual aids or standardized work for the operation of their QMS.

GETTING STARTED

Although ISO 9001:2015 doesn't require specific documented information that would be consistent with procedures, it's entirely reasonable to think that documented procedures would be required for an effective and sustainable QMS. It's important that organizations consider when procedures might be needed to maintain the integrity of the QMS.

Procedure writing is a critical part of every business. If an organization doesn't have procedures that can be understood or followed, there's the potential for mistakes that could cause nonconforming product, safety issues, or unmet customer expectations. That's why it's important to write procedures that are not only understood but that also cannot be *misunderstood*.

Before starting down the path of writing procedures, remember that there are a number of myths that exist about procedures. These myths can either lead an organization down the wrong path or cause it to fall into a false sense of security. Figure 17.1 outlines two of the most common myths.

Each organization needs to keep these myths in mind to make the right decisions about documenting procedures. The organization must also avoid documenting so many processes that the business cannot operate or is inefficient.

Determine if your organization needs documented procedures

It's important to emphasize that most compliance standards don't prescribe the level of detail to which instructions are written. There are typically some minimum requirements that must be considered. ISO 9001:2015 doesn't require specific documented procedures. However, if documented procedures exist, they must be followed and are subject to audit. For that reason, caution should be exercised in ensuring that your QMS doesn't become bureaucratic or difficult to follow. For ex-

Figure 17.1 — Procedure Writing: Myth vs. Reality

Myth	Reality
ISO 9001:2015 doesn't require organizations to have documented procedures.	It is true that there are no procedural requirements in ISO 9001:2015. However, organizations must determine what level of documentation is necessary for their organization to ensure that processes achieve the desired results and employees are able to meet requirements consistently.
If I use/copy procedures from another ISO-certified QMS, it will be easier to get certified.	Copying procedures from another system will work only if your organization plans to perform the task in exactly the same manner. It's better to use examples from other organizations as a benchmark or a starting point for your organization.

ample, if a procedure says you have to obtain five signatures for a purchasing requisition to be approved, you have to comply because it's a procedural requirement. However, due to past experience, findings from assessments, or corrective actions, it may be quite necessary to obtain these signatures. This procedural requirement would then be subject to audit. Hence, it's always a balance of documenting enough to ensure clarity and consistency while also ensuring that it's not over-documented and a source of errors or inefficiencies.

Considerations for an organization determining whether it needs a documented procedure include:
- Would the lack of a procedure adversely affect quality?
- Is the requirement global in nature and applicable to many employees?
- If the person who routinely performs this task isn't available, would another employee be able to adequately perform the task without a written procedure?

How much detail?

Once an organization determines that a documented procedure is needed, the next consideration is its level of detail. Organizations should consider the experience of the users, the frequency of the task being performed, and the criticality and complexity of the task.

Keep in mind that the level of detail goes directly to users. When a procedure doesn't have enough detail, the user may spend a lot of time looking for procedural details and feel pressed for time. When a procedure has too many details, the user may spend time reading non-value-added details. It may even be a source of confusion. This detracts from the user actually completing the task.

Procedure writers should exercise caution to avoid writing procedures that are too complex. When possible, procedures should be limited to three to five pages. These types of procedures are easier to read and more useful when searching for needed information. Limiting the number of pages can easily be achieved by focusing on a specific topic. Procedures that have many different concepts can lead to a heavy demand on the user and cause performance errors. If you can't limit a procedure to a manageable number of pages, it may be a good indication that it's too complex. It could be made into separate, more understandable procedures. It may also be reasonable to assume that supplemental training may be needed for complex procedures.

Procedure writers should also limit cross-references to other procedures. When one procedure references another and subsequently leads to another procedure, users will become frustrated and quit looking for the information they need.

Experience of users

When a procedure writing team gets started, it must gather as much information as possible about potential users. This includes the training level of the users and how long the user has or will perform a specific job activity. The procedure only needs to provide enough detail to ensure that the task is performed accurately and efficiently. It's important to note that procedures need to be written for the user with the least amount of experience.

Frequency of the task

Some tasks in an organization are performed every day; other tasks are performed once or twice a year. Additionally, the same task may be performed at different frequencies by different people. There are some tasks that certain employees perform on a daily basis; other employees may perform the same tasks only occasionally. This makes writing a balanced documented procedure more challenging. If you write for employees who perform the task daily, they will tend not to refer to the procedure once they're trained. Therefore, the focus can be more on ensuring that the person who performs the task less frequently has the level of detail necessary to perform the task.

The following can typically be applied based on the frequency that a task is performed.

- *Frequent tasks.* Low level of detail required.
- *Infrequent tasks.* High level of detail required.

Complexity of the task

Procedure writers should also consider the complexity of the task. Complex tasks are typically more likely to be performed inaccurately and incompletely than simple tasks. For example, it's more likely that a procedure would be needed for how to control nonconforming product or perform a specific inspection test than to fill out a simple form. As the procedure owner, you need to interview users to get an idea of the level of detail needed. Procedure owners also need to be conscious of including steps that seem natural to experienced users but may be unknown to novice users.

How critical is the task?

When determining if a procedure is needed, consideration should also be given to the potential consequences if the actions of the task result in noncompliance or a nonconformity. Critical tasks might include those that could end in personal injury, equipment damage, or significant product loss. Each of these tasks would be an indicator for a higher level of detail in a documented procedure.

Once an organization determines that it needs documented procedures and the level of detail that should be included, the documents must meet the requirements in subclause 7.5, Documented information. Some of the needed controls for procedures can also be implemented as best business practices. Organizations should consider the following:

- *Controls for approval.* What mechanisms are used to ensure that the procedure is reviewed for adequacy prior to use? Approval of a procedure is typically the "sign-off" by the procedure owner. Additionally, some organizations have peer reviews as part of the approval process. These may be used to determine cross-functional suitability or other change management aspects prior to the formal approval. Although many organizations require multiple signature levels for approval, ISO 9001:2015 only requires that the approval process be documented. Organizations that use fewer signature levels find that their procedures have shorter cycle times to release a document. The key is to assign the right approver.
- *Review and approval.* When it comes to reviewing procedures, many organizations require some type of ongoing review cycle. However, this cycle differs from one organization to another. Organizations typically set a cycle from one to three years. ISO 9001:2015 requires that documents be reviewed as necessary. A simple approach for implementing this requirement is to state in the documented procedure that owners are responsible for reviewing procedures when process changes are made. The documented procedure must also address what

approvals are required when changes are made. This is usually the same person who owns the procedure.
- *Identification and description.* Organizations must determine how their documented procedures would be identified. Many organizations are familiar with using revision levels such as "Document 123, Revision A." Although this method is acceptable, organizations may choose to implement a simpler version, such as the date of the procedure. With the growing availability of electronic information, many organizations are making only the most current version available electronically. Organizations that use this technique must make sure that previous versions of electronic procedures are maintained. This is accomplished with some type of archive that only the person responsible for maintaining controls of documented procedures can access.

    Another method for controlling the versions of procedures is to choose a date when the procedures become obsolete or paper versions are considered working copies. Many organizations will use a footer on their document that states something such as the following:
    - ✓ Electronic versions of this document take precedence over printed versions.
    - ✓ Valid through date

- *Versions available where used.* Organizations must ensure that documented procedures are available where and when needed. When an organization determines what method it will use to ensure that documents are available at points of use, it might consider the following, specifically for electronic documents:
    - ✓ Availability of computers for employees to access (e.g., for employees that don't work on-site)
    - ✓ Return on investment for implementing an electronic system
    - ✓ How obsolete documents and/or versions will be controlled

Maintaining your procedures

Once documented procedures exist, they must be maintained. Many organizations establish strong procedures during the early stages of implementation but struggle with keeping them current and relevant.

At first glance, your procedure system may appear strong. After further review, the system may show signs of fatigue. In fact, there are several reasons that an organization may want to do a comprehensive review of procedures:

- Procedures were written when there was a different workload. This might include growth in the organization through employees or product lines.
- Changes in organization structure or complexity, such as mergers, acquisitions, or significant staff changes.

- The organization begins to see an increase in the number of findings. This can be an indication that the procedures are not current or correct.
- There is a shift in user experience. The organization may have had a shift in employees from those who have been with the organization for a significant amount of time to a large number of new hire employees.

WRITING PROCEDURES

Not only is it important to have the right level of detail in documented procedures, but they also must be developed in a manner that adds value to your organization.

Assign the right procedure owner

Having the right procedure owner assigned to document a process is critical to the accurate documentation and success of the QMS. Each organization should develop responsibilities for their procedure owners that make sense to them. Because procedure owners are the gatekeepers to the management system, they should exhibit the following characteristics:

- *Subject matter expert.* The procedure owner needs be perceived as the person who has the organizational authority for the subject matter or knows the most about the topic he or she is writing about. If the procedure owner doesn't have the ability to set policy for specific requirements, he or she isn't the right owner.
- *Technical accuracy of procedures.* Procedure owners, in addition to writing and/or approving procedures, must ensure that the procedure is correct and can be followed.
- *Review/validate documentation to requirements.* Procedure owners need to follow up and make sure that the requirements have been written clearly and are understood. This can be done by having other employees review or walk through the procedure.
- *Integrating change.* When the organization receives new or revised requirements, the procedure owner is responsible for making sure this change is adequately integrated into the procedure.

Sometimes employees feel uncomfortable writing procedures. In this scenario, top management needs to provide a resource to help the employee write the procedure. If you use someone other than the subject matter expert to write the procedure, it's critical that users verify/validate the procedure prior to publication.

Form good teams

Procedure owners can write procedures on their own, but some procedures are naturally complex in nature or cross department lines. In this case, a team might be better suited for writing the procedure. Procedures written by teams also encourage buy-in by all users and ensure that the process is correctly documented.

Train procedure owners/teams

The procedure owners and critical team members need to be trained on the procedure format that the organization selects. This includes any writing styles, formats to be followed, and required approvals. This training provides consistency among different procedure writers and the final output.

Know requirements

The procedure owners need to know the requirements they are responsible for documenting. This could include ISO 9001:2015 requirements, customer requirements, laws (e.g., statutory and regulatory requirements), internal company requirements, or other compliance standards.

Map the process

Process mapping is not a requirement of ISO 9001:2015, other compliance documents, or for writing procedures. Regardless, many organizations find this tool an efficient way to document their operations. In fact, some organizations use these process maps as the documented procedure itself. When mapping, the following should be kept in mind:
- *Know where your process begins and ends.* This helps reduce redundant procedures or requirements from owner to owner.
- *Use a cross-functional team.* This helps the procedure owner with knowing all of the steps of the process are addressed.
- *Map your process without looking at existing documentation.* This keeps the procedure writing team from only focusing on those steps that have already been documented.

Gap analysis

Once the process is mapped, the procedure owner and/or team needs to determine if a procedure is required, keeping in mind the criteria discussed previously.

If the organization has existing procedures, the procedure owner needs to conduct a gap analysis to identify whether there are any contradictions between the process map and existing procedures. Based on the complexity of the process and competence of the personnel, procedures may not be required.

Procedure owners need to remember that the failure to understand the relationship of their process to other processes can lead to duplication, omission, or conflict. The key to success is to do your homework prior to beginning documentation.

Drafting the procedure

From the time we are in elementary school, we are taught to be creative in our writing. We shouldn't start paragraphs with the same words, and we should use different language to describe similar situations. When it comes to drafting procedures, this couldn't be further from the truth.

Procedure writing is not creative writing. Wherever possible, similar language should be used for ease of understanding by users. When considering a word choice, procedure writers should also consider the user's ability, experience, and reading levels. The simplest word choice should be used wherever possible, except where standard terms or technical words are necessary to define or clarify the subject.

Procedure writers should also be careful to avoid audit traps by not using ambiguous or prescriptive words. These words can be considered absolutes. For example, if a procedure states that something needs to be done "every" time, there is no flexibility even when there might be good rationale for not completing the task. Examples of these words include, but are not limited to:

- Should
- Significant
- As appropriate
- All
- Never
- Might
- Avoid
- As necessary
- May
- As required

Other tips

Procedure writers often have a tendency to write a procedure the way they think it needs to be written. They omit steps because they think they're known. Listed below is a list of questions to consider to mitigate these traps. These questions can also be used when writing procedures for others or when reviewing procedures for accuracy. They frequently assist with eliminating steps that have been forgotten, reducing bureaucracy, or making sure procedures are flexible enough to address unique situations.

- What do you do?
- What are the steps that you follow?
- Are you able to do it the way you define it?
- Is it the right way to do it?
- Does it always happen that way?
- How does your next customer (internal) react when you do this step/don't do this step?
- What happens next?
- Who does that step?
- Does it really happen this way?
- Does something happen before this step?
- When everything goes wrong, what happens?
- Have you included administrative issues and steps (e.g., paperwork)?
- When you have a rush job, what do you do?

VERIFYING PROCEDURES

Procedure writers should allow time after drafting to review procedures. Verifying procedures typically relates to a desktop review. Procedure owners should keep in mind that trying to objectively review a procedure immediately after its creation is more difficult. It reduces the chances of being an objective evaluator because the ideas developed are still fresh. For this reason, the writer may need a "cooling off" period to objectively evaluate a message. The procedure owner may also want to engage an independent reviewer.

Quality of procedures

The quality of procedures can give an impression to third-party auditors, customers, or other interested parties of the level of attention the organization gives to the QMS. Procedures with typos and formatting errors are indicators that an organization isn't adequately reviewing its documents or taking care to ensure they are correct. Procedure owners should review their procedures to avoid these types of errors prior to publication. Items to review when verifying documents include:

- Ensure procedure format has been followed (formatting errors removed/corrected).

- Language is clear and concise.
- Terms are defined.
- Documents are spellchecked.
- Electronic documents can be viewed through delivery software, including diagrams and maps.
- Review references to forms, procedures, reports, and records to verify that they:
  - ✓ Exist, are standardized, and correct.
  - ✓ Exactly match numbers and formats of the referenced document.
  - ✓ Appear in the document (there is no need to list documents that are not directly referenced in the document).
  - ✓ Validate positions and/or departments referenced in the procedure.

Process validation

It's important that procedures be evaluated by users with different experience levels to determine if the process can be followed as written.

There are several techniques that a procedure owner can use when validating procedures:

- *User review.* Users of the procedure follow the procedure to determine if it is correct.
- *Walk through the process.* Step through the actual procedure in the work environment where it's going to be used.
- *Structured reading.* Compare the draft to objective criteria. Audit your draft against criteria.

Provide training

Before a validated procedure is released, employees must be trained so they can follow it. Consider the following training levels based on the nature of the change:

- *Formal training.* This type of training is typically provided for new processes or for users with limited experience.
- *Information sharing.* Some procedures may require that you notify users that there is a change to a document but the change can be understood without formal training. In this situation, an e-mail to the users asking them to review the procedure will suffice.
- *Read only.* No notification is necessary. Users can review procedures at their convenience.

Integrating change

One of the most important methods of maintaining the integrity of the business management system and procedures is managing change when it occurs.

Changes that need to be made to procedures can be driven by different reasons:
- *New requirements.* Customer, ISO 9001, ISO 14001, laws, or other compliance documents
- *Audit findings.* Procedure doesn't reflect current work practices.
- *New program implementation.* Software or product line
- *Process improvement.* New activities resulting from continual improvement teams
- *Work activities.* Cannot be conducted according to existing procedures.

In all of these scenarios, it's important to remember that wherever possible changes should be planned, coordinated with other procedure owners where other procedures could be affected, and that the appropriate level of training is provided.

Once the change is identified there are several steps that a procedure owner should take:

1. *Conduct a gap analysis of existing procedures.* Consider whether this is the way the organization does business. Does it meet customer and other requirements? Does it contradict other existing procedures?
2. *Determine if change is required.* This could include determining where the change fits, if it exists already, or if it is really needed.
3. *Conduct interviews/validate with users.* Experienced users can identify potential problems. Novice users can identify the need for additional detail.
4. *Write change.* Actually draft the words of the change.
5. *Coordinate change with other procedure owners.* Consider the effect on other users and make sure these procedure owners revise their documents as necessary.
6. *Provide appropriate level of training to users.* This training needs to be based on the effect of the change on users.
7. *Communicate thoroughly.* It's important to communicate to all affected persons throughout the process of making the change.

DEVIATING FROM PROCEDURES

Organizations should consider how they will handle situations where employees cannot follow procedures for one reason or another. Although it would never be the preference of the organization to deviate from controlled procedures, at times it may be necessary. Having this mechanism in place could allow the organization to avoid having audit traps. In addition, if this system is in place and documented, deviations can be controlled.

A documented procedure is not required. A process must be established that identifies the controls for potential deviation. The organization may want to implement a system that considers the following:
- What criteria must the deviation meet in order to be considered?
- Will it allow deviations on a temporary basis (60 or 90 days)?
- How is the deviation controlled (formal procedure system or other method)?
- Who approves the deviation?
- How is the deviation recalled upon termination?

IDENTIFYING GAPS TO PROCEDURES

Gaps to procedures can be found in many different ways. To find them, employees must be fully engaged. The employees are ultimately responsible for stopping work when they cannot follow procedures because they cannot find a procedure or a procedure is incorrect.

Other ways that gaps can be identified include:
- Audits (internal, customer, third party)
- Self-assessment by procedure owner
- Implementation of new requirements
- Implementation of a pilot program in a specific area/department

Procedure writing is one of those things in business that we think anyone can do. In reality, procedure writing is an art form. A well-written procedure should:
- Include the right amount of detail so employees can follow the process.
- Limit the amount of detail to avoid complicated instructions that employees cannot follow.
- Assign the person who understands the process the best.

Finding the right balance in your organization will not only ensure that work is being performed according to requirements but also that the procedures add value to the business.

CHAPTER 18

Internal Audit Process

Internal audits are a requirement of ISO 9001:2015. They can be implemented with a basic approach that meets the intent of the standard or systematically to help the organization improve. This chapter provides a general framework for conducting internal audits and includes the different stages of the internal audit process as well as tips on to how to conduct more effective audits. Don't use this chapter without considering the requirements for internal audits found in ISO 9001:2015, clause 9, Performance evaluation. ISO 19011, Guidelines for auditing management systems, also provides guidance on how to implement an internal audit program.

Figure 18.1 illustrates the steps in an internal audit process. Some of these stages could be completed in a different sequence or combined together. The key is to establish a process that works for your organization and drives consistency among internal audits.

DEVELOP AN INTERNAL AUDIT SCHEDULE

The organization needs to plan the internal audits for the year at a specific point in time. The frequency of how often and when to conduct the audits is up to the organization. Consider the complexity of the process as well as past performance when scheduling. Performance might be reflected through objectives or the results from the previous audit.

Auditors should be deliberately assigned to specific audits on the internal audit schedule. Whenever possible, auditors should not audit their own work. In situations when this isn't possible, specifically for small and medium enterprises, impartiality of the audit process should still be maintained. This could include using a

Figure 18.1	Internal Audit Process
Schedule internal audits.	
Initiate the audit.	
Conduct document review.	
Develop checklist (if used).	
Schedule audit.	
Conduct opening meeting.	
Conduct audit.	
Develop report.	
Conduct closing meeting.	
Follow-up corrective actions.	

team to conduct the audit or having a manager review the internal audit report to ensure that it is objective.

Organizations need to ensure that auditors meet the competence requirements and that documented information is being retained to provide objective evidence.

INITIATE THE AUDIT

Internal audits tend to be more informal than second- or third-party audits. Therefore, the basic steps that are part of initiating the audit are often overlooked. This stage should focus on developing the audit objective. For internal audits, it's possible that the objective could be the same for every audit. It could simply state that the objective is to evaluate the organization's QMS for conformance to ISO 9001:2015 requirements, statutory and regulatory requirements, and customer requirements. Some organizations use internal audits to assess conformance to more than one standard, so the internal audit might also include evaluation of conformance to other standards such as ISO 14001:2015.

The internal auditor should review the results from the previous audit to determine areas that need to be included in the audit for follow-up. This might include assessing the effectiveness of any actions taken as corrective action on nonconformities identified during the last audit.

The audit scope should be determined during this initiation stage. This might have been determined when establishing the internal audit schedule. However, it should be confirmed by determining the processes and activities, departments, and physical locations to be audited when there is more than one site. The duration of the audit as well as the time it will be conducted should also be established.

CONDUCT DOCUMENT REVIEW

This step is focused on being prepared for the internal audit. Many internal auditors take a minimal approach to this stage because they believe they are familiar enough with the organization not to conduct this review. In fact, some internal auditors simply audit off of memory and not to requirements.

Prior to actually conducting the audit, the internal auditor should review any necessary documented information. This could include documented procedures and policies, statutory and regulatory requirements, specific documented information that is being retained as objective evidence that a requirement is being fulfilled, any manuals that document business practices, results from previous audits, and requirements from existing standards.

It's possible that some organizations may have a minimal amount of documentation based on the size of the organization or the complexity of the processes. In this case, the internal auditor should prepare questions to ask to confirm conformance.

The internal auditor will need to ask questions about how the processes operate. This could be done at the management level or with process owners and confirmed with those who actually perform the process. The actual work should conform to the process that was explained during the interview. If confirmation cannot be made, then a nonconformity should be raised.

Reviewing documented information prior to the internal audit helps to ensure a current understanding of the organization. However, it shouldn't be used as the sole means of conducting the audit because this document review doesn't provide objective evidence that the documented information has been effectively implemented.

DEVELOP A CHECKLIST OR SAMPLING PLAN

Checklists aren't a requirement for conducting ISO 9001:2015 internal audits. However, many organizations choose to use a checklist to conduct internal audits. There are a variety of reasons for using checklists, including the lack of experience of the internal auditor, as a reference to trigger questions, to help plan the audit, as a document to record results, to help manage time during the audit, and as a tool that gives a consistent approach during the internal audit.

There are two types of checklists. The first is used by all of the internal auditors. To be most effective, it should include all of the relevant requirements including ISO 9001:2015, customer, statutory and regulatory, and internal documented information (procedures).

The second type of checklist is audit specific. With this type of checklist, the internal auditor prepares a list of questions to ask based on the area being audited and the relevant requirements in the area.

If checklists will be used to assist in the internal audit process, the checklists should include specific evidence that has been reviewed in order to avoid a "check the box" audit.

Internal auditors should be trained on how to use checklists or they can lose their effectiveness.

Checklists can be intimidating to the auditee or too narrow in scope to identify problem areas. If internal auditors become too reliant on them, they might be unable to improvise and audit an area that isn't included in the checklist.

Whether checklists are used or not, the internal audit needs to focus on obtaining evidence of conformance. Audit techniques should be consistently reviewed and modified as internal auditors gain experience or the organization learns what works best.

OPENING MEETING

Many organizations skip opening meetings for internal audits. They view them as too formal and not necessary. However, this part of the process helps to set the tone of the importance of the internal audit process. In addition, in some larger organizations it's possible that the auditee may not know the internal auditor, so the opening meeting can help facilitate introductions.

Some organizations—specifically small organizations—might determine that an opening meeting isn't necessary. If this decision is made, then at a minimum, an e-mail should be sent out that includes the information that would have been discussed at the meeting.

Prior to the opening meeting, the internal auditor should have developed the audit schedule and selected the processes, areas, and departments to audit. This information should be reviewed along with the audit objectives and scope of the audit. The internal auditor should introduce him or herself and any team members.

The internal auditor should establish the time he or she wishes to conduct the audit. This time should be agreed upon during the opening meeting. It's important that this time is mutually agreeable to all parties involved to complete the audit on time. Emphasis should be placed on the need to limit interruptions during the audit. Internal audits are frequently difficult to conduct because auditees are easily distracted. They might leave to attend a meeting, handle an issue, or simply not wish to participate.

It should be understood that unplanned circumstances can arise during the audit, but these should be limited. At the same time, it's important for internal auditors to realize that they can't expect auditees to be available if they arrive unannounced. This is one of the reasons why audit planning is so critical.

Although internal auditors are part of the organization, issues related to confidentiality can still come into play. For example, the internal auditor may need to access the training records for other employees and in some cases actually see employees' personnel records. Many organizations are reluctant to share this information. In cases where these types of records are accessed, it should be emphasized that the information will be treated as confidential.

If the internal auditor is conducting the audit at a different geographic location than his or her regular office, he or she should let the auditee know of any resource needs. This could include an office and access to online systems. However, this most likely would have been agreed to during the planning stage.

The internal auditor should explain any techniques that will be used during the audit, including interviews and sampling methods. This helps to manage expectations and helps to gain buy-in on the results and output of the audit.

Communication during the internal audit process is key to avoiding an adversarial relationship. Internal auditors should indicate to the auditees during the opening meeting how they will keep them informed. For shorter audits, it's not necessary to have opening meetings, but to avoid potential disagreements in the closing meeting, it's recommended that any nonconformities that are determined during the audit are immediately shared with the manager, supervisor, or process owner.

CONDUCT THE AUDIT

After the opening meeting, it's time to actually conduct the audit. During the planning and initiation stages, the auditor reviews documented information and relevant requirements for the organization. It's now time to confirm conformance to these requirements.

Internal audits are conducted on a sampling basis, which means not every possible example in every possible area of the organization is assessed. The sample size should be larger than one if there are more samples available. Some internal auditors will establish their sample size during the planning stage while others may make a determination based on the results. The internal auditor may want to consider expanding the sample size if a nonconformity is determined. This allows a determination of whether the nonconformity is an isolated or systemic issue.

Results should be based upon evidence, not opinion. For example, an auditor might believe that a process isn't being followed either through working knowledge of the organization or an overall feeling. However, there needs to be evidence, gathered either through interviews or records, that a nonconformity exists. Additionally, the internal auditor shouldn't take conformance at face value. If an auditee explains an activity that demonstrates conformance, such as a completed document, the auditor should ask to see the record of the activity to verify conformance.

Evidence of conformance can be gained through various methods. These include interviews, observations in the area, documented information, customer complaints and feedback, and evaluations for external providers.

CONDUCTING AN INTERVIEW

One of the most critical components of internal auditing is the interview. Interviews are one of the best ways to get information about the level of conformance in the QMS. Therefore, extraordinary efforts should be taken to ensure the process is as effective as it can be. This requires certain auditor etiquette whether you know the person you are interviewing or not. Of course, when the auditor and the auditee know each other, it's reasonable that some of the steps might not be required.

- *Introduce yourself.* If you already know the person, introduce yourself in the context of the internal audit process. Explain the purpose of the interview and the reason you will be taking notes. Whenever possible, the interviewee's supervisor should observe the interview to ensure there is an understanding of any nonconformity that might come up and to provide support.
- *Make the interviewee comfortable.* It's OK to have a brief conversation about something that's not audit related to break the ice. If you know the interviewee, it could be inquiring about his or her family or a hobby. If you don't know the auditee, you could inquire about a picture in the area or a T-shirt with a sports team's logo they might be wearing. Whenever possible, the auditor and auditee should be at the same level. If the auditee is seated, then ask for a chair to eliminate a sense of domination by standing over him or her.
- *Interview the person in his or her work environment.* This is especially true when the person being interviewed is providing the product or delivering the service, but this approach should be used for all potential auditees. It's possible that some interviews could be conducted in a conference room where documented information is available online. However, it's typically easier for interviewees to access information from their own workstations where they are familiar with computer shortcuts and mapped drives.
- *Use language that's familiar to the person being interviewed.* ISO 9001:2015 sometimes uses language that doesn't match the language an organization uses to refer to certain processes or activities. For example, an organization may

continue to use the word "supplier" and not "external provider" or it may use "documents" and "records" instead of "documented information." If the internal auditor uses unfamiliar language, the auditee might not understand the question being asked. Ensure the auditee upfront that you are happy to rephrase any question if necessary.

- *Ask relevant questions.* The questions should be appropriate to the person being interviewed. The auditor shouldn't ask the auditee to explain a process that he or she isn't involved in. If the auditor realizes that an auditee doesn't have the necessary background to answer a question after it has been asked, it should be withdrawn.
- *Ask questions that provide information.* The internal auditor should ask questions that require an explanation (open questions) as opposed to questions with yes or no answers (closed questions). Avoid asking leading questions that provide the evidence as an internal auditor based on either your knowledge of the process or documented information. Here are examples of each:
  - ✓ *Closed.* Do you control nonconforming output?
  - ✓ *Open.* Show me how you control nonconforming output.
  - ✓ *Leading.* So you control nonconforming output by identifying it and segregating it in a red bin, correct?

- *Observe.* Many interviewees get nervous when questions are being asked. A good technique to use with nervous interviewees is to simply observe them performing the activity in question. This can provide a great deal of information about the level of nonconformity. The internal auditor can observe using standardized work or a work order and then ask follow-up questions as needed.
- *Use good time management.* If a specific time has been scheduled to conduct the audit, show up on time and only stay the amount of time allocated unless a longer stay is agreed to. If there is an urgent activity in the area, such as meeting a customer deadline, it might be necessary to reschedule. It's important to balance between urgent business needs without compromising the integrity of a robust and timely audit.
- *Avoid organization politics.* The internal auditor shouldn't engage in gossip about internal issues and let these influence the audit. At times, there might be a need for the internal auditor to audit someone that they have previously had a conflict with. Whenever possible, another internal auditor should be used. However, if this cannot be coordinated, then the internal auditor should focus on ensuring that the results are based on evidence reviewed.
- *Avoid assumptions.* When interviewing a person that the internal auditor knows, avoid the philosophy that since the interviewee is known the process is being

followed. The internal auditor is required to maintain impartiality and audit as if the person and process are unknown.

- *Focus the interview on the process and not the person.* At times during the interview process, a nonconformity is identified. This can result in the interviewee becoming uncomfortable and either assuming the blame or feeling like he or she will be blamed. The internal auditor should continually assure the auditee that the process is being audited not the person.
- *If a nonconformity is identified, it should be discussed at the time of discovery.* Ensure the auditee understands the issue. Reviewing the nonconformity at a later time doesn't allow for discussion and clarification of the issue. At times, the auditee might have additional information that could clarify the nonconformity. It also helps to ensure that there is better understanding of any issues prior to the closing meeting.
- *Thank the auditee.* Being audited is never a fun activity. Make sure you thank the person and provide positive feedback when warranted. This could include complimenting the auditee on an activity that he or she did well or the way questions were answered during the interview.

Every internal auditor will need to develop his or her own unique style for conducting audits. However, this is an area where practice makes perfect. So, it makes sense that the auditor might need to practice before conducting an internal audit without assistance. Therefore, conducting mock audits as a step in an internal auditor achieving competence helps to ensure that auditors are well-equipped.

AUDIT RESULTS

The purpose of an internal audit is to verify conformance. However, there is a tendency to focus on nonconformance. This can be a result of the audit, but it shouldn't detract from the positive areas of conformance.

During or after the interview activity, the internal auditor will have results from the evidence that has been reviewed. Any conclusions that are reached need to be based on this evidence and not the auditor's opinion. Nonconformities must reference a specific requirement—customer, statutory, regulatory, ISO 9001, other standard, or internal documented information—to be valid. If there is no requirement, there is no nonconformity. In this case, the internal auditor might document an observation or opportunity for improvement.

It's important that the internal auditor share any potential nonconformities during the internal audit with the auditee so that there are no surprises. This provides an opportunity to resolve any issues or get additional objective evidence if needed. There may be times where the internal auditor needs to confer with either an audit team or manager. If a final conclusion cannot be made then, the internal auditor should provide the initial conclusions and indicate the results are pending discussion. If a conclusion is made at the time of the interview, then acknowledgment should be obtained from the auditee and the manager in the area if possible.

When a nonconformity is identified, a standard format should be used to consistently convey the results of the audit. Many organizations adopt a format that specifies the requirement that the organization isn't in conformance with, a statement of nonconformity, and the evidence.

The following is an example of a nonconformity that references the requirement and the evidence:
- *Requirement.* Procedure 123: The company president shall approve all customer contracts over $50,000.
- *Nonconformity.* The president is not approving contracts over $50,000 as required by procedure 123.
- *Evidence.* The following contracts over $50,000 were not approved by the president: contract 45678 and contract 12345.

The audit results will be included in an audit report.

AUDIT REPORT

The organization should establish a report format that is suitable to its operations. Reporting results is a requirement of ISO 9001:2015, but specific sections of information are not required. Sections that an organization might want to include in its audit report include:
- Executive summary
- Nonconformities
- Follow-up plan
- Noteworthy efforts
- Observations
- Opportunities for improvement

Some organizations choose to develop a format where the results are reported and where responses to any nonconformities can be made. Other organizations choose to use the checklist as their audit report. However, this format isn't very friendly for management or anyone else who is not familiar with how the checklist was developed or completed.

Creating a report format that includes a summary, such as the number of nonconformities and some general analysis of the results, provides an easy method for management to review audit results without the need to read the entire report. Some organizations choose to post internal audit reports in a system where anyone in the organization can access them, which provides an opportunity to take action in similar areas based on the audit results.

CLOSING MEETING

The purpose of the closing meeting is to review the audit results and ensure that there is agreement on any conclusions and the time frame required for corrective actions. At a minimum, auditees and members of management who will need to respond should be invited. In some cases, not all auditees may be able to attend, but whenever possible this helps to ensure a comprehensive review of the results.

A best management practice is for the internal auditor to provide a copy of the audit report to the participants prior to the closing meeting. This gives them time to review the information and be prepared with any additional information that might need to be provided at the meeting and eliminates surprises.

The lead internal audit report should review the audit results and present them in the context of the requirement, the determined nonconformity, and confirming evidence. Ideally, agreement should be achieved regarding audit results. However, if agreement isn't achieved, conflicting viewpoints should be captured in the meeting minutes.

Distribution of the audit report can be used in lieu of a closing meeting. However, the report should be acknowledged by the recipients to ensure the results are understood and acknowledged.

VIRTUAL AUDITING

As organizations obtain more technology and more employees work remotely, organizations need to consider alternative approaches to face-to-face audits that still add value.

To solve the issue of remote employees or locations, organizations are adopting remote or virtual auditing techniques. This type of audit allows the auditor to not be physically present with the auditee or at the location being audited. This is different than what is called a conference room audit, which is where an internal auditor conducts an audit from a conference room and does not visit other areas of the organization.

Remote auditing isn't appropriate for all types of internal audits, but in some cases it can be used where objective evidence is generally retained in an online system that can be accessed from any location. This could include design engineering, software, or some service organizations. Manufacturing processes would be difficult to audit remotely, but some of the support processes or service organizations could be audited in this manner.

During a remote audit, web meetings can be used to conduct the audit. The relevant persons of the organization should participate in interviews. In this scenario, the internal auditor is required to follow the same internal audit process with all of the same reporting requirements.

CHAPTER 19

Adding Value to the Quality Management System

The perceptions that come with a quality management system (QMS) are in many cases just that—perceptions. There is the perception that ISO 9001 adds costs and drives bureaucracy in organizations. These claims originated with the first version of ISO 9001 and have continued in some shape or form with every revision.

This chapter focuses on how to add value to your QMS by seeing it as a framework for doing business and not just a list of requirements. This can be accomplished by examining the methods used to meet requirements. This chapter will also provide details on how to manage costs—perceived and real—in the QMS.

ADDING VALUE WITH MANAGEMENT REVIEW

Progress has been made in recent years with understanding the integration of ISO 9001 requirements into the overall management system of the organization. However, there remains some level of referring to activities that relate to an ISO 9001 requirement as the "ISO system," implying that there is another system that addresses actual operations. Organizations that take this approach frequently treat certain activities as a rubber stamp, where the requirement is fulfilled but at no value to the organization.

ISO 9001's management review requirement outlines how the organization takes the results from analysis and evaluation, determines trends, and makes decisions about the performance and effectiveness of the QMS. If you review the list of inputs, these are typically issues that organizations routinely discuss. They're not something that is peculiar only to the QMS.

Most organizations would not independently call this type of meeting "management review." In fact, the methods that are used to conduct a management review, such as frequency and how the information is presented, can lead management to be discouraged with the process. Consider that when management review was first introduced as a concept in ISO 9001, the technology and the ability to analyze data were not what they are today. At that time, it might have taken an organization two or three weeks to gather the needed information for management review. In today's business environment, access to data that provides information on the effectiveness of the QMS is available almost instantaneously. Therefore, analyzing performance on a delayed time frame doesn't make sense to most organizations and leads to the impression that the management review activity doesn't add value.

Hearing someone in top management refer to management review as a waste of time or as an "ISO 9001 meeting" is a good indication that management review isn't adding value to the organization. This is because some organizations treat management review as separate from the meetings used to review the organization's performance. For example, an organization might conduct monthly business reviews where it analyzes the organization's performance, but once a year conducts a management review to meet the "ISO 9001 requirement." Some organizations consider management review as simply a report card of how the organization performed last year. This certainly isn't the spirit in which the requirement was planned.

Some organizations follow this path of implementation because it makes it easier to provide objective evidence that all of the necessary inputs and outputs have been addressed. Others use this approach because the person responsible for ensuring that the management review requirements are fulfilled isn't necessarily involved in existing "business" meetings. Other organizations don't want to maintain action items on a more frequent basis or simply don't understand that management review doesn't need to be separate from regular business activities.

ISO 9001:2015 references management review as an event that should be conducted in alignment with the strategic direction of the organization. This was incorporated in ISO 9001:2015 to emphasize that this meeting should not be separate and to imply integration into the business processes.

There are several actions the organization can take to add value to the management review process, including:

- *Engage management in establishing an approach for management review.* At times those involved in management review may not be aware of the purpose of management review or that there are options in conducting management review. One of the best options for engaging management is to determine what adds value to them. Consider gathering management together and discussing the management review requirements and let the management team determine an approach that would meet their needs.

- *Integrate management review inputs into existing meetings.* Determine if there are existing meetings that can be adapted to cover management review and if there are ways to ensure that the right people are involved to ensure requirements are met. Many organizations conduct regular organizational performance reviews where actions are taken on a timelier basis. Because these meetings are already required by management, this potentially eliminates the need to conduct a stand-alone management review. In this approach, organizations may conduct the reviews either daily or weekly. Some inputs might not be discussed at the same frequency as other inputs because information might not be updated so frequently. For example, the organization might discuss process performance and product conformity, which could include information about quality objectives such as on-time delivery or scrap on a daily basis, but only discuss information about external providers weekly. Other inputs that might be discussed less frequently include internal audits, changes in internal and external issues, and actions to address risks and opportunities.

    Some organizations supplement a daily or weekly meeting review with a periodic review where a more comprehensive review is conducted. Using this approach, the organization would look at trends over several months, allowing discussion of inputs that don't require as frequent review.

- *Share ownership of management review.* Many organizations fall into the trap of having quality professionals present all of the inputs to management review even if they're not the process owners. They may or may not have all of the necessary details and typically would not have decision-making authority. This can give the impression that management review is a quality initiative and not a review of the entire management system.

    When management review inputs are presented by the process owners, the emphasis is placed on reviewing the data and not because it's an ISO 9001:2015 requirement.

The key to increasing the value of management review is transitioning from the philosophy of something the organization has to do to something the organization wants to do by adopting practices that lead to this while still meeting the intent of the requirement. This can be done at no added cost and may ultimately lead to a reduction in meeting costs.

ADDING VALUE TO YOUR INTERNAL AUDIT PROCESS

There are many reasons to emphasize the value of internal audits: They identify areas of nonconformity and reduce the potential of customer dissatisfaction, they can help an organization ensure changes are effectively implemented, and they can confirm that the persons of the organization are performing their jobs according to established requirements. Let's look at how to add value to the internal audit process.

One of the ongoing discussions in the quality world revolves around the value of internal audits. Many of the viewpoints are derived from the fact that most organizations develop an internal audit program not because they want to but because they are *required* to. When an organization perceives that internal audits are simply an ISO 9001:2015 requirement, it considers them as causing more problems than solutions, thereby limiting the effectiveness of the internal audit process.

In addition to this perception, the organization might not see the value in the internal audit process due to the methods by which it has been established and are being maintained. Here are some of the common reasons an internal audit program may struggle and add to the paradigms that exist.

- *Internal auditors don't have enough time to conduct the audit.* In many organizations, internal auditing is performed as a part-time activity; therefore, time isn't always properly allocated to conduct the audit. In other cases, the organization simply doesn't schedule enough time for the audit. For example, some organizations will audit their entire system in one day, which might not be enough time based on the size of the organization or the number of persons assigned to conduct the audit. In these situations, the internal auditor might not go deep enough, thereby not identifying nonconformities in the organization and conducting a "check the box" audit.

  Organizations should ensure that internal auditors have the time to conduct audits separate from their daily work activities. They should also ensure that auditees make themselves available to allow for timely completion of audits.

- *The internal auditor hasn't received proper training.* Internal auditors should receive training in two different areas: requirements (e.g., ISO 9001, customer, regulatory) and conducting internal audits. Lack of training on requirements can lead to audit findings based on personal opinion instead of a specific requirement or documented information. There is also the potential for the auditor to write very basic nonconformities due to his or her level of understanding of the QMS, such as identifying an incorrect reference in a procedure.

  Although an incorrect reference in a procedure is technically a nonconformity, the time and effort of going through the corrective action process would not equal the severity of the nonconformity. Inadequate training on audit techniques can also lead to ineffective communication on the results of audits, which can frustrate the auditee. In fact, when the internal auditor doesn't communicate that a finding has been identified until the report is distributed, this can create an adversarial relationship and diminish the value of the audit for the organization.

It's important to realize that internal auditor training is an investment. Not all training needs to be classroom training, nor does it need to be provided by an outside source. Internal auditors can serve as audit team members prior to serving as an internal auditor themselves. However, because many organizations use internal auditors in a part-time role, they frequently don't have the experience in understanding a specific standard or set of requirements to deliver the training effectively. There are many resources available—many of which are available at no cost—that can provide internal auditors with information on how to conduct audits. One of the best resources available to internal auditors that are conducting ISO 9001 audits is the work developed by the Auditing Practices Group.

The Auditing Practices Group is an ad hoc group of QMS experts, auditors, and practitioners drawn from ISO/TC 176 (the committee responsible for the ISO 9000 standard series) and the International Accreditation Forum (IAF). It has developed a number of guidance papers and presentations that contain ideas, examples, and explanations about QMS auditing. These reflect the process-based approach that is essential for auditing to the requirements of an ISO 9001:2015-based QMS and provide methods not only on how to conduct audits, but also on how to consider specific requirements. These papers can be found at *www.iso.org/tc176/ISO9001AuditingPracticesGroup*.

To gain experience, internal auditors can also participate as guides during certification body activities. This provides the internal auditor an opportunity to learn methods for sampling and interview techniques.

- *Internal audit reports contain limited information.* Based on the level of detail in the internal audit report, there can be limited information that the organization can use to improve. There are a variety of reasons why internal audit reports don't contain the right amount of information, including lack of time by the internal auditor or a format that doesn't require that information be provided regarding conformance as well as nonconformance.

  When organizations choose to implement a checklist as their report, they might find that the internal auditor has only checked "yes" or "no" for conformance. With such limited information, the organization doesn't have an opportunity to make improvements. This type of report also makes it unclear as to whether the internal auditor sampled any processes or simply conducted a desktop review.

The organization should establish a report format that includes enough information to allow the reader to take any needed action.

Consider requiring an executive summary that provides quick details regarding the audit. This provides management the ability to review the information quickly and see the audit results at a higher level. The organization should also consider circulating the results of the audit report to other departments and managers. Providing audit reports for others to review allows employees to take proactive action in their respective work areas. It also provides an opportunity to eliminate a potential nonconformity before it occurs.

- *Communication during internal audits.* Sometimes organizations choose internal auditors not based on their ability but as fill-in work or as a reassignment when the employee isn't performing other duties. Organizations that make these types of assignments may find that the internal auditor doesn't have the right personality to conduct audits, which can result in adversarial relationships during the audit. This can ultimately lead to conflict and minimizes the opportunity to use internal audits to help the organization improve.

  Providing ongoing communication during the audit such as conducting an opening and closing meeting can help set the stage for open dialogue. Many organizations may think of these meetings as a luxury reserved for external audits, but the same benefits translate to the internal audit. The opening meeting helps those involved understand the process and scope for the internal audit. The closing meeting offers an opportunity to discuss the findings and ensure understanding of the issues by both the internal auditor and auditee. In addition, internal auditors should be trained to provide feedback to the auditee during the audit any time an issue is identified. The auditee shouldn't be surprised at the closing meeting with any results. Using these simple communication methods can improve value by eliminating misunderstandings and provide a method for partnering to improve the performance of the organization.

To develop an internal program that management and employees see as contributing to the business, it's important to identify issues that are within the organization's control and that it has the ability to change. In today's environment, where organizations continue to be conservative when managing costs, there might be a limited budget available to provide training or increase the number of auditors. However, there are some things an organization can do while minimizing the cost.

Develop an action plan to improve the internal audit process and add value to the organization. Without a plan, you won't know what needs to change, thereby minimizing your opportunity to improve. Don't assume you know what management and other internal auditor customers need. Conduct a brainstorming meeting and determine the expectations from management and then add these expectations to your plan. Once an approach to meeting expectations is developed, it's important to follow through with management to ensure enough time is available to conduct internal audits. Expectations can be set, but without the necessary resources, improvements cannot be made.

Organizations that experience tough economic times may reduce their internal audit program either by reducing the number of internal auditors or the number of audits conducted. They might also choose not to provide training on an ongoing basis to ensure that auditors have the right skills to provide audits. It's important to emphasize to the management team that internal audits become an important tool to ensure conformance when processes are being changed, employees are changing positions, and procedures are being modified. Instead of cutting internal audits, they should consider increasing them. When changes are made, the cost of an internal audit is minimal compared to the cost of a process change that doesn't meet customer expectations.

The organization can also conduct audits based on risk and using management to help develop the internal audit schedule to obtain their buy-in. Many organizations audit every department or every requirement in a specific standard during the calendar year. However, many standards, including ISO 9001:2015, indicate that internal audits can be scheduled taking into consideration the results of past audits and the importance of the area to the organization. Processes or departments that aren't performing well should be audited more frequently than organizations that are performing well. Processes related to providing the product or delivering the service are generally more critical to audit than management processes. If an organization is struggling to meet its internal audit schedule, considering risk in developing the schedule will allow more time in fewer areas, which will ensure the department is adequately covered.

Although there are many opportunities for the internal audit process to add value, the responsible parties for conducting audits should select and focus on a few key activities and then continue to improve. Internal audits are one of the cornerstones on which a management system is based. A little investment into creating an improved program can yield better results, thus improving value to the organization.

MANAGING COSTS IN YOUR QUALITY MANAGEMENT SYSTEM

Since ISO 9001 first came into existence, there have been claims related to the costs associated with conformance to the standard's requirements. These costs include the certification body performing a third-party audit and the associated travel expenses for the auditors. They might also be associated with the resources needed to perform activities such as internal auditing.

Audit expenses can also be "perceived" costs, which are typically associated with a requirement that the organization believes is a derivative of the QMS. An example of such costs is a belief that the QMS increases bureaucracy by adding requirements. It's frequently based on a philosophy that "ISO makes us do it." This is a lack of understanding that ISO 9001:2015 requirements simply provide a framework for the organization's QMS. There may also be a lack of understanding that ISO 9001:2015 doesn't prescribe the level of implementation or control for a specific requirement. Some of these specific requirements would still be expectations of customers or relevant interested parties even if the organization didn't implement ISO 9001:2015. Therefore, the true incremental costs of conformance to ISO 9001:2015 may be minimal.

With that said, today's business environment continues to drive a focus on managing costs. Organizations may be challenged with economic shortfalls due to lost business, which can result in layoffs or business decisions that can take their toll on the QMS.

When an organization is faced with financial problems, indirect costs are often scrutinized. These are frequently directed at employees as well as the cost of maintaining the ISO 9001:2015 certification.

Because the management team doesn't always have all the information related to real vs. perceived costs, steps should be taken to ensure the integrity of the QMS is maintained during economic challenges. First, make sure the management team understands the concerns with managing costs. Although quality professionals won't always be involved in decisions related to the budget, it's important for them to provide the background necessary to management so that they can make fact-based decisions. Doing this at a time when the organization is not faced with an economic challenge allows the information to be considered at a later time and not when the information could be perceived as defensive.

The following list includes tips to help manage costs in a QMS:

- *Help management understand the relationship between ISO 9001:2015 requirements and customer, regulatory, and statutory requirements.* ISO 9001:2015 requirements are just one type of requirement that an organization must meet.

    It's not always apparent to the management team that most if not all of the requirements in ISO 9001:2015 are either customer, statutory, or regulatory requirements. Depending on the organization, examples may include the cost of controlling nonconforming products or the cost of training employees to be competent in their respective jobs.

    Therefore, eliminating the ISO 9001:2015 certication doesn't always eliminate requirements or their associated costs. For example, ISO 9001:2015 requires the control of nonconforming outputs. Even if the ISO 9001:2015 requirements were not in place, the customer would have an expectation that these controls would be in place.

To help with understanding, the management team should be encouraged to read ISO 9001:2015. Providing examples to management of customer, statutory, and regulatory requirements compared to ISO 9001 requirements also helps to illustrate this. This basic understanding can help show the relationship and demonstrate that the third-party or certification body audits help to evaluate conformity to customer requirements.

- *Use caution when making decisions to reduce costs.* It's critical when managing costs that you don't arbitrarily make changes. It's understandable that organizations need to make adjustments to reduce costs. However, not analyzing or understanding these changes can potentially jeopardize an organization's ability to provide products and deliver services that meet customer requirements.

  For example, an organization could cut training costs by 25 percent. However, there could be some processes (e.g., departments) in the organization where there is a greater need for training than others. Yes, it requires more analysis but in this scenario you are more assured that necessary personnel received their recertification training.

  This same approach needs to be considered when reducing head count. Organizations need to consider what roles are needed. If an organization has a reduction in force and is focused on reducing indirect roles, which frequently include the quality organization, there is a potential that the level of resources cannot support the QMS.

- *Challenge your QMS to determine if it is over-implemented.* Although ISO 9001:2015, customer, statutory, and regulatory requirements cannot be eliminated, at times the methods used to implement these requirements increase costs. For example, documented information requires approval. However, it's up to your organization to determine the method of approval. It can be as simple as an online review or an e-mail message or as complicated as circulating the document for approval through three levels of management. As you look for opportunities to reduce costs, examine the requirements, review how you have implemented them, and then consider if there are methods of conformance that you have in place that could be simplified or streamlined. Many organizations have "lean" or continuous improvement departments that can help analyze the processes to streamline and find inefficiencies.

- *Conduct certification audits annually, wherever practical or possible.* Although the number of audit days doesn't decrease from an audit conducted every six months to once a year, savings on travel costs can be realized when you only pay for airfare and travel time once a year. As a reminder, audit days are mandated by the International Accreditation Forum and adhered to by certification bodies.

Some certification bodies might allow reductions based on the complexity of the processes, maturity of the QMS, and determination of requirements that don't apply. However, these are strictly limited and heavily scrutinized by the certification body's accreditation body. Because the goal is to have the audit add value to the organization, this should not be a primary area where an organization looks to cut costs.

- *Seek a local auditor from your certification body.* Local auditors have less distance to travel, saving travel costs. Because certification body auditors must meet competence requirements, there might be an auditor in your geographic area who can't audit your organization because he or she isn't competent in your industry.

  You could discuss with the certification body if there are options for the requested auditor to achieve the necessary competence. This might not be possible in all situations, but the discussion will allow your oganization to be involved in the selection of auditors for its site and drive the focus of cost management to the certification body.

- *Share travel costs.* Frequently, certification body auditors travel to the same geographic location multiple times over the course of a year. Determine if your audit can be synchronized with another organization in your location. This would allow you to share travel costs with another company.

  At times the level of coordination needed between the two sites is difficult and won't always work because each organization could have conflicting activities.

- *Determine if resources are available in your state.* In some states, there are resources that are available to help organizations either achieve or sustain ISO 9001:2015 certification. Grants and financial assistance programs aren't consistent from state to state, but there are some programs that provide a stipend to assist with the cost of the initial certification. This could be reimbursing the organization for consulting services, covering certification costs, or funding training. It's important to research what resources you might have at your disposal. Sources to check include your state's economic development department, local technical or community colleges, or your local Manufacturing Extension Partnership (MEP). Small businesses should also check with the local Small Business Administration to determine if programs are available.

  Although technical schools or community colleges might not provide reimbursement, they frequently offer affordable services. Many of them also have programs where students are being trained as internal auditors. As part of the student's course curriculum, they are required to conduct audits and these audits are offered to local businesses at a reduced fee.

- *Host training at your location.* The cost of training frequently prohibits all the necessary persons of the organization from getting the training they need to be competent in their job. Hosting a training course at the organization site at times allows a group rate and avoids travel costs.

    In addition, consider inviting other organizations to participate. This provides a great opportunity to network with other organizations while sharing the training costs.
- *Trade internal auditor resources.* Some organizations trade internal auditor resources. Each organization borrows auditor resources to conduct their internal audits. This is especially helpful for smaller organizations that frequently have to hire contractors to conduct their audits to maintain impartiality of the audit process.

The reality is that there are some costs to implementing QMS requirements. However, the level of costs is easily managed if you think outside the box and look for opportunities to make changes without affecting conformance to the QMS. The key is to make those changes that balance reducing costs and maintaining a strong QMS. It's a tightrope, but with a little creative thinking you can demonstrate to management that the QMS can add value and be cost effective at the same time.

SECTION IV

Transition

This section gives readers an understanding of what is needed to move from an ISO 9001:2008 quality management system to meet the requirements of ISO 9001:2015.

CHAPTER 20

ISO 9001:2008 to ISO 9001:2015 Transition

ISO 9001:2015 is the standard's first major revision since 2000. There are some similarities in the level of revision, with the introduction of a new structure and changes in specific terminology. Another similarity is that many of the concerns with this revision are the same ones voiced during the 2000 revision: "This requirement is not auditable," "This will require me to make changes our organization doesn't need to the quality management system," and "How do I demonstrate conformance when there isn't required documented information (e.g., procedures)?"

These concerns can be directly linked to a lack of understanding of ISO 9001:2015's requirements and a fear of the unknown. The steps outlined in this chapter provide a foundation of understanding that will help ensure a successful transition. They should be used along with the clause-by-clause analysis in section II to understand the requirements to conduct the gap analysis.

The following steps will help ensure a successful transition to ISO 9001:2015:

1. *Read ISO 9001:2015 and ISO 9000:2015.* It's essential to have a clear understanding of the requirements in ISO 9001:2015 and of the terminology used in ISO 9000:2015, the normative reference for ISO 9001:2015, to effectively implement those requirements.
2. *Conduct training.* Although the established guidelines for an organization to achieve conformance to ISO 9001:2015 don't include specific training requirements, it's assumed that some level of training will be required for certain employees. Groups that might need training include quality personnel, internal au-

ditors, and management. The training can be developed internally or obtained from an external provider.

3. *Perform a gap analysis.* Organizations need to determine whether they meet ISO 9001:2015's requirements. This can be done by conducting a gap analysis of the existing management system to the revised standard. This activity can also be performed as an internal audit. This is an excellent opportunity to confirm not only conformance with new requirements but also existing requirements.

   The organization is likely performing many of the "new" requirements in ISO 9001:2015. Organizations need to scrutinize existing methods to establish conformance prior to determining there is a gap in the system.

   Organizations should also ensure they are assessing to requirements in the standard and not specific terms. For example, many organizations will note that the terms "quality manual" or "management representative" are no longer used in ISO 9001:2015. However, the standard does include similar requirements without using the same terminology. Subclause 4.3 includes requirements that are similar to the previous requirements for the quality manual requirements, and subclause 5.3 includes requirements that are similar to management representative requirements in ISO 9001:2008.

   Once the gaps are determined, organizations should take actions to address the areas where change is required.

4. *Talk to your certification body.* It's important to communicate with your certification body regarding the transition process it will use to ensure you take any specific steps it will be looking for when it audits your organization to ISO 9001:2015.

5. *Consider other customer, statutory, and regulatory requirements.* ISO 9001:2015 has made changes to specific requirements that might lead you to make a change such as using a method other than a quality manual for providing documented information. However, if there is a customer, statutory, or regulatory requirement that the organization is required to meet for a quality manual, the organization always has to meet the more stringent requirement.

6. *Develop an implementation plan.* Once the gap analysis has been completed, an organization should develop its implementation plan considering the date it wishes to transition. Specific actions to address gaps should be included in the implementation plan as well as training and other communication steps.

7. *Establish a transition date.* The most frequent question asked by organizations is "What will be the plan for organizations to transition from ISO 9001:2008 to ISO 9001:2015?" Organizations have until September 2018 to transition to ISO 9001:2015.

   Organizations will need to conduct specific activities or make certain considerations when establishing a transition date. The level of change that will be required will vary based on the maturity of an organization's quality management system (QMS) and past approaches to implementation. Therefore, some organizations may find a minimal amount of change is required while others will see the need for more substantial change.

Organizations that are due for recertification prior to the expiration of the three-year transition might choose to wait until that time. Consideration should be given to the fact that if the expiration date of an organization's certificate is too close to the expiration of the three-year period, the organization could be challenged with establishing a satisfactory date for their audit based on the schedules of auditors from certification bodies.

ISO 9001:2008 TO ISO 9001:2015 CORRELATION MATRIX

Chapter 21 includes the correlation matrix from ISO 9001:2008 to ISO 9001:2015 that can be used as a quick reference for organizations that currently conform to the requirements of ISO 9001:2008.

Chapter 21

ISO 9001:2008 to ISO 9001:2015 Correlation

ISO 9001:2008	ISO 9001:2015
4 Quality management system	4 Context of the organization
4.1 General requirements	4.4 Quality management system and its processes
4.2 Documentation requirements	7.5 Documented information
4.2.1 General	7.5.1 General
4.2.2 Quality manual	4.3 Determining the scope of the quality management system 7.5.1 General 4.4 Quality management system and its processes
4.2.3 Control of documents	7.5.2 Creating and updating 7.5.3 Control of documented information
4.2.4 Control of records	7.5.2 Creating and updating 7.5.3 Control of documented information
5 Management responsibility	5 Leadership

ISO 9001:2008	ISO 9001:2015
5.1 Management commitment	5.1 Leadership and commitment 5.1.1 General
5.2 Customer focus	5.1.2 Customer focus
5.3 Quality policy	5.2 Policy 5.2.1 Establishing the quality policy 5.2.2 Communicating the quality policy
5.4 Planning	6 Planning
5.4.1 Quality objectives	6.2 Quality objectives and planning to achieve them
5.4.2 Quality management system planning	6 Planning 6.1 Actions to address risks and opportunities 6.3 Planning of changes
5.5 Responsibility, authority, and communication	5 Leadership
5.5.1 Responsibility and authority	5.3 Organizational roles, responsibilities, and authorities
5.5.2 Management representative	NOTE: Title removed 5.3 Organizational roles, responsibilities, and authorities
5.5.3 Internal communication	7.4 Communication
5.6 Management review	9.3 Management review
5.6.1 General	9.3.1 General
5.6.2 Review input	9.3.2 Management review inputs
5.6.3 Review output	9.3.3 Management review outputs
6 Resource management	7.1 Resources
6.1 Provision of resources	7.1.1 General 7.1.2 People
6.2 Human resources	NOTE: Title removed 7.2 Competence
6.2.1 General	7.2 Competence

ISO 9001:2008	ISO 9001:2015
6.2.2 Competence, training, and awareness	7.2 Competence 7.3 Awareness
6.3 Infrastructure	7.1.3 Infrastructure
6.4 Work environment	7.1.4 Environment for the operation of processes
7 Product realization	8 Operation
7.1 Planning of product realization	8.1 Operational planning and control
7.2 Customer-related processes	8.2 Requirements for products and services
7.2.1 Determination of requirements related to the product	8.2.2 Determining the requirements for products and services
7.2.2 Review of requirements related to the product	8.2.3 Review of the requirements for products and services 8.2.4 Changes to requirements for products and services
7.2.3 Customer communication	8.2.1 Customer communication
7.3 Design and development	8.5 Production and service provision
7.3.1 Design and development planning	8.3 Design and development of products and services 8.3.1 General 8.3.2 Design and development planning
7.3.2 Design and development inputs	8.3.3 Design and development inputs
7.3.3 Design and development outputs	8.3.5 Design and development outputs
7.3.4 Design and development review	8.3.4 Design and development controls
7.3.5 Design and development outputs	8.3.4 Design and development controls
7.3.6 Design and development validation	8.3.4 Design and development controls
7.3.7 Control of design and development changes	8.3.6 Design and development changes

ISO 9001:2008	ISO 9001:2015
7.4 Purchasing	8.4 Control of externally provided processes, products, and services
7.4.1 Purchasing process	8.4.1 General 8.4.2 Type and extent of control
7.4.2 Purchasing information	8.4.3 Information for external providers
7.4.3 Verification of purchased product	8.6 Release of products and services
7.5 Production and service provision	8.5 Production and service provision
7.5.1 Control of production and service provision	8.5.1 Control of production and service provision 8.5.5 Post-delivery activities
7.5.2 Validation of processes for production and service provision	8.5.1 Control of production and service provision
7.5.3 Identification and traceability	8.5.2 Identification and traceability
7.5.4 Customer property	8.5.3 Property belonging to customers or external providers
7.5.5 Preservation of product	8.5.4 Preservation
7.6 Control of monitoring and measuring equipment	7.1.5 Monitoring and measuring resources
8 Measurement, analysis, and improvement	9.1 Monitoring, measurement, analysis, and evaluation
8.1 General	9.1.1 General
8.2 Monitoring and measurement	9.1 Monitoring, measurement, analysis, and evaluation
8.2.1 Customer satisfaction	9.1.2 Customer satisfaction
8.2.2 Internal audit	9.2 Internal audit
8.2.3 Monitoring and measurement of processes	9.1.1 General
8.2.4 Monitoring and measurement of product	8.6 Release of products and services
8.3 Control of nonconforming product	8.7 Control of nonconforming outputs

ISO 9001:2008	ISO 9001:2015
8.4 Analysis of data	9.1.3 Analysis and evaluation
8.5 Improvement	10 Improvement
8.5.1 Continual improvement	10.1 General 10.3 Continual improvement
8.5.2 Corrective action	10.2 Nonconformity and corrective action
8.5.3 Preventive action	NOTE: Clause removed 6.1 Actions to address risks and opportunities

Section V

Appendices

This section provides additional information that's helpful to understanding ISO 9001:2015 and its relationship to other standards and other excellence models, as well as more information on the entire ISO 9000 family of standards. We've also included a sample quality management system checklist.

Appendix A

Integrated Management System Standards

As companies look for ways to become more effective and efficient in how they conduct business, there is always a call to reduce redundancies while looking for ways to increase points of alignment and integration. This is particularly evident in large organizations with differing systems. These systems are evident in functional departments such as finance; supply chain; environmental, health and safety; quality; information technology; and others. All too often, however, they are run as separate entities.

Of course it's not a new concept that organizations need to tear down silos of activities. There are calls for cross-functional teams that make their way into various expectations, guidelines, and even standards. Although cross-functional teams can be incredibly valuable and important to any company, they're not the ultimate answer to all the organization's problems. Integrated management systems, however, can extract the full potential and value of all of the key functions aligned and integrated to support the organization's strategy, mission, and vision.

So how does an organization go about integrating the work of the various functions? Begin by understanding what needs to take place. Although there are a lot of articles that can be found with a simple internet search, there is no foolproof recipe. Start by identifying the management systems within the organization and take stock of their roles.

MANAGEMENT SYSTEM STANDARDS

At its base level, a system is simply a set of connected parts that are performing a function within the overall strategies of an organization. ISO 9001:2015 draws on the analogy of the systems that work together within an organism, such as a human being. The systems all have a function that when integrated and fulfilling their role serve to help sustain the organism or organization.

In a general sense, management systems stretch to multiple aspects within an organization. When speaking of management system standards, the following are the management systems with associated standards that are most often cited:

- *Quality management system (QMS).* A QMS can be described as a set of policies, processes, and practices required for the planning and execution of an organization's quality objectives. As well over 1 million ISO 9001 certificates have been issued, it's safe to say that a significant number of organizations will continue to use ISO 9001:2015 as the basis for their QMS.

    Examples of QMS standards include:
    - ✓ ISO 9001
    - ✓ AS9100 for the aerospace and defense sector
    - ✓ ISO 13485 for the medical devices sector
    - ✓ ISO/TS 16949 for the automotive sector

- *Environmental management system (EMS).* An EMS determines the policies, processes, and practices required for planning, execution, and improvement of an organization's environmental position and performance. The primary environmental management system standard is ISO 14001.

- *Health and safety management system.* An occupational health and safety management system determines the policies, processes, and practices required for planning, execution, and improvement of an organization's health and safety position and performance.

    Examples of health and safety management system standards include:
    - ✓ OHSAS 18001
    - ✓ ISO 45001 (under development)

- *Energy management system.* The primary energy management system standard is ISO 50001, Energy management systems—Requirements with guidance for use.

- *Information security management system.* The primary information security management system standard is ISO/IEC 27001, Information technology—Security techniques—Information security management systems—Requirements.

- *Food Safety Management System.* The primary food safety management system standard is ISO 22000, Food safety management systems—Requirements for any organization in the food chain.

BENEFITS OF INTEGRATED MANAGEMENT SYSTEMS

As with any other aspect of a business, the effective use of resources is of the utmost concern. Beyond the maximization of resources through the removal of redundancies, there are added benefits in having the major systems of an organization all aligned toward common strategies and objectives. It provides clarity to the organization by having all functions working together. Although it's clear that there may be some specific market, industry, or sector requirements that may make it difficult to integrate management systems, the potential benefits make exploring integration a valuable activity.

The reduction in duplication of efforts is clear in that there are consistent elements that are expected from the management systems within an organization. The following are some examples of areas that are clear for integration between the various management systems:

- Control of documented information
- Process approach
- Internal audits
- Analysis of key measures of performance
- Competence
- Corrective action
- Management review
- Risk-based thinking

The realization of the common elements between management systems and the potential efficiency gains through integration was one of the primary inputs to developing Annex SL. With the development of Annex SL within the ISO Directives, every new management system standard developed by a technical committee (TC) within ISO must comply with the high-level structure and wording within Annex SL unless a justification to deviate is approved. Although Annex SL creates limitations on the drafters of the individual ISO management system standards, the basic intent is to make it easier for a company intending to integrate its management systems.

As an organization integrates any formal management system standard, additional consideration must be taken if any of those management systems are currently under a third-party certification. There are many certification bodies that claim that they will conduct integrated assessments. It is, however, suggested that the organization be cautious in understanding what the certification body means by "integrated assessment." It should mean more than just having experts in multiple disciplines within one certification body. It requires significant planning and coordination to gain the full value of an integrated approach to auditing. Finally, the organization should clearly understand if there are restrictions that are placed upon the actual conduct of the assessment by the organization's customers. A specific example are the requirements within the certification scheme for the automotive sector QMS requirements, ISO/TS 16949.

Additional guidance on the integration of ISO management systems standards can be found in a book published by ISO titled, "The integrated use of management system standards." Work is ongoing within ISO to continue to provide guidance on the integration of management systems, as well as updating the ISO Directives and Annex SL.

Appendix B

The Relationship Between ISO 9001 and ISO 14001

The International Organization for Standardization (ISO) has developed many management system standards. There are, however, two that are more closely aligned than other standards. ISO 14001, Environmental management systems—Requirements with guidance for use, is probably the second-most implemented management system standard next to ISO 9001. This chapter outlines some of the similarities and differences between ISO 9001 and ISO 14001.

For the first time since ISO 14001 was developed, the projects to revise ISO 9001 and ISO 14001 were aligned. This created a unique situation where both working groups had the opportunity to exchange drafts and provide feedback. In many cases, a common approach was adopted to ensure consistency between the standards. This includes the use of "maintain" and "retain" for documented information.

Early in 2012, both revision projects were initiated based on the high-level structure of management system standards (as outlined in Annex SL of the ISO Directives, Part 2). This means that both standards have the same structure with the same numbering scheme and some identical text with common definitions.

This results in a better alignment between the standards. However, quality management and environmental management have their own specific aspects that are maintained in the final versions of ISO 9001:2015 and ISO 14001:2015.

During the development of ISO 9001:2015, some minor deviations from the common text (as outlined in Annex SL of the ISO Directives, Part 2) were incorporated. These deviations were not always considered in the development of ISO 14001:2015 and could be perceived as a difference. However, in many instances the differences between the two standards are due to the different disciplines of quality and environment.

Although these differences exist, it's important to note that an organization that implements an ISO 14001:2015 system will find it beneficial when in implementing some of the discipline-specific requirements of ISO 9001:2015.

Although ISO 9001:2015 and ISO 14001:2015 share some common elements as part of their scope, they both have their own intent.

The following provides an overview of some of the key differences between the two standards, including a clause-by-clause overview:

SCOPE

Figure B.1 includes the scopes for ISO 9001:2015 and ISO 14001:2015. ISO 9001:2015 is focused on delivering products and services that meet applicable requirements while ISO 14001 is focused on performance, compliance, and meeting objectives of the environmental management system (EMS). These different scopes illustrate the need for discipline-specific requirements for each management system.

Figure B.1	Scope of ISO 14001:2015, ISO 9001:2015
ISO 14001:2015	
Consistent with the organization's environmental policy, the intended outcomes of an environmental management system include: — enhancement of environmental performance; — fulfilment of compliance obligations; — achievement of environmental objectives.	
ISO 9001:2015	
This International Standard specifies requirements for a quality management system when an organization: a) needs to demonstrate its ability to consistently provide products and services that meet customer and applicable statutory and regulatory requirements, and b) aims to enhance customer satisfaction through the effective application of the system, including processes for improvement of the system and the assurance of conformity to customer and applicable statutory and regulatory requirements.	

TERMS AND DEFINITIONS

ISO 9001:2015 uses ISO 9000:2015 as normative reference; ISO 14001 does not have any normative reference. There are some variations in the use of concepts and terminology. This is why it is critical that organizations review the terminology for each document to ensure the best understanding of the requirements.

4 CONTEXT OF THE ORGANIZATION

Many of the requirements in clause 4 are new to both ISO 9001:2015 and ISO 14001:2015. These requirements have similar text, but will end up being implemented in different ways because of the nature of each management system. For example, ISO 14001 has always included a consideration of interested parties. ISO 9001 has typically focused on customers. For this reason, the interested parties might be somewhat different when implementing more than one system.

The requirements related to the management system and its processes are also different.

Since the 2000 version, ISO 9001 has incorporated the process approach into its requirements. In the past, ISO 14001 did not include any consideration of process. However, with the 2015 revision, ISO 14001 considers processes in most of its requirements. There still remains a difference in the process approach. ISO 9001:2015 includes more detailed requirements in subclause 4.4, which are not included in ISO 14001:2015. It also does not use the process approach as the foundation for its requirements.

However, if an organization has a robust process approach based on ISO 9001, any other management system standard or initiative can be implemented without major difficulties. For example, subclause 4.4.1(e) requires responsibilities and authorities to be assigned for every process. This requirement can be considered when implementing ISO 14001:2015. The process owner can have specific roles for both management systems.

5 LEADERSHIP

Both standards are fairly consistent in their intent, but organizations should realize that the focus on leadership and its commitment may vary from a QMS to an EMS. ISO 9001:2015 includes specific requirements with respect to customer focus and expands the requirements for management commitment.

6 PLANNING

Both standards have a common set of requirements regarding actions to address risks and opportunities (see subclause 6.1).

There are differences in the use of the concepts of risks and opportunities and this can be perceived as a major difference between the two standards. The definition of risk is consistent between both standards. However, ISO 14001:2015 has a definition for "risks and opportunities" where ISO 9001:2015 does not and focuses instead on risk-based thinking.

ISO 14001:2015 considers the environmental aspects and compliance obligations as part of the actions for determining risks and opportunities. These considerations are very specific in the context of the EMS.

The other difference between the two standards is that ISO 9001:2015 includes a set of requirements for planning of changes where ISO 14001:2015 does not.

7 SUPPORT

ISO 14001:2015 has a very generic requirement for considering resources for the EMS. This differs from ISO 9001:2015, which has more prescriptive requirements covering persons, infrastructure, work environment, and organizational knowledge.

The resources included in ISO 9001:2015 can be considered for the implementation of the generic requirements of ISO 14001:2015 due to their correlation to the operation of the EMS infrastructure and work environment, which can be subject to specific environmental controls.

For example, a plating process in which a zinc coating is applied to a steel wire has several environmental aspects to consider that can have a significant effect on the environment (including the persons operating the process). In this scenario, the tanks containing the zinc are a critical infrastructure to be considered for both the QMS and EMS. The coating can represent a critical quality characteristic that needs to be controlled to ensure that product meets requirements while any spill of zinc can have a major environmental impact.

The other difference in clause 7 between the two standards is that ISO 14001:2015 is more prescriptive in its communication requirements than ISO 9001:2015. This is due in part to the nature of the management system. Because ISO 14001:2015 focuses on environmental issues, it can be expected that there is a need for more specific communication.

8 OPERATION

Clause 8 is one of the areas where there are major difference between the two standards. This is due to the requirements in clause 8 that are specific to the operation of the management system. It would be expected that there would be different approaches to these requirements.

ISO 14001:2015 is generic regarding operational control. To meet the EMS requirements, operating criteria needs to be established for the process(es) and control of the process(es) needs to be implemented according the operating criteria.

ISO 14001:2015 also provides specific requirements for consideration of life cycle in design and development of the product, procurement, communication, and post-delivery activities. Specific requirements are included for emergency preparedness and response because the significant aspects identified in the EMS could result in a disaster or emergency in the organization.

Although ISO 14001:2015 is very specific to the operation of the EMS, ISO 9001:2015 provides a complete set of requirements that are consistent with the way any organization operates regardless of the process or activity. For this reason, the requirements of ISO 14001:2015 can also be considered in the following ISO 9001:2015 clauses:
- 8.3 Design and development of products and services
- 8.4 Control of externally provided processes, products and services
- 8.5 Production and service provision
- 8.7 Control of nonconforming outputs

9 PERFORMANCE EVALUATION

The requirements in clause 9 are fairly similar for both standards. They both include specific requirements based on the discipline of the management system for management review. ISO 14001:2015 also includes in its subclause 9.1 requirements related to measuring equipment, the communication of relevant environmental performance information and evaluation of compliance. ISO 9001:2015 includes requirements for measuring resources and communication in clause 7. ISO 9001:2015 also includes requirements for analysis and evaluation that are not included in ISO 14001:2015.

10 IMPROVEMENT

One of the differences between the two standards is simply the philosophy of improvement vs. continual improvement. ISO 9001:2015 uses continual improvement only in subclause 10.3; ISO 14001:2015 uses continual improvement throughout the standard. This difference in philosophy should not cause any confusion when implementing the two standards.

ANNEXES

Both standards include annexes that are meant to assist users in understanding their requirements. ISO 14001:2015 provides specific guidance on the use of the standard. This is one reason why there are less prescriptive requirements in the standard. ISO 9001:2015 doesn't include any guidance in the document itself. It does include an annex that provides some points of clarification from the 2008 to 2015 versions of the standard. A guidance standard for ISO 9001:2015 is under development and will be published as ISO/TS 9002 during 2016.

Although the requirements of these two standards are more similar than ever, it's still important to note that organizations may be deliberate in their approaches to implementing these standards to ensure that the nuances between the two are maintained. The differences can also be used to strengthen the aspects of the other management system.

The common structure (Annex SL) has addressed many past user concerns. But, ultimately, the differences are there for a reason.

Appendix C

Compliance Standards vs. Excellence Models

There have been plenty of articles and conversations questioning the continued relevance of ISO 9001 in the marketplace. Many examine the relationship between conformance standards and various performance excellence models. The benefits and utility of a conformance standard is more about the organization and its intent than solely about the standard. A standard such ISO 9001:2015 is intended to provide assurance that any organization claiming conformance meets a minimum set of requirements that can be demonstrated through internal or external assessment. Beyond that, it's up to the organization to use its quality management system (QMS) in a way that advances its mission, vision, and objectives.

Is there a place for ISO 9001:2015 in an organization that wants to utilize an excellence model? Can they work together? From a very practical standpoint and individual experience, the answer is yes. However, it's up to the individual organization to determine the best way to integrate them.

Of course, fervent believers, users, and those heavily invested will have their opinions and defenders. However, does it have to be an either/or proposition? It can certainly be a benefit for an organization to think of how having an ISO 9001-based QMS can take advantage of an excellence model addressing the complete business. One of the statements that often gets put forward in quality discussions is that a QMS must be fully integrated into the overall business operating system to be most successful. Therefore, building the ISO 9001-based QMS within a framework of an excellence model is one way to achieve this goal.

Through each successive revision of ISO 9001 there has been a call to push the "output matters" concept. Yet, there are many certificate holders who pursue ISO 9001 for external factors only, rather than on balance with the internal value drivers that can be achieved. Most of the excellence models put a strong emphasis on linking and aligning the outputs of processes to the strategic planning of the organization. Studies show the effect of ISO 9001 deployment on the overall success of the organization. The conclusions have been varied as to the results. However, it's clear that for any implementation to be transformative, it needs to have a strong root in internal needs rather than simply external demands.

Although there was no stated goal to make ISO 9001:2015 align with popular excellence models, there are many features that do just that. Some examples include emphasis on concepts such as customer focus, context of the organization, and relevant interested parties. However, there are also some differences. One key example is in the audit process within ISO 9001. It's in place to ensure that the organization conducts audits (internally and third party) to assure conformance with a series of requirements. Within excellence models, the assessment is in place to assess the extent to which the organization has achieved the intended results that support its strategy and focus on organizational learning for future results.

The intent isn't to compare or contrast the benefits of ISO 9001 or the various excellence models. The premise is that there are tangible benefits to using them in a complementary fashion.

We've already explored ISO 9001:2015 in depth in this book. So, we will now take a look at the most popular excellence models to provide a basis for understanding and comparison.

OVERVIEW OF EXCELLENCE MODELS

Although there are many excellence models in the international marketplace, we will focus on several of the more well-known models. It's clear that there are many commonalities between the models. We will first review the overall content of some models. Then, we will spend some additional focus on the two most widely known: the European Foundation for Quality Management (EFQM) and the Malcolm Baldrige National Quality Award (MBNQA).

Malcolm Baldrige Criteria for Performance Excellence
www.nist.gov/baldrige/

The Malcolm Baldrige National Quality Award process is administered by the American Society for Quality (ASQ) and managed by the National Institute of Standards and Technology (NIST), an agency of the U.S. Department of Commerce. Many other excellence models are based directly or in part on this model.

The model consists of seven categories:
- Leadership
- Strategy
- Customers
- Measurement, analysis, and knowledge management
- Workforce
- Operations
- Results

EFQM Excellence Model
www.efqm.org

The European Business Excellence Award is run by the European Foundation for Quality Management (EFQM). This framework is used as the basis for national business excellence and quality awards across Europe.

There are nine categories within the model:
- Leadership
- Strategy
- People
- Partnerships and resources
- Processes, products, and services
- Customer results
- People results
- Society results
- Business results

Canadian Framework for Business Excellence
www.excellence.ca/en/knowledge-centre/products-and-tools/canadian-framework-for-business-excellence2

The Canadian Framework for Business Excellence is used as a management model for organizational excellence within Canada. The framework is administered by Excellence Canada.

The framework consists of seven categories:
- Leadership
- Planning
- Customer focus

- People focus
- Process management
- Supplier/partner focus
- Business performance

Australian Business Excellence Framework

www.saiglobal.com/Improve/ExcellenceModels/BusinessExcellenceFramework

The Australian Business Excellence Framework provides the criteria for the Australian Business Excellence Awards. The framework is administered by SAI Global.

The framework consists of seven categories:
- Leadership
- Customers and stakeholders
- Strategy and planning
- People
- Information and knowledge
- Process management, improvement, and innovation
- Results and sustainable performance

MBNQA AND EFQM

During the 1980s, there was a growing emphasis on quality in the United States after it was perceived that Japan had surged ahead in manufacturing quality. In 1987, the U.S. Congress established the Malcolm Baldrige National Quality Award to promote a greater awareness of the effect of quality on the overall success of organizations. Although the name of the award has quality in it, the emphasis is on overall business excellence, not just the silo of the quality department.

The framework for the Baldrige Award lists a series of core values and concepts that are fundamental to the criteria:
- Systems perspective
- Visionary leadership
- Customer-focused excellence
- Valuing people
- Organizational learning and agility
- Focus on success
- Managing for innovation
- Management by fact
- Societal responsibility

- Ethics and transparency
- Delivering value and results

NIST administers the Baldrige Award process along with ASQ. Since its introduction, there have been many outstanding organizations that have won the award, resulting in significant benefits. According to the NIST website, "An October 2001 study of the economic impact of the Baldrige Program, prepared for NIST by Albert N. Link and John T. Scott, conservatively estimated the net private benefits associated with the program to the economy as a whole at $24.65 billion. When compared to the social costs of the program of $119 million, the Baldrige Program's social benefit-to-cost ratio was 207-to-1. A December 2011 study by Link and Scott of the Baldrige Program's value to U.S. organizations found an even greater benefit-to-cost ratio of 820-to-1."

The EFQM is a nonprofit foundation based in Brussels that was formed in 1988 by a group of major European organizations. EFQM administers the EFQM Business Excellence Model. According to EFQM, one of the primary reasons to use its excellence model is that an organization striving for excellence will seek solutions to problems that will enhance long-term performance that will help sustain it. As EFQM states on its website, "The Balanced Score Card (BSC) provides a framework for monitoring KPIs, ISO 9001 secures a robust quality management system, ISO 26000 provides guidance for corporate social responsibility (CSR), Lean helps eliminate waste and streamline processes." It is then put forward that the EFQM Excellence Model is one way to capture and deploy resources working within the various management systems to optimize the performance toward the organization's strategy and mission.

It's clear that the excellence models put forward by the various organizations that administer them have many more similarities than differences. Each of them provides a robust framework that organizations can use to seek excellence. The act of planning, deployment, self-assessment, and recognition within any of the models can be a significant drain on resources. However, it's equally clear that having a definite excellence framework helps to ensure that all components of the management system are aligned. Long story short, there is absolutely a complementary position to be had by any organization choosing to have both an ISO 9001-based QMS and an award-based excellence model.

Appendix D

ISO 9000 Family of Standards

One of the least known facts about ISO/TC 176 is that not only is it responsible for ISO 9001, but it also has a portfolio of standards that provide guidance on a variety of requirements in ISO 9001. There are three subcommittees (SCs) responsible for this portfolio:
- SC1 Concepts and terminology
- SC2 Quality systems
- SC3 Supporting technologies

The standards developed by these subcommittees are included in Annex B of ISO 9001:2015 along with an explanation of how each standard can be used. The following list includes the standards in the portfolio grouped by how they might be used. Additional ISO guides are available at www.iso.org. This is also a good source of information to check the current status of a standard or guidance document.
- Core standards:
  - ✓ ISO 9000:2015, Quality management systems—fundamentals and vocabulary
  - ✓ ISO 9001:2015, Quality management systems—requirements
  - ✓ ISO 9004:2009, Managing for the sustained success of an organization—A quality management approach

- Auditing
  - ✓ ISO 19011:2011, Guidelines for auditing management systems
- Documentation
  - ✓ ISO 10005:2005, Quality management systems—Guidelines for quality plans

- ✓ ISO/TR 10013:2001, Guidelines for quality management system documentation

- Project management
  - ✓ ISO 10006:2003, Quality management systems—Guidelines for quality management in projects

- Configuration management
  - ✓ ISO 10007:2003, Quality management systems—Guidelines for configuration management

- Customer Satisfaction
  - ✓ ISO 10001:2007, Quality management—Customer satisfaction—Guidelines for codes of conduct for organizations
  - ✓ ISO 10002:2014, Quality management—Customer satisfaction—Guidelines for complaints handling in organizations
  - ✓ ISO 10003:2007, Quality management—Customer satisfaction—Guidelines for dispute resolution external to organizations
  - ✓ ISO 10004:2012 Quality management—Customer satisfaction—Guidelines for monitoring and measuring
  - ✓ ISO 10008:2013, Quality management—Customer satisfaction—Guidelines for business-to-consumer electronic commerce transactions

- Training/people
  - ✓ ISO 10015:1999, Quality management—Guidelines for training
  - ✓ ISO 10018:2012, Quality management—Guidelines on people involvement and competence

- Other standards
  - ✓ ISO 10012:2003, Measurement management system—Requirements for measurement processes and measuring equipment
  - ✓ ISO 10014:2006, Quality management—Guidelines for realizing financial and economic benefits
  - ✓ ISO/TR 10017:2003, Guidance on statistical techniques for ISO 9001:2000
  - ✓ ISO 10019:2005, Guidelines for the selection of quality management system consultants and use of their services

Appendix E

Quality Management System Checklist

There are many actions that an organization needs to consider when implementing a quality management system (QMS) that conforms to the requirements of ISO 9001:2015. The following checklist includes actions that were outlined in section III, Implementation. This checklist can be used in developing an implementation plan or be used as a quick reference to track status.

Figure E.1	QMS Checklist
Action	
Read ISO 9000 and ISO 9001	
Assign responsibilities and authorities	
Implementation team training	
Management overview training	
Internal auditor training	
Employee awareness	
Determine scope of QMS	
Conduct gap analysis	
Develop implementation plan	
Determine external and internal issues	
Determine relevant interested parties	

Determine requirements for relevant interested parties	
Determine/map processes	
Establish quality policy	
Develop quality objectives	
Ensure required documented information requirements are in place • Maintain documented information • Retain documented information	
Develop additional documented information as necessary	
Determine competence requirements for persons of the organization	
Conduct management review	
Initiate internal audits—audit all ISO 9001 requirements prior to initial audit	
Implement corrective actions	
Select certification body	
Schedule third-party audits	
Complete corrective action	
Registration audit	
Complete corrective action	
Celebrate	
Ongoing maintenance and improvement	

Index

A
accreditation 174
actions to address risks and opportunities 65-68
adding value 231-241
advanced product quality planning 102
American Society for Quality (ASQ) 268-269, 271
analysis and evaluation 144-146
Annex A 31-32
Annex B 32
Annex SL 6-8, 259-261, 266
appeals process 179
applicability 9
APQP 102
AS9100 258
audit planning 176
audit report 227-228, 235
audit results 226-227
audit schedule 202
Australian Business Excellence Framework 270
awareness 16, 87-88

B
balanced score card 271

C
calibration 79-81
Canadian Framework for Business Excellence 269-270
celebrations 203
certification 173-180
certification
  scope of 196-197
  third-party 201-203
certification audits 176-177
certification body 201-202, 246
changes
  control of 134-136
  planning of 71-72
checklist 221-222
clause/subject matter expert 192
closing meeting 228
coaches 186
communication 17, 56, 88-90, 102-103, 236
communication plan 194-196
competence 16, 83-87
complaints 102-103
compliance standards 267-271
concession 139
consultants 186
context of the organization 15, 41-52, 263
continual improvement 164-165
contractors 86
control of changes 134-136
control of external provider and its resulting output 121
control of externally provided processes, products, and services 117-123
control of nonconforming outputs 138-140
control of processes 121
control of production and service provision 124-128
correction 139, 152, 161-164, 177
corrective action 152, 161-164, 177, 183, 201-202
customer communication 102-103
customer feedback 102-103
customer focus 18, 58-59, 63

customer property 102-103
customer satisfaction 142-144
customer surveys 143
customers 130-131, 188-189, 195-196

D

declaration of conformity 173-180
Deming Prize 184
design and development 108-116
    changes 116-117
    controls 113-114
    inputs 112-113
    outputs 114-116
    planning 109-111
    products and services 108-116
determination of requirements for products and services 102-107
determining the scope of the quality management system 45-47
document review 221
documented information 10-11, 67-69, 79, 86, 90-98, 101, 106, 125, 163-164, 198-200
    control of 95-98
    creating and updating 93-95
    examples of 86
documented procedures 200, 205-217

E

effectiveness 35
efficiency 35
electronic documents 96
employee awareness 193
employees 188, 195
energy management system
    definition 258
engagement of people 18
environment 77-78
environment for the operation of processes 77-78
environmental management system 258, 261-266
    definition 258
equipment 80-81

European Business Excellence Award 269, 271
European Foundation for Quality Management (EFQM) 269, 271
evidence-based decision making 19
Excellence Canada 269-270
excellence models 267-271
external providers 117-124, 130-131, 189
    information for 122-124
externally provided processes, products, and services 117-123
    control of 117-123
externally provided products and services 12
    control of 12

F

feedback 143
food safety management system
    definition 259

G

gap analysis 187, 197-198, 212-213, 216, 246

H

handling 80-81, 131-132
handling and storage 80-81
health and safety management system
    definition 258
human error 126
human resources 75

I

identification 131-132
identification and traceability 128-129
identification of processes 198-200
implementation 181-204
    approaches to 184-187
    benefits of 188-190
implementation plan 186-187, 246
    developing 186-187
implementation team 190-191
improvement 18-19, 159-165, 265

Index

information for external providers 122-124
information security management system
    definition 258
infrastructure 75-76, 125
integrated management system standards 257-260
interested party 8-9, 15, 43
internal audit 146-153, 183, 201, 219-229
    adding value 234-237
    audit criteria and audit scope 151-152
    audit report 227-228
    changes affecting the organization 149
    closing meeting 228
    conducting 223-224
    corrective action 152
    documented information 153
    frequency 148
    methods 148
    observation 150-151
    planning requirements 149
    process 219-229
    reporting 150
    report to relevant management 152
    responsibilities 149
    results from previous audits 149-150
    results of 226-227
    schedule 219-220
internal auditor 194
International Accreditation Forum 174
Interviews
    conducting 224-226
ISO 10005 102
ISO 13485 258
ISO 14001 258, 261-266
ISO 19011 146
ISO 22000 259
ISO 45001 258
ISO 50001 258
ISO 9000:2015
    overview 13-23
    format of 13
ISO 9001 coordinator 192-193

ISO standards development process 25-30
ISO Technical Management Board 6
ISO/IEC 27001 258
ISO/TS 16949 258-260
ISO/TS 9002 266

J

job descriptions 84

K

kaizen 57, 160

L

leadership 18, 53-64, 169-172, 182, 189, 195, 263
leadership and commitment 53-57
lean 184
learning organizations 170
Link, Albert N. 271

M

maintenance 203-204
major nonconformity 177
Malcolm Baldrige National Quality Award 184, 268-270
management commitment 190
management overview 193
management review 57, 63, 67, 124-125, 153-158, 201, 231-233
    inputs 155-157
    outputs 157-158
management sponsor 192
management system standards 257-260
managing costs 237-241
Manufacturing Extension Partnership 240
measurement traceability 79-81
mentors 191
minor nonconformity 177
monitoring and measuring 78-81, 125 78-81
monitoring, measurement, analysis, and evaluation 141-146

Multilateral Recognition Arrangement 174

N

National Institute of Standards and Technology (NIST) 268-269, 271
nonconforming outputs
    control of 138-140
nonconformity
    major 177
    minor 177
nonconformity and corrective action 161-164

O

objective 35
OHSAS 18001 258
opening meetings 222-223
operation 264-265
operation of processes 125
operational planning and control 99-102
operational processes 101
operations 99-140
opportunities for improvement 157-158
organizational chart 169
organizational knowledge 11, 81-83
organizational roles, responsibilities, and authorities 62-64
output 33

P

packaging 131-132
Papakostantinu, Peter v
PDCA cycle 33, 37
people 16-18, 75
    engagement of 18
performance 35
performance evaluation 141-158, 265
person of the organization 84
plan-do-check-act cycle 33, 37
planning 65-72, 263-264
planning audits 176
planning of changes 71-72
policy 59-61

post-delivery activities 133-134
pre-certification activities 175
preservation 131-132
preventive action 67
preventive maintenance 76
procedure writing 205-217
procedures 205-217
    drafting 213
    deviating from 216-217
    identifying gaps 217
    quality of 214-215
    verifying 214-216
process 33
process approach 18, 33-37, 48, 55-56, 215
processes
    control of 121
    identification of 198-200
production and service provision 124-136
    control of 124-128
products and services 8, 136-134
    release of 136-134
property belonging to customers or external providers 130-131
protection 131-132
providers 117-123, 196

Q

QMS development 20-21
QMS model 20
quality 14
quality management principles 14-22
quality management system 15, 258
    definition 258
quality management system and its processes 47-52
quality objectives 55, 60, 68-71, 87-88
    planning to achieve them 68-71
quality plans 102
quality policy 55, 59-61, 87-88
    communicating 60-61

R

recertification 178
relationship management 19
release of products and services 136-138
remote auditing 228-229
reputation 170
resource needs 158
resources 56, 73-83
results 56-57
revalidation 126
rework 88
risk 35, 65
risk-based thinking 10, 33-37, 55-56, 65
risks and opportunities 182

S

SAI Global 270
sampling plan 221-222
scope of certification 196-197
    example 197
Scott, John T. 271
scrap 88
Six Sigma 57, 184
Small Business Administration 240
special processes 125-126
standards development process 29-30
statutory and regulatory requirements
    104-105, 107
storage 131-132
suppliers 117-123
support 73-98, 264
surveillance audit 178
sustaining a QMS 204
SWOT analysis 43
system 33

T

temporary employees 86
terms and definitions 22
third-party certification 201-203
top management 58-59, 153-158, 169-172
training 192-194, 215-216, 234-235, 245-246

transition 245-247

date 246-247

U

U.S. Department of Commerce 269
understanding the needs and expectations of interested parties 43-45
understanding the organization and its context 42-43

V

virtual auditing 228-229

Z

zero defects 170

Printed in Poland
by Amazon Fulfillment
Poland Sp. z o.o., Wrocław